NELSON'S

Arthur William Devis, *The Death of Nelson* (National Maritime Museum)

Nelson's Surgeon

*William Beatty, Naval Medicine,
and the Battle of Trafalgar*

LAURENCE BROCKLISS

JOHN CARDWELL

and

MICHAEL MOSS

OXFORD

UNIVERSITY PRESS

OXFORD

UNIVERSITY PRESS

Great Clarendon Street, Oxford OX2 6DP

Oxford University Press is a department of the University of Oxford.
It furthers the University's objective of excellence in research, scholarship,
and education by publishing worldwide in

Oxford New York

Auckland Cape Town Dar es Salaam Hong Kong Karachi
Kuala Lumpur Madrid Melbourne Mexico City Nairobi
New Delhi Shanghai Taipei Toronto

With offices in

Argentina Austria Brazil Chile Czech Republic France Greece
Guatemala Hungary Italy Japan Poland Portugal Singapore
South Korea Switzerland Thailand Turkey Ukraine Vietnam

Oxford is a registered trade mark of Oxford University Press
in the UK and in certain other countries

Published in the United States
by Oxford University Press Inc., New York

© Laurence Brockliss, John Cardwell, and Michael Moss 2005

The moral rights of the authors have been asserted
Database right Oxford University Press (maker)

First published 2005
First published in paperback 2008

British Library Cataloguing in Publication Data

Data available

Library of Congress Cataloging in Publication Data

Data available

Typeset by SPI Publisher Services, Pondicherry, India
Printed in Great Britain
by
Biddles Ltd., King's Lynn, Norfolk

ISBN 978–0–19–928742–0 (Hbk.)   978–0–19–954135–5 (Pbk.)

1 3 5 7 9 10 8 6 4 2

To Alison, Lynne, and Stella

Preface

For more than twenty years, from 1793 to 1815, Britain was at war with France and her allies, the long years of conflict punctuated only by the short peace negotiated at Amiens in 1802 and the temporary restoration of the Bourbons in 1814. According to the rhetoric of the politicians, this began as a war to defend our national way of life against the irreligious and demagogic principles of the French revolutionaries and became a struggle to free the peoples of Europe from the tyrannical grip of Napoleon. To more reflective historians it has been seen as the culmination of a conflict that had lasted a hundred years between Britain and France to decide the mastery of the world. Regardless of its cause, this was a war which Britain ultimately won, thereby establishing her status for most of the nineteenth century as the world's only superpower. Among the many victories over the enemy at sea, none has been accorded a greater significance than the Battle of Trafalgar fought off Cadiz against the combined fleets of France and Spain on 21 October 1805, which purportedly saved the United Kingdom from the threat of invasion and gave her dominion of the seas. The daring tactics of the British fleet's commanding officer, Admiral Lord Nelson, and his death at the moment of victory have also ensured that no other battle in the long war, then or since, has so fired the public imagination. London's Trafalgar Square, a number of Nelson's columns dotted about the country, and the preservation of the admiral's flagship, HMS *Victory,* at Portsmouth bear powerful witness to the continued belief that the battle was a defining moment in the nation's history.

This book is a professional biography of one of the countless unsung heroes of the British fleet at Trafalgar. William Beatty was the chief surgeon on board Nelson's flagship. During the battle he remained confined for many hours below the waterline in the dark, hot, airless, and swaying cockpit, attending to the continual stream of wounded and dying while the cannon roared overhead. In the course of a long afternoon he and his two assistant surgeons, aided by other non-combatants, treated 100 of the *Victory's* approximately 820 crew. By the time darkness fell he had seen his best friend, who had been mortally wounded in the fight, expire in front of his eyes, then nursed the dying Nelson through his agony. Throughout the ordeal he remained calmly in control, clamping, probing, sawing, and bandaging. He ended the day by preserving the admiral's body, so that it could be brought back to England. Beatty was 32. Although he had been in the navy since 1791, this was the first major action he had served in. Trafalgar was his baptism by fire.

Unlike most of the officers and crew of the *Victory*, Beatty has not completely slipped from the historical memory. After Trafalgar he went on to have a distinguished career in the naval medical service and eventually became physician to Greenwich Hospital in 1822. An FRS, a Licentiate of the Royal College of Physicians, and a knight of the realm, when he died in 1842 he was a figure of importance in the world of London medicine, who inevitably, like many of those involved in the great sea battle, received a short notice at the end of the nineteenth century in the *Dictionary of National Biography*. Beatty's physical likeness, too, has survived, captured on canvas in several publicly displayed portraits and historical reconstructions. In Arthur Devis's famous *Death of Nelson,* painted in 1806–7, the surgeon is the fresh-faced, dark-haired young man on the right of the picture taking the dying hero's pulse. In the weeks after the victory Nelson came to be seen as a Christlike figure, saviour of the nation, if not the world. In Devis's painting Beatty hovers over the prostrate hero, like Mary Magdalene over the body of Christ in paintings of the Deposition (see the Frontispiece).

Nonetheless, William Beatty remains a cardboard and largely neglected figure. Unlike some army and navy surgeons who served during the wars, he left no autobiography or account of his experiences. Nor, unlike others, was he accorded a detailed biographical notice in the press when he died. Nor, too, since he was always a bachelor, was his memory honoured by his sons and daughters in a published eulogy. There is not even a gravestone, for Beatty was buried in an unmarked tomb in a vault in Kensal Green cemetery. All that the public knows of the man is his public life. The notices in both the original and *Oxford Dictionary of National Biography* merely cite the main milestones of his naval career: they contain several errors and say nothing about his background, training, or personality. The official *Victory* website, which lists the nationality of all the officers and men on board the ship at Trafalgar, calls him Scottish, presumably on the strength of his surname: in fact he hailed from Londonderry. In some accounts of the battle Beatty is even confused with the chaplain, Alexander John Scott, who was one of Nelson's secretaries.[1]

---

[1] To confuse matters, Nelson's other secretary was John Scott, who was killed early on in the battle. http://www.hms-victory.com (Feb. 2005).

In this bicentennial year of the Battle of Trafalgar the public will inevitably be deluged with a plethora of books, TV programmes, and exhibitions devoted to the lives and loves of Lord Nelson and his famous victory. The battle will be fought and refought in an attempt to understand why the allies in their more powerful ships were so easily defeated, and historians will argue over the significance of the British victory and Nelson's standing among the great commanders. Were the British gunners so much better trained than their rivals? Was Nelson's opposite number, Admiral Villeneuve, an incompetent, as the French believe? Did Trafalgar really ensure that Napoleon could not invade England? Did the battle successfully clear the seas of enemy warships for the rest of the French war? Was Nelson a naval genius, or a lucky gambler? These and other questions deserve to be put and analysed, as we celebrate a great moment in the history of Britain and the British Empire or pick over the rags of a national myth—depending on our point of view. But in the age of the common man, and in the midst of another war where ordinary young men and women have once more been sent to fight, supposedly, in defence of our national security, it seems right to give proper space on the public stage to some of the lesser actors in the battle, who obeyed Nelson's final signal and did their duty.

In choosing to write a professional biography about a naval surgeon, we intend not only to bring to life the medical career of an unsung hero but also to ensure that the naval medical service receives its proper due in any assessment of the Trafalgar campaign. The battle was won in part because the crews of the British fleet were healthier than their foes, and in consequence could fire broadsides and manoeuvre their ships more quickly. In the course of the war the navy had at last begun to win the fight against disease, owing to the new emphasis placed on hygiene and prophylaxis. While many of Villeneuve's sailors were ill and weak, Nelson commanded crews which were healthy and fit, thanks in particular to the conquest of scurvy through regularly drinking lemon juice and eating onions. When the *Victory* briefly returned to Spithead in August 1805, after two years at sea and chasing the combined fleet across the Atlantic and back, the ship's surgeon could report with pride that there was not a single man in the sick bay. Beatty's achievements, though, were matched by the hundreds of other young surgeons who served in the Royal Navy during the twenty-year war with France. He was efficient and dedicated, but not an exceptional doctor. Although he ultimately rose higher in the service than most, he was not a pioneer. His professional biography, then, can stand as a figure for the whole service.[2]

On the other hand, Beatty's career deserves reconstructing more than the large majority of his peers', albeit their contribution to the health and morale of the navy was just as great. Beatty was not just a surgeon. He was also a myth-maker. As the surgeon who attended the dying hero and later performed the autopsy on the body, Beatty understandably made the most of his good fortune, publishing in early 1807 his *Authentic Narrative of the Death of Lord Nelson*. It was principally through this text that the British public and the world learnt for the first time of the mortally wounded admiral's selflessness and stoicism, his request that Hardy should kiss him as the captain took his leave, and his constantly repeated dying words: 'Thank God I have done my duty.' Beatty's narrative was the stuff of which legends are made, and generations of historians have uncritically pillaged the text ever since. In an important respect, then, Beatty forged the myth of the dying Nelson. Much more than Devis, whose painting is not widely known among today's public, it was Nelson's surgeon who eternally placed the death of the hero in the minds of the British nation and created a word-image which would be honoured unto parody.

This biography is underpinned by an ongoing prosopographical study of nearly 900 army and navy surgeons who served in the British armed forces during the French wars.[3] The story of Beatty's personal career, therefore, is securely grounded in its professional context.[4] The details of his life are

---

[2] The only work in recent years to make more than passing reference to the fitness of the British crews during the long French war is Stephen R. Bown, *The Age of Scurvy: How a Surgeon, a Mariner and a Gentleman Helped Britain Win the Battle of Trafalgar* (Chichester, 2003), ch. 9. Sadly, it is not based on archival sources.

[3] The starting-points for the prosopography are two sets of service records which exist in the National Archive, Kew. The first, TNA W025/3904–11, consists of a collection of pro-forma documents distributed by the Army Medical Board to army surgeons in service or on half-pay in the years following the end of the French wars, where they were asked to record details of their place of origin, education, and army career to date. The second set, TNA ADM 104/12–14, comprises a collection of service records proper drawn up in 1835 for all active and inactive navy surgeons who had joined the service between 1774 and 1815. Except for giving the surgeon's age in 1835, they provide no details about background or education, but, since they were thereafter updated, they do contain valuable information about the surgeons' later life, including often their wives' names. The prosopography is based on a random sample of 454 army and 430 navy surgeons, between a third and a half of the total recorded. From this starting-point, and using many other archival and printed sources, it has been possible over the last five years to build up a detailed portrait of the origins, education, military and civilian career, family fortunes, wealth, and intellectual interests of the men who staffed the army and navy medical services during the French wars.

[4] The chief conclusions of this study will appear in Marcus Ackroyd *et al.*, *Advancing with the Army: Professionalization and Social Mobility in the Army Medical Corps 1790–1850* (Oxford, 2006).

largely drawn from letters and documents in the National Archive, British Library, National Maritime Museum, the Royal Naval Museum Portsmouth, and the Wellcome Institute Library, and to a lesser extent from material in provincial libraries and archives in England, Scotland, and Northern Ireland. The book attempts to cover the whole of Beatty's life from his birth in Londonderry in 1773 to his death in London in 1842. Particular attention, however, is given to Beatty's service with the Mediterranean Fleet in 1804–5, his role at the Battle of Trafalgar, and the part that he subsequently played in preparing the body for Nelson's state funeral and stabilizing the narrative of Nelson's death. This emphasis seems legitimate for several reasons. Not only was this the one period in his life when Beatty was caught up in events of peculiar national importance, but Trafalgar and its aftermath were formative moments in his life and career. It was his privileged position as surgeon on the *Victory* that gave him the opportunity to present a narrative of Nelson's death which would command national consent. The book, then, does not just emphasize Beatty's role as a myth-maker, but explores the myth's construction. It builds on the important insights into the deification of Nelson in Andrew Lambert's recent biography, but goes further in questioning the reliability of even the hero's famous last words. Lambert says much about the apotheosis of Nelson in art, but nothing about the construction of Beatty's *Authentic Narrative,* which is accepted as gospel.[5]

This book could not have been written without the assistance of a large number of enthusiastic naval, local, and family historians, archivists, and librarians in Britain and Ireland, who painstakingly assisted our relentless enquiries for information about Beatty and his family. We owe them an enormous debt of gratitude, particularly Brian Mitchell of the Derry Genealogical Centre, Freya McClements, Tim Clayton, and the staff of the Londonderry Public Library. Our thanks too must go to the surgeon's collateral descendant, Peter Beattie, who allowed us to find our way through the complex maze of the Beatty family website, to the National Maritime Museum in allowing us to reproduce a number of its paintings, engravings, and photographs, to the HBOS archive in Edinburgh for allowing us to view the minute books of the Clerical, Medical there, to Matthew Sheldon of the Royal Naval Museum, Portsmouth, to the Bank of England archives, to Peter Drew of Pembroke Interactive for permitting us to use the images of the *Victory,* and to Lord Digby for allowing us to consult the papers of Admiral

---

[5] Andrew Lambert, *Nelson: Britannia's God of War* (London, 2004), pt. iv.

Sir Henry Digby. Our research was financed primarily by the Wellcome Trust, who provided a grant to support John Cardwell for the year 2003–4. The Trust's generosity and enthusiastic backing for our desire to place medicine at the centre of the Trafalgar campaign ultimately made the book possible. This simple acknowledgement of the Trust's contribution cannot do justice to our continued appreciation of its support.

Laurence Brockliss
John Cardwell
Michael Moss

McFarlane Library,
Magdalen College
31 January 2005

Contents

List of Illustrations

Cover and Frontispiece: Arthur William Devis, *The Death of Nelson* (1807) (by kind permission of the National Maritime Museum, London)

1. The Sick Bay on the *Victory* (by kind permission of the Commanding Officer of HMS *Victory*, Portsmouth)

2. Arthur William Devis, *William Beatty: Portrait as Physician of the Fleet*, (*c*.1806) (by kind permission of the National Maritime Museum, London)

3. Beatty's Examination for the Position of Naval Surgeon, 1795 (by kind permission of the Royal College of Surgeons, London)

4. The Court Martial Verdict, 1795 (by kind permission of The National Archive, Kew)

5. Thomas Whitcombe, *Capture of the Santa Brigida by the Alcmene* (1800) (Courtauld Institute of Art, London: Photographic Survey of Private Collections)

6. The Cockpit of the *Victory* (by kind permission of the Commanding Officer of HMS *Victory*, Portsmouth)

7. Beatty's Surgical Instruments (by kind permission of the Royal College of Physicians and Surgeons, Glasgow)

8. The *Victory*'s Casualty List at the Battle of Trafalgar (by kind permission of The National Archive, Kew)

9. Beatty's Autopsy Report, December 1805 (by kind permission of the Wellcome Library, London)

10. The Bullet Which Killed Nelson (by kind permission of The Royal Collection, Windsor)

11. Benjamin West, *Death of Nelson* (1806) (by kind permission of the Walker Art Gallery, Liverpool)

12. Arthur William Devis, *Lord Viscount Nelson . . . in the dress he wore when he received his mortal wound* (engraving, 1806; printed in William Beatty, *Authentic Narrative of the Death of Lord Nelson*, 1807) (by kind permission of the National Maritime Museum, London)

13. Benjamin West, *Death of Lord Nelson in the Cockpit of the Victory* (1809) (by kind permission of the National Maritime Museum, London, Greenwich Hospital Collection)

List of Maps, Table, and Figure

Maps

Table

Figure

List of Abbreviations

Add. MSS	Additional Manuscripts
ADM	Admiralty
BL	British Library, London
CGM	Clerical, General and Medical Life Assurance Archives, Bristol
DNB	*Oxford Dictionary of National Biography*
GRO	General Registry Office, London
HO	Home Office
IGI	International Genealogical Index (website)
IR	Inland Revenue
KCL	King's College, London
Minterne	Minterne Magna, Papers of Sir Henry Digby, Dorset
NAS	National Archives of Scotland, Edinburgh
NAI	National Archives of Ireland, Dublin
NLI	National Library of Ireland, Dublin
NC	*Naval Chronicle*
NMM	National Maritime Museum, Greenwich
NMP	Royal Naval Museum, Portsmouth
Prob	Probate
PRONI	Public Record Office of Northern Ireland, Belfast
RAMC	Royal Army Medical Corps

TNA   The National Archive (formerly the Public Record Office), Kew

WL   The Wellcome Library, London

WO   War Office

Note

The dates of army and navy surgeons where known are given in the text when an individual is first mentioned.

During the French Revolutionary and Napoleonic Wars, Royal Navy warships were divided into rates according to the number of their guns as follows:

First   100–120
Second   90 and 98
Third   64–84
Fourth   50–60
Fifth   30–44
Sixth   20–28

First and Second Rates had three guns decks, and Third and Fourth Rates had two. These classes were described as ships of the line for their ability to fight in the line of battle. By this time, only Fourth Rates mounting sixty or more guns were considered powerful enough to lie in the line of battle. Frigates, sloops and brigs were smaller, cruising warships.[1]

[1] N. A. M. Rodger, *The Command of the Ocean: A Naval History of Britain: 1649–1815* (London, 2004), xxvi–xxvii.

[The Naval Surgeon]

Oft let me, too, at morning hours, be near
The sick man's friend, immersed in useful care;
Serious yet cheerful; of unruffled mind;
Fixed in his purpose; resolute yet kind;
Humane in manners; blest with ready skill
That traces to its source each latent ill.
See, as he walks his round in sober state,
And anxious expectations on him wait,
Neatness and order follow in his train,
Attend his beck and smooth the couch of pain.
With unobtrusive eye, yet glancing keen,
Th'acute expression scarce a moment seen,
He marks as flitting o'er the averted cheek,
His torture though the sufferer scorns to speak:
While danger claims the firm unshrinking hand,
He softens anguish with attentions bland,
And haply mingles praise. Thrice grateful sound!
The sweetest balm that soothes a sailor's wound.

Or where out-stretched, yon form unnervate lies,
While half dissevered seem all earthly ties,
In silent languor on the feverous bed,
Where reason wavering stays, where hope has fled;—
What trembling joy the death pale visage shows,
As from the lips th'auspicious presage flows!
A lust'rous beam lights up the vacant eye,
The fleeting visions of despondence fly:
And life, and strength, and circling years, and taste
Of future bliss, in fancy bright are traced.

(Thomas Downey, *Naval Poems*
(London, 1813), 60–2: from
'Pleasures of the Naval Life', canto II)

(Downey had by then been a naval
surgeon for eighteen years; William
Beatty subscribed to the volume.)

1

The Naval Surgeon During the French Wars

THE MEDICAL PROFESSION AT THE TURN OF THE NINETEENTH CENTURY

At the turn of the nineteenth century there was no medical profession in the new United Kingdom of Britain and Ireland, as the term would be understood today.[1] Until parliament passed the Medical Act in 1858 and established a register of licensed practitioners, most doctors were uncertificated and had never had their competence examined. To all intents and purposes, there was no constraint on anyone setting up as a medical practitioner, beyond the fear of being prosecuted under the criminal law by disillusioned patients and their relatives when treatment went wrong. In most continental countries medicine over the centuries had gradually become a regulated corporative craft. Distinction was carefully made between physicians, who treated internal diseases, surgeons, who looked after external lesions, and apothecaries, who supplied the remedies. Each had its separate system of training and certification, physicians being deemed superior to the other two on the grounds that they had to study medicine at university and take a degree. Certificated practitioners alone could legally proffer medical assistance, their monopoly backed up in most parts of Europe by the presence of guilds or professional associations which controlled and organized medical practice in the towns and surrounding countryside.[2] In the British Isles, in

---

[1] Penelope J. Corfield, *Power and the Professions in Britain 1700–1850* (London, 1995), ch. 6; Irvine Loudon, *Medical Care and the General Practitioner, 1750–1850* (Oxford, 1986); Roy and Dorothy Porter, *The Patients' Progress: Doctors and Doctoring in Eighteenth-Century England* (Cambridge, 1989); Anne Digby, *Making a Medical Living: Doctors and Patients in the English Market for Medicine, 1720–1911* (Cambridge, 1994).

[2] Mary Lindemann, *Medicine and Society in Early Modern Europe* (Cambridge, 1999), esp. ch. 6; Laurence Brockliss, 'Organisation, Training and the Medical Marketplace in the Eighteenth Century', in Peter Elmer (ed.), *The Healing Arts: Health, Society and Disease in Europe 1500–1800* (Manchester, 2004), 346–71.

contrast, the state had never decreed that medical practice should be confined to licensed practitioners and the guild system had never properly developed. In the eighteenth century only London, Edinburgh, Dublin, and Glasgow had medical guilds representing the three medical arts. Although they too in the past had been granted, and attempted to establish, a monopoly of practice in their respective cities—or in the case of the Dublin corporations over the whole island of Ireland—their power to enforce compliance had begun to be eroded. The Dublin apothecaries continued to fight to stop anyone in Ireland dispensing medicines who was not a member of their Society, but the other guilds had largely thrown in the towel. In consequence, interloping was rife, especially in London, where only a minority of practitioners belonged to the established corporations, and where members of the Apothecaries' Company in particular no longer stuck to their appointed last.

Nonetheless, if medical practice in the British Isles was largely carried on in an unregulated marketplace, an important boundary divided the trained from the untrained practitioner, however much their method of healing was often the same. Many—perhaps most—Britons when sick sought medical advice, if they sought any at all, from the plethora of Ladies-Bountiful, wise-women, blacksmiths, bone-setters, hangmen, and quacks whose nostrums and potions were readily available in virtually every village and town. These untrained, often part-time practitioners, however, need to be distinguished from doctors who had served a formal medical apprenticeship of three to five years with a properly trained surgeon-apothecary, and who had been taught how to mix medicines, dress wounds, set fractures, deliver babies, and treat common-or-garden ailments. Such men were not uncultured bores but had usually received a good classical education before beginning their medical training in their early to mid teens. From the mid-eighteenth century, too, an increasing number of these so-called general practitioners had pursued their medical studies more deeply after serving their apprenticeships, rather than setting up their plate immediately.

Historically, the universities of Britain and Ireland had offered little opportunity for medical study, and doctors who wanted an academic training had been forced to go abroad, particularly to Leiden.[3] As a result, only a small proportion had enjoyed such a training. In the course of the eighteenth century, on the other hand, the thirst for a fuller understanding of anatomy, surgery, and patient-care in the Age of Enlightenment became so great, and

---

[3] E. Ashworth Underwood, *Boerhaave's Men at Leyden and After* (Edinburgh, 1977), esp. chs. 1–4.

the numbers striving to study abroad so large, that proper facilities were inevitably developed at home. By the end of the eighteenth century Glasgow and Dublin universities were only on the point of developing their own successful medical schools, but Edinburgh already possessed one of the leading faculties of medicine in Europe. It offered high-quality teaching in all branches of the science, and only awarded a doctorate after a rigorous examination whose chief component was an original dissertation in Latin. London, too, was already a vibrant centre of medical education. Although as yet without a university, the capital had a growing number of hospitals to service its huge number of poor, staffed by physicians and surgeons eager to cash in on the new interest in medical learning. In consequence, by the end of the eighteenth century the leading London hospitals were in turn becoming medical schools, offering prospective practitioners the chance to watch complex operations, gain experience in dissection, and study a cross-section of diseases. And the more courses on offer, the greater the demand. What had begun as a minority preference had become by the early nineteenth century *de rigueur*. By 1815 Edinburgh had 2,000 medical students and London 400 walking the wards.[4]

A second, if less significant, boundary divided the certificated from the uncertificated trained practitioner. The large majority of medical students at the turn of the nineteenth century spent one or two years at one or more of the burgeoning medical schools and then went home without submitting themselves to an examination. A small but growing proportion, in contrast, completed their studies by taking a degree or gaining a diploma or licence from one of the medical corporations. Traditionally, few had done so. Holding a medical doctorate always gave the practitioner a certain social cachet, since it meant he could call himself a physician and stand apart from his peers; but before the development of the Edinburgh medical school this does not seem to have been a good enough incentive for doctors to obtain a medical degree in any numbers, even when a diploma could be obtained fairly easily in certain continental universities, such as Rheims.[5] Similarly,

[4] Lisa Rosner, *Medical Education in the Age of Improvement* (Edinburgh, 1991); Guenter Risse, *Hospital Life in Enlightenment Scotland* (Cambridge, 1986); Susan Lawrence, *Charitable Knowledge: Hospital Pupils and Practitioners in Eighteenth-Century London* (Cambridge, 1996); Derek Dow and Michael Moss, 'The Medical Curriculum at Glasgow in the Early Nineteenth Century', *History of Universities*, 7 (1988), 227–58.

[5] Laurence Brockliss, 'Medicine and the Small University in Eighteenth-Century France', in G. P. Brizzi and Jacques Verger (eds.), *Le università minori in Europa (secoli XV–XIX)* (Soveria Mannelli, 1998), 263–4 (medical doctorates bestowed on graduates from the British Isles, 1600–1800).

those who gained a qualification from one of the medical corporations were usually only people who aspired to join the local medical elite and occupy the highest echelons of the profession. They were not common-or-garden provincial doctors.

The power of the medical corporations at the turn of the nineteenth century was real, but it was social rather than legal.[6] By tradition, they were filled with the wealthiest and most important practitioners in the local medical community. Moreover, the corporations of physicians and surgeons in London, Edinburgh, and Dublin were royal institutions, whose status and authority were strengthened by Crown patronage. Membership guaranteed a socially prominent clientele, perhaps even access to court and government circles. Not surprisingly, entry could be expensive, the conditions of entry were strict, and nepotism was rife. No one could become a fellow of a college of physicians without gaining a medical degree from the local university, while no one could enter any of the corporations without being examined for its diploma or licence. As London had no university, the Royal College of Physicians in the capital insisted that its fellows have medical degrees from the non-teaching faculties of Oxford and Cambridge, a particularly expensive and onerous condition which effectively restricted membership to members of the Church of England because the two English universities were con-fessionally closed.[7] Candidates with doctorates from other universities could only become licentiates of the college and could not sit on the governing body. Traditionally, therefore, for most trained practitioners the difficulties in joining a medical corporation made the game not worth the candle.

In the later Georgian age, however, practitioners who had no intention of residing in the city in question or limiting their practice to the relevant spe-cialism started to seek membership of the medical corporations, especially the colleges of surgeons. Equally, from the middle of the eighteenth century the numbers seeking medical degrees, often late in their career, began to rise. In both cases the practitioners presumably aimed to raise their status locally. As the number of trained medical practitioners seems to have grown rapidly in this period, this made perfect sense as a career move: the ambitious general practitioner needed to distinguish himself from the herd. The corporations, in

---

[6] There are a number of solid but old-fashioned histories of the Royal Colleges, notably Sir George Clark, *A History of the Royal College of Physicians of London*, 2 vols. (London, 1964). The only recent study is J. Geyer-Gordesch *Physicians and Surgeons in Glasgow: A History of the Royal College of Physicians and Surgeons of Glasgow, c. 1599–1868* (London, 1999).

[7] Non-Anglicans could not take degrees at Oxford and Cambridge until the 1850s.

response, placed no obstacles in the way of the surge of applicants but grate-fully pocketed the fees. The universities too did nothing to halt the trend by making a doctorate more difficult to obtain. Indeed, the universities of Aberdeen and St Andrews, whose medical faculties were all but dormant, only encouraged the development: they happily oiled the wheels of the changing market demand by selling applicants a medical degree by post, provided the request was supported by one or two respected physicians.[8] All the same, before the end of the French war the enthusiasm for certification was always limited. The trickle of applications only became a flood in 1815 when parliament passed the Apothecaries' Act, which declared that no one could be a general practitioner in England who had not been licensed by the London Society of Apothecaries, unless he held a medical diploma from another corporation or university, or had served as a medical officer in the army or navy.[9]

THE NAVAL MEDICAL SERVICE

Surgeons have sailed with the Royal Navy since its inception in the reign of Henry VIII.[10] Although sea battles were infrequent and usually brief—the week-long engagement with the Spanish Armada in the English Channel in 1588 was very much an exception—naval service for both ratings and officers was always hazardous. Surgeons had to be constantly on hand to deal with the broken limbs, strains, and sores which were the daily companions of life at sea in the age of sail, where accidents were commonplace, discipline severe, and sexual behaviour often lax. From the mid-seventeenth century, too, as the navy's ships stayed longer at sea and moved out of the Channel to augment and defend Britain's burgeoning empire, the surgeon also had to be a physician. The navy of the eighteenth and first half of the nineteenth centuries was continually hit by lethal epidemics of dysentery, typhus, scurvy, malaria, and yellow fever. Although through better hygiene and diet the annual death rate greatly improved in the Nelsonian era—from 1 in 42 in 1779 to 1 in 143 in

---

[8] One famous surgeon to buy a degree was the Gloucestershire practitioner and father of vaccination Edward Jenner (1749–1823), who became a St Andrews MD in 1792.

[9] Loudon, *Medical care*, 159–88.

[10] Unless otherwise stated, this section relies heavily on vol. 3 of Christopher Lloyd and J. L. S. Coulter, *Medicine and the Navy 1200–1900*, 4 vols. (Edinburgh, 1961). The most recent study of the Royal Navy during the century-long struggle with France, N. A. M. Rodger's, *The Command of the Ocean: A Naval History of Britain, 1649–1815* (London, 2004), provides limited information about naval medicine.

1813—only scurvy, caused by a deficiency in vitamin C, was successfully (if not completely) brought under control, thanks to the introduction of lemon juice in all the fleets in the mid-1790s. Nelson himself, already weakened by disease when he joined the navy aged 12, was a prey to malaria throughout his career, while he nearly died from the yellow fever that he contracted in 1780 during his service in Central America.

The duties of the naval surgeon at the turn of the nineteenth century were laid down in the *Regulations and Instructions Relating to His Majesty's Service at Sea*, initially published in 1731. Throughout the eighteenth century the regulations were no more than a brief series of articles, but it was a sign of the growing importance of the medical service to the navy that they were greatly extended in 1806.[11] Essentially, the surgeon was expected to visit the sick twice a day, present a daily sick list to the captain, and keep a log of his activities. Minor injuries and ailments were quickly dealt with at the daily sick muster, but more serious cases were confined to the ship's sick berth where the sailors could be isolated from the rest of the crew. Traditionally, the sick berth had been no more than a canvas cubicle between two gun ports, situated anywhere in the vessel where there was room, and often unhygienic and airless. While commander-in-chief of the Channel Fleet, however, Admiral Earl St Vincent, who was the government minister in charge of the navy as first lord of the Admiralty from 1801 to 1804, had been so impressed by the sick berth set up by Adam Markham, captain of the *Centaur*, that he ordered that henceforth it should be located in all ships on the upper deck under the forecastle, for maximum ventilation. The sick berth on the *Victory* at the time of Trafalgar was in consequence an upper deck wing-berth, and no longer a death-trap (see Ill. 1).

The sick bay was only intended to accommodate a handful of men. When a ship was struck by an epidemic, a much larger area had to be commandeered. The sick bay, too, was not used during engagements, when the surgeon was required by the 1731 regulations to retreat to the hold or orlop deck, which were located below the waterline, and keep himself safe. In smaller vessels makeshift operating theatres were erected in the cable tier, the section of the orlop where the ship's cables were stored, before action commenced, but in ships of the line the surgeon set up an operating platform and laid out his instruments in the cockpit, the area of the orlop immediately behind the cable tier, in which the midshipmen, master's mates, and surgeon's

---

[11] *Regulations and Instructions relating to his Majesty's Service at Sea* (London, 1731), 129–32; *Regulations and Instructions* (London, 1806), 265–86.

mates were usually quartered. This was far from ideal. Unbearably hot, lit only by lanterns, and often close to the magazine, it was far too small. At the Battle of Camperdown on 11 October 1797, Robert Young, surgeon on the *Ardent*, was completely swamped by the number of casualties:

Ninety wounded were brought down during the action. The whole cockpit deck, cabins, wing berths and part of the cable tier, together with my platform and my preparations for dressing were covered with them. So that for a time they were laid on each other at the foot of the ladder where they were brought down, and I was obliged to go on deck to the Commanding Officer to state the situation and apply for men to go down the main hatchway and move the foremost of the wounded into the tiers and wings, and thus make room in the cockpit.[12]

By the end of the long war with France the navy had some one thousand ships in commission and employed 140,000 officers and men. Most ships of the line, including twenty-four of the twenty-seven which fought at Trafalgar, carried crews of more than 500 men. Few warships, however, and especially the larger line-of-battle ships, had a medical establishment commensurate with their needs. By the end of the seventeenth century it had become accepted that each ship in service, whatever her size, had to carry a surgeon's mate lest the crew be left with no medical assistance if the surgeon died. At the same time, it was established that surgeons in the largest ships of the line were entitled to extra assistants. In Nelson's day, however, provision was far from liberal. Under an Order in Council of 23 January 1805, only fourth-rates and above were allowed more than one mate, and even the largest ships of the line were only entitled to three. But these were optimum levels of staffing, and were seldom met. It was not uncommon for ships of the line to sail without a surgeon's mate and for small ships to put to sea without a surgeon at all. Even the *Victory* at Trafalgar, with her 100 guns and approximately 820 officers and men, did not have her full complement of mates. Beatty only had the services of two trained assistants, Neil Smith (d. 1819) and William Westenburg. Like other naval surgeons, in and out of battle, he had to rely on the support of other members of the crew, released from their normal duties. The nursing staff were usually pressed landsmen who showed next to no aptitude for the rigours of a seafaring life and were

---

[12] TNA, ADM 101/85: Young's log.

known as 'loblolly boys'. But sometimes the nurses were women, since many captains allowed a few warrant officers and men to have their wives on board. Although frowned upon by Evangelical Protestants (of whom there were many among the navy's officer corps) and disciplinarians, it was a useful way of supplementing the meagre medical establishment. Few of these women have left any record of their existence, for their names were not included on the ship's books, but one Christiaan White, who was present at the Battle of the Nile, has left an account of her experiences.[13]

The Nelsonian navy could cope reasonably well with only a handful of medical men on even its largest ships, because over the previous century it had developed an effective back-up service. From the time of the Third Dutch War (1672–4), it was common for each fleet to be supported by a hospital ship, to which the long-term sick could be transferred. The model in the eighteenth century was the *Blenheim*, which had its upper and lower decks converted in 1743 to take 255 patients, who were segregated into four areas according to whether they were suffering from skin irritations, simple fever, dysentery, or malaria. Although never purpose-built and usually vessels about to be decommissioned, most of these ships seem to have fulfilled their function reasonably satisfactorily. In April 1797, when the sailors of the Channel Fleet mutinied at Sheerness over the conditions of service and asked the lords of the Admiralty that they 'will be pleased seriously to look into the state of the sick on board H. M. Ships',[14] their target was the disease-ridden flagship the *Sandwich*, overcrowded with new recruits. The mutineers had no complaint about the Channel Fleet's hospital ship, the *Spanker*, besides the quality of the food.

The hospital ship was the medical command centre of a naval fleet. While its medical personnel, according to the 1805 Order in Council, was to consist of a surgeon and three assistants, it was also the customary quarters of the 'physician of the fleet'. This was a senior medical practitioner, normally with a university degree, who was responsible for the overall health of the crews. He was expected to visit the other ships in the fleet, inspect the surgeons' medical chests and journals, and prepare a weekly health report for the benefit of the admiral. Although he had no direct authority over the ships' surgeons, who answered in the first instance to their captain, he was intended to be proactive and encourage medical best practice. Under the new naval regulations

---

[13] WL, MS 3677.   [14] Lloyd and Coulter, *Medicine and the Navy*, iii. 162.

of 1808 he was also given the power to recommend surgeons for promotion. Most physicians of the fleet had begun as surgeons' mates and had long experience of life at sea. They played an important role in reducing the mortality-rate in the Nelsonian era, none more so than Thomas Trotter (1760–1832), who was physician of the Channel Fleet in the mid-1790s under Admiral Viscount Howe. Trotter joined the navy at 19, then nine years later took a degree at Edinburgh. An indefatigable reformer, who bombarded the Admiralty with suggestions for improving seamen's health and the surgeons' conditions of service, he published his experience on board the hospital ship *Charon* in the form of a three-volume manual entitled *Medicina Nautica*, which appeared between 1797 and 1802.[15]

By the early nineteenth century, moreover, the facilities of the hospital ships were supplemented by the growing number of purpose-built land hospitals, which often received the sick and injured directly. In the seventeenth century the navy had had no hospital of its own, but had relied on the local mayor to find board, lodging, and medical care for the sick and wounded landed in the Channel ports. The two old London hospitals, Bart's and St Thomas's, had also been forced to set aside beds for sailors. In the course of the eighteenth century, on the other hand, the navy gained a permanent medical presence on shore. The first and most famous naval hospital was opened at Greenwich in 1705, in buildings designed by Sir Christopher Wren. Greenwich, though, was never intended to house officers and men on active service. Like the earlier army hospital sited at Chelsea, it was a refuge for the retired, although after 1771 it did have its own infirmary (today the Dreadnought Seamen's Hospital).[16] It was only from the middle of the century that the navy had hospitals for its serving personnel, with the foundation of Haslar at Portsmouth, occupied from 1754, and the infirmary at Plymouth, completed in 1762.

Haslar, designed by John Turner and Theodore Jacobsen, was and is a gigantic three-sided building, which cost £100,000 to build and some £14,000 per annum to maintain. By the end of the eighteenth century it could accommodate nearly 2,000 patients. Plymouth Infirmary, built around a quadrangle, could only take 1,250, but was nearly as expensive to run.

[15] Thomas Trotter, *Medicina Nautica: An Essay on the Diseases of Seamen*, 3 vols. (London, 1797–1802). The preface was to Admiral Howe. Despite Trotter's significance, there is no biography. He was chary of using lemon juice as a general prophylactic against scurvy.

[16] The most recent study is John Bold, *An Architectural History of the Royal Hospital for Seamen and the Queen's House* (London, 2000).

Both had a large medical establishment. At Haslar in the 1780s there was a physician, two surgeons, a dispenser (or apothecary in charge of the drugs), seven surgeons' mates, and three further assistants, plus a large number of female nurses. By 1805 the roll had doubled. Both too were initially set up to be administered by the medical staff without any assistance from regular naval officers. Thus, at Haslar, the effective governor of the institution from 1758 to 1783, and the man responsible for drawing up the detailed regulations under which it came to operate from December 1777, was its first chief physician, James Lind—the naval surgeon who had first promoted the use of citrus fruits as a prophylactic against scurvy.[17]

In the first years of the war neither establishment came up to the exacting standards of Thomas Trotter, second physician at Haslar in the early 1790s, who had concentrated on improving cleanliness. The medical practitioners were underpaid, the finances chaotic and the patients ill-disciplined. As a result, in 1794 Admiral Howe, on Trotter's prompting, set up a Board of Inquiry, and the following year an Order in Council of 3 July 1795 placed the administration in the hands of a post-captain and three lieutenants. Even then there remained problems, especially in the realm of patient-care. The Devon hospital, complained Trotter, still lacked a purpose-built operating theatre, and the medical staff paid too much attention to earning money on the side from civilian patients, whom they looked after at the expense of seamen:

At the beginning of this war a seaman fell from the top of a ship fitting at Plymouth, and was wounded dreadfully. He was immediately conveyed on shore, but nobody could be found to open the gate of the hospital. At last access was obtained; but not a surgeon could be found; he was attending a gentleman of great fortune in Cornwall. It is to be added, the man died of haemorrhage from his wounds.[18]

The situation presumably improved dramatically after 1805, when hospital staff were forbidden to maintain a civilian practice. But Trotter never obtained satisfaction on a further issue—the development of Haslar as a training school for junior naval surgeons. In his view, Haslar could become the Mecca of European medical practice: he called for the establishment of a library and the introduction of clinical instruction. In this, though, he was

---

[17] Lind (1716–94) had been on active service overseas in the late 1730s and 1740s. Lacking a proper understanding of the cause of scurvy, he had initially suggested a number of remedies for the disease, including spruce beer. This was tried with disastrous results at Quebec in the winter of 1759–60: see Erica Charters, ' "The Most Inveterate Scurvy": Disease and the British Garrison at Quebec, 1754–1780' unpublished paper (2004).   [18] Trotter, *Medicina Nautica*, iii. 18–20.

over-optimistic. Although he himself seems to have given a clinical course in the hospital, it would be 1827 before either dream was properly fulfilled.

Haslar and Plymouth remained the two principal naval hospitals during the wars. But others were established temporarily at Deal, Sheerness, Yarmouth, and Dartmouth to cope with the large numbers of sick in the Channel and North Sea fleets. More significantly, naval hospitals in this period came to be founded on British territories all over the globe, to serve the other squadrons far from home. Typical was the hospital set up on Malta in 1804, the Mediterranean island formerly owned by the Knights of St John, which was occupied by the British at the turn of the nineteenth century. Intended for 150 sailors of the Mediterranean Fleet, the first physician appointed to the hospital was Dr Leonard Gillespie (1758–1842). Gillespie, a native of Armagh, had been surgeon on the *Majestic* at the Glorious First of June—the name later given to Admiral Howe's defeat of the French fleet on that day 1794 out in the Atlantic—and had later served in the West Indies. The publication in 1800 of his observations of the yellow fever epidemic which hit the army and navy in 1794–6 marked him out as another dynamic member of the medical service dedicated to improving the sailors' lot.[19] Instead of going to Malta, however, he was appointed physician of the Mediterranean Fleet under Nelson, the post that he occupied until shortly before Trafalgar.

The size of the naval medical service during the conflict cannot be properly known until the publication of the first official *Navy List* in 1814. According to *Steel's Navy List*, which was published privately from 1782, there were 550 naval surgeons in 1793 and 720 in 1806, but it only records the names of full surgeons and not their mates or assistants. The first official list reveals that the navy had more than 1,400 medical practitioners on its books by the end of the war: fourteen physicians, 850 surgeons, 500 assistant surgeons, twenty-five dispensers or apothecaries, and fifty hospital mates.[20] At this stage, although numbers were soon to be severely reduced (there were only 450 on active duty in 1838), the navy had a greater number of surgeons than the army, a much larger service.[21] Unlike the army, however, it lacked a separate medical department in overall charge of appointments and standards.

---

[19] L. Gillespie, *Observations on the Diseases which Prevailed on Board a part of His Majesty's Squadron, on the Leeward Island Station, between Nov. 1794 and April 1796* (London, 1800).

[20] *Steel's Original and Correct List of the Royal Navy, sub annis*; *Navy List*, 1814.

[21] There were 1,274 army surgeons in 1814: see Ackroyd *et al.*, *Advancing with the Army*, table 1.2.

Throughout the war the service was run by subcommittees of the Navy Board which had a number of duties.

At the outset the medics came under the authority of the Commissioners of the Sick and Hurt Board. This was a Board first established in 1664 and made permanent in 1702. Besides overseeing the health of seamen, it administered navy pensions, supported the widows and orphans of men who had died in service, and looked after prisoners of war. The number of commissioners varied over time, but from 1779 was fixed at five and in the 1790s included four physicians and one civilian, Sir William Gibbons, who each received £300 per year. From 1800 they were also assisted in fulfilling their medical duties by a separate inspector of hospitals, a post that the first lord of the Admiralty, St Vincent, had created for the former surgeon of his flagship, Dr Andrew Baird. In 1806, however, subsequent to the report of the thirteenth Parliamentary Commission of Naval Inquiry which revealed fiscal mismanagement over many years, the Sick and Hurt Board was subsumed in another subcommittee of the Navy Board, the Transport Board, which dealt with the movement of troops by sea. Thereafter, the medical service was basically run by one man, for the only one of the seven commissioners who had a medical background was Dr John Harness, a former physician of the fleet. Harness effectively controlled the service until 1817, when the Transport Board was merged in turn with the Victualling Board, which was responsible for the whole commissariat. This board again had one medical commissioner, Dr John Weir, who was already employed as a second inspector of naval hospitals. It was only in 1832 that an independent naval medical department was finally created under Sir William Burnett (1779–1861), who had served as a ship's surgeon at the battles of St Vincent, the Nile, and Trafalgar, and had been physician of the Mediterranean Fleet from 1810 to 1813.

The absence of a separate medical department during the French wars, however, did not mean that the navy was less well served than its sister service. In fact, the Army Medical Board was itself the subject of a parliamentary commission of inquiry in 1808 and its members roundly chastised for waste and favouritism. At the same time, the authors of the report praised the naval medical service for its comparative professionalism.[22] This positive verdict owed much to the reforming energy of the physician, Sir Gilbert Blane (1749–1834), who was a commissioner of the Sick and Hurt Board from

[22] *Fifth Report of the Commissioners of Military Enquiry: Army Medical Deparment* (London, 1808), 35–7, 57–8.

1795 to 1802. Unlike Trotter, Blane had never been a humble naval surgeon, but as Admiral George Rodney's personal doctor he had been made a physician of the fleet during the War of American Independence, and had continued to take an interest in naval medicine while physician at St Thomas' Hospital in London. Blane was a great collector of illness and mortality statistics, and would be the co-author of a paper on the human cost of the war which was published in 1815 in the leading medical journal of the period, the *Medico-Chirurgical Transactions*.[23] More importantly, from his observations while serving with Rodney, he was a convinced supporter of the value of lemon juice in the fight against scurvy. In consequence, when he joined the Board he was able to press the case of the anti-scorbutic much more forcibly than ever before. It was principally due to Blane, therefore, that Lind's discovery was finally adopted by the navy.[24]

THE SURGEONS

Like their counterparts in the British army, recruits to the naval medical service throughout the French war were mainly simple general practitioners who had recently finished their training. There was no requirement that recruits should have obtained a formal medical qualification before applying to enter the service, nor any demand that they should have already gained practical experience. The Admiralty insisted that their competence be assessed before they were warranted, but the examination was oral and entrants were not expected to offer a practical demonstration of their skill. As a result, most recruits were in their early twenties and wet behind the ears. All were volunteers. Unlike the French, the British armed forces did not attempt to conscript medical practitioners, though naval surgeons had been pressed in the seventeenth century.

Would-be naval medical officers normally first appeared before the board that was at that time in charge of the service, where they would be quizzed on their background and training. If satisfactory, they next received a letter addressed to the College of Surgeons in Lincoln's Inn Fields requesting that they be examined in their competence in surgery. The College, formerly the Company of Barber Surgeons of London, had the right to license surgeons for the navy, army, and East India Company, a privilege that in the first case

[23] Gilbert Blane, 'Statement of the Comparative Health of the British Navy from the Year 1774 to the Year 1814', *Medico-Chirurgical Transactions*, 6 (1815).   [24] Bown, *The Age of Scurvy*.

went back to Tudor times. From 1788, however, it had to share its monopoly with the Royal Colleges of Surgeons of Edinburgh and Dublin, which allowed Scottish and Irish recruits and English expatriates the chance, if they wished, to be initially examined locally before attending the Board.[25] Having passed the examination in surgery, the applicant had to take another in physic. Until 1799 this was conducted by the physician of Greenwich Hospital, but thereafter the task was devolved to the commissioners of the Sick and Hurt and their successors, and became the responsibility of one of the medical delegates or inspectors of hospitals.[26]

Candidates could be examined for the position of mate or surgeon, and were passed fit to serve in vessels of a particular rate according to their abilities. To gain promotion or move to a larger ship, therefore, many naval surgeons had to resit the examination a second or even third time. When Thomas Longmore of Blackfriars, whose warrants and letters home survive in the London Wellcome Library, joined the service as a surgeon's mate at the beginning of 1799, he was deemed sufficiently able in physic to serve as an assistant on any ship, but in surgery he was judged worthy of no better post than that of second mate on a third-rate. Six months later, after a period of service afloat on the gun vessel *Contest*, he qualified as a surgeon. Again, he demonstrated a sound knowledge of physic and was found good enough to serve on a second-rate. But his surgery still let him down, and the best that he could manage was to qualify for a fourth. [27]

The examiners' ability to judge an applicant's competence so precisely was not based on lengthy enquiry, for the oral examinations in physic and surgery, though testing, seldom lasted more than an hour. At Surgeons Hall candidates were dealt with in batches of six and seven, and each applicant was assigned to a particular examiner. If the experience in 1789 of Peter Cullen, a distant relative of the distinguished Edinburgh professor and nosologist William, is any guide, the occasion was one of dignified informality:

The examiners were seated at a semi-circular table, where were two or more candidates standing before it, and answering such questions as were put to them.

---

[25] Details about the examinations taken by individual applicants can be found in the archives of the three colleges.

[26] Army surgeons did not have to take an exam in physic until 1796. Cf. the favourable comments in this regard in Robert Hamilton, *The Duties of a Regimental Surgeon Considered*, 2 vols. (London, 1787), ii. 171–3.

[27] WL, RAMC, Longmore Papers, L6/1–4. Longmore's son later rose to the top of the army medical service.

Mr Cullen [his narrative is in the third person] having walked up to the table and made his bow, was asked his name, from whence he came, and for what purpose he meant to be examined? On answering that it was for the Naval Service, one of the examiners arose, and taking Mr Cullen to the side of the room, enquired his age, his apprenticeship, studies and practice in his profession. To all these Mr Cullen having returned a satisfactory reply, the examiner proceeded to question him on anatomy, physiology and surgery. Then stated some of the more important surgical cases or diseases, and how he would treat them. This gentleman was quite satisfied with Mr Cullen's proficiency, and taking him up to the centre of the table, where the President was sitting, said 'I find this young gentleman fully qualified as an Assistant Surgeon for His Majesty's Navy'. The President bowed to Mr Cullen, and desired him to pay one guinea as a fee.[28]

Once qualified, the new recruit received from the Board his certificate and warrant, then awaited his first posting. His specific qualification had no effect on his pay and status.

For the first part of the war the pay and conditions of naval surgeons were poor in comparison with their army counterparts. From the beginning, regimental surgeons were commissioned officers with the rank of captain, entitled to a smart red uniform and regimental buttons, had the prospect of earning 10–12 shillings a day after serving a number of years, and were guaranteed half-pay when their services were no longer required. From 1796, too, their assistants enjoyed similar benefits.[29] Naval surgeons, in contrast, received a flat salary of £5 per month and their assistants a mere £2–£3, while only the senior 320 surgeons were eligible for half-pay.[30] Moreover, they were only un-uniformed warrant officers so could not eat and drink in the wardroom by right. Rather, full surgeons had their own cabin off the gunroom where they lived with the master, purser, and chaplain, while their assistants messed with the midshipmen, slinging their hammock alongside boys possibly half their age. In addition, to add insult to injury, the surgeons had to purchase their own instruments and medicines, the latter supplied at high prices by the Navy Stock Company, an offshoot of the London Society of Apothecaries.

Not surprisingly, naval doctors resented their comparative inferiority and lobbied the Admiralty for an improvement in their position, and their fury became all the greater in 1804 when army surgeons received a considerable

[28] 'Memoirs of Peter Cullen', in *Five Naval Journals, 1789–1817*, ed. H. G. Thursfield, Navy Records Society (London, 1951), 49.
[29] Ackroyd *et al.*, *Advancing with the Army*, tables 1.3. and 1.4.
[30] The complex half-pay rules are laid down in *Steel's List of the Royal Navy*: e.g. Steel (1802), 52.

The Naval Surgeon During the French Wars

Table 1. Daily rates of pay for naval surgeons from 1805 (shillings/pence)

	Active service	Active service (after 10 years)	Active service (after 20 years)	Half-pay	Half-pay (after 10 years)	Retirement (after 20 years)	Retirement (after 30 years)
Assistant surgeons	6s. 6d.			2s.–3s.[a]			15s.
Surgeons	10s.	14s.[b]	18s.[c]	6s.		6s.[d]	15s.
Physicans	21s.	29s.		10s. 6d.	21s.		
Hospital surgeons	15s.	20s.					

Note: [a] More than two years service to qualify. After three years service = 3s. per day; [b] Includes service as assistant surgeon; [c] Includes service as assistant surgeon; [d] If forced to retire on grounds of ill-health, then entitled to 10s. per day.

Surgeons on active service were entitled to free provisions. Physicians not lodged in a hospital or serving afloat received a 21s. a week housing allowance. Hospital surgeons not accommodated in the hospital were given 15s. per week for housing. Widows of medical personnel who died in service were entitled to a pension which was assessed according to need. A new pay scale was established by Order in Council of 10 August 1840 but did not make major changes, except that assistant surgeons were thereafter paid on a sliding scale according to length of service ranging from 7s. to 10s. and could look forward to half-pay from 3s. to 5s. Surgeons now began at 11s. per day, and the sliding scale was more complicated but otherwise the full-pay and half-pay range was the same. Physicians, rechristened inspectors and deputy inspectors of Fleets and Hospitals, were a little better rewarded.

Sources: Charles Dunne, *The Chirurgical Candidate* (London, 1808), 89–97. TNA, ADM 105/39: pay scales (printed) 1840 and 1843.

pay rise. Among the petitions consequently forwarded was one from the surgeons of the Mediterranean Fleet, which was presented in October to Henry Dundas, Viscount Melville, first lord of the Admiralty 1804–5, with a supporting letter from their commander-in-chief, Lord Nelson. ' ... As the particular case of so valuable and so respectable a body of men is no doubt well known to your Lordship, it is not necessary for me to make any comments on the justice of their request.'[31]

Nelson's backing of the surgeons' campaign presumably carried considerable weight, and a few months later, in January 1805, an Order in Council gave the petitioners most of what they desired.[32] In the future naval surgeons were to be paid on a sliding scale, at a rate of 10s. a day when first posted to 18s. a day after twenty years of continuous service. Only their mates, now called assistants and given a daily wage of 6s. 6d., would continue to receive a

[31] Sir Nicholas Harris Nicolas (ed.), *The Dispatches and Letters of Lord Nelson*, 7 vols (London, 1845–6), vi. 237.

[32] Charles Dunne, *The Chirurgical Candidate* (London, 1808), 89–102: full details (part of a longer discussion of service as a naval surgeon). Dunne had served in the navy.

fixed salary. In addition, all members of the service would now be eligible for half-pay if they had served for at least two years, and surgeons who remained in the service for thirty years could look forward to a lucrative pension of 15*s.* per day or £273. 15*s.* per year. This was an enviable sum, for the average annual stipend of a minister in the Church of England in the first half of the nineteenth century was only £200.³³

More importantly for their pride, in a service where officers had a regulation dress but ordinary seamen did not, all naval doctors were to be 'allowed to wear a distinguishing uniform and to have similar rank with the officers of the same class in Your Majesty's land forces'.³⁴ Henceforth, surgeons were to wear a blue cloth coat, white or blue cloth waistcoat and breeches, and a plain hat, those at sea sporting a button bearing a plain anchor. Surgeons with the rank of physician would be differentiated by the two rows of gold lace round their coat cuffs (see Ill. 2). Three years later, moreover, full surgeons became 'warrant officers of wardroom rank', in effect essentially equal to commissioned officers, although they had to wait until 1843 to be awarded the formal privilege of holding a commission.

The official justification for the 1805 reform was that the Royal Navy had 'suffered materially in the present war from want of Surgeons and Surgeons' Mates', and that 'the difficulty in procuring qualified persons' was 'in great measure to be attributed to the more liberal provision made for the description of officers in Your Majesty's land forces'.³⁵ The negative picture of the navy surgeon painted by contemporaries, especially in the first half of the war, would suggest that an initiative to boost the quality of recruitment was badly needed. According to the Edinburgh surgeon John Bell (1763–1820), in a pamphlet printed in 1800 which had been addressed several years before to Earl Spencer, first lord of the Admiralty 1794–1801, the medical practitioner who joined either branch of the armed services in the 1790s cut a sorry figure. In his opinion, the recruit was socially disadvantaged and ignorant, and had gained admittance simply by passing 'a slight examination', thanks to learning 'by rote to answer the common questions'. In addition, Bell maintained, he was friendless. 'Thrown from childhood almost orphan on the world', his choice of a military career reflected lack of family support: 'Very

---

³³ Eric Evans, *The Forging of the Modern State: Early Industrial Britain 1783–1870* (London, 1983), 425 (table). In 1833 34% of Church of England benefices produced an income of less than £150.

³⁴ Order in Council, 23 Jan. 1805, preamble: cited in Lloyd and Coulter, *Medicine and the Navy*, iii. 32.   ³⁵ Ibid. iii. 32.

slender are his appointments; his education is limited and imperfect; he finds himself oppressive to his friends, and enters at once into the service from hard necessity and the difficulty of pursuing his studies; he enters, my lord, into the public service, not from enthusiasm for that service, but in despair.'[36] Such recruits, Bell believed, were murderers, not doctors. Among the navy's mates, he declared, there was not one who could perform the great operations of surgery.

A similar view was voiced by a number of surgeons in the service. In the same year Alexander Whyte, surgeon of the *Atlas*, had nothing but contempt for his three assistants. The third mate knew no Latin and could not spell common English words, while the first mate was even more ignorant and incompetent. And as for the second mate, an Irish BA, 'he could neither perform a simple operation of venesection [i.e. opening a vein to let blood], nor make up the most common medical preparations'.[37] Charles Dunne in 1808 went one better and claimed to have encountered a complete illiterate. 'While I was serving at the royal hospital at Haslar, I met with an assistant surgeon of the royal navy, there, who, on being ordered to write the case of a sick man he brought from his ship, was under the necessity, after much controversy, to confess he could not write at all.'[38]

At first sight this unflattering picture of the young naval surgeon in the first years of service does not seem implausible. This was an age when it would be expected that the tyro medical practitioner would return to his native hearth on completing his training rather than volunteer for the dangers and discomforts of service in the armed forces. That a surgeon chose the second option would suggest that he lacked the family connections and wealth to establish a lucrative practice at home, or that he had had an insufficient education to cut the mustard in a competitive marketplace. Arguably, the navy, even more than the army, would have had to scrape the bottom of the professional barrel to find its surgeons. Until 1805, as we saw, their pay was less and their status lower, while their chances of using the service as a launch-pad for a successful civilian career in later life were poor, as Trotter explained in his *Medicina Nautica*. Army surgeons were 'quartered in great towns' and had 'intercourse with polished society'. If interested in pursuing their studies, 'they are not cut off from information to be obtained from books; and their situation affords them opportunities to cultivate acquaintance with literary

[36] John Bell, *Memorial Concerning the Present State of Military and Naval Surgery* (Edinburgh, 1800), 6, 11, 15.   [37] Lloyd and Coulter, *Medicine and the Navy*, iii. 31.
[38] Dunne, *Chirurgical Candidate*, 26.

characters and the general progress of medicine'. A naval surgeon, on the other hand, was confined on board ship, where he developed 'a disposition of mind, that unfits him for the exercise of his profession in private practice'. At the same time, 'his naval servitude, in the prime of youth, had prevented him from making friends and forming connections, that would have been favourable to his future prospects in medical rank and reputation'. As a result, he was destined to end his days in a 'state of precarious dependence.'[39] It was little wonder, Trotter concluded, that the entry qualifications were so undemanding.

Too much attention, however, should not be paid to contemporary jeremiads. Most were part of a concerted campaign to improve the pay and conditions of naval surgeons or, in Bell's case, to establish a military medical school, where entrants to the two services could receive specialist training in dealing with battle wounds and epidemic diseases. In fact, most military surgeons recruited during the wars sprang from respectable backgrounds and had received a state-of-the-art medical education.

Army surgeons during the French wars came from a mix of middling backgrounds. A few had fathers who were clerics; many belonged to medical families; while the majority were the sons of merchants and small landowners or tenant farmers.[40] Although information about naval surgeons is more limited, there is no reason to believe that their social origins were very different.[41] Sir David Dickson (1780–1850), who joined the service in 1799 and became physician at Plymouth in 1824, was the son of a Presbyterian minister in Roxburghshire; John Harness's grandfather was a medical practitioner whose first cousin was Dr Frank Nicholls, professor of anatomy at Oxford; while Sir Benjamin Fonseca Outram (1774–1856), who entered the service at the beginning of the war and rose to the rank of inspector of fleets and of hospitals, was the son of a captain in the merchant navy: three of his father's five brothers were minor gentry in the East Riding of Yorkshire, another was a merchant-manufacturer and lord mayor of Hull, and the last a shopkeeper.[42] Less successful surgeons emerged from much the same sort of milieu. Peter Wilson (1791–1863), who was appointed assistant surgeon in

---

[39] Trotter, *Medicina Nautica*, i. 14–15.

[40] Ackroyd *et al.*, *Advancing with the Army*, ch. 2, sec. 2, esp. table 2.2.

[41] In our ongoing prosopographical study of army and navy surgeons referred to in the Preface, above, we have uncovered the social origin of a nearly a quarter of the army but less than an eighth of the naval cohort.

[42] *British Biographical Archive*, *sub* Dickson; William Nisbet, *Authentic Memoirs, Biographical, Critical and Literary, of the Most Eminent Physicians and Surgeons of Great Britain* (London, 1818), 387–8; Google search, *sub* Outram, 11 Sept. 2004. All the brothers were baptized at Burton Agnes,

1811 and later settled in New Zealand, was the son of a merchant and farmer at Dunbar.[43] Thomas Longmore, another recruit in 1799, came from London mercantile stock: his family, which hailed from Kidderminster, appropriately dealt in carpets from a shop in Blackfriars.[44] Several naval surgeons belonged to seriously upwardly mobile families reminiscent of the Wordsworths and the Coleridges. William Porter (1774–1850), who was warranted surgeon in 1794 and ended his days in Bristol, was the son of a surgeon in the Enniskillen Dragoon Guards. One of his brothers, John, was an army colonel, while another, three years his junior, Sir Robert Ker (1777–1842), was an artist who specialized in history paintings and landscapes and eventually became British consul in Venezuela. To add to this, he had two younger sisters, Anna Maria (1780–1832) and Jane (1776–1850), who were both successful novelists.[45]

Similarly, army and navy surgeons largely shared a common educational background and scarcely deserved to be labelled ignorant.[46] True, they seldom held a university degree or a qualification from one of the medical colleges before they joined the service. This was a luxury that they either forewent altogether, like most of their peers, or delayed until they had been in the service some time or placed on half-pay. But this did not mean that they had not had a good education (as understood by contemporaries). Despite the complaints about illiteracy, many recruits had enjoyed a sound introduction to modern and classical languages and literature. Otherwise so many could not have gone on to publish their observations and experiences, or take a degree at Edinburgh in later life, where candidates had to write a dissertation in Latin.[47] Most would have attended the local grammar school, as did Burnett at Montrose and John Weir at Lesmahgo, County Lanark. Others would have been tutored privately, like Harness, who owed his knowledge of Latin and Greek to a Revd Birkhead of Watlington, Oxfordshire.[48] Some,

---

a village outside Hull: see IGI, *sub* John, Joseph, William, Benjamin, Samuel, and Thomas Outram (year range: 1734–43; county: Yorkshire).

[43] Gail Lambert, *Peter Wilson: Colonial Surgeon* (Palmerston North, NZ, 1981), 17: this is the only modern biography of a naval surgeon in the French wars, but is primarily interested in his later career.

[44] WL, RAMC, Longmore Papers L19/1–106: letters home 1799–1806: references to the carpet trade, *passim*, and mother's occasional visits to Worcestershire.

[45] Memorial to William Porter, Bristol Cathedral cloisters; *DNB*, *sub* Anna Marie, Jane and Sir Robert Ker.   [46] Ackroyd *et al.*, *Advancing with the Army*, ch. 3.

[47] A quarter of army surgeons and an eighth of naval surgeons gained an Edinburgh degree. This information is often given in their service record and can be verified through the printed degree list.

[48] *Lancet* (July–Dec. 1850), 558 ff.: Burnett, biography; Nisbet, *Memoirs*, 541, 387.

too, even went on to study the humanities and philosophy at university, like the hapless second surgeon's mate of the *Atlas* whom Whyte castigated for his medical ineptitude. Sir James Clark (1788–1870), who joined the navy in 1809 and found fame in later life as a court physician, completed his liberal education by taking an MA at Aberdeen, as did Sir James McGrigor (1771–1858), the future head of the Army Medical Service.[49]

Most military surgeons, though, left school in their early to mid-teens and began to train for a medical career. To start with, they virtually all served the customary three-to-five year apprenticeship with a surgeon-apothecary in order to learn the medical ropes, a move that would easily have cost their parents the not-insignificant sum of £50 to £100, or even more if the practitioner was a fashionable London doctor. Normally they were apprenticed locally, often to a relative, but sometimes they were sent far from the family hearth to serve their time with a practitioner who was highly respected or one with the right religious and moral credentials. The navy surgeon Outram, born in 1774, was apprenticed to two surgeon-apothecaries, a Mr Coleman and William Harris at Gravesend, the town where he was baptized and presumably raised. The army doctor, Joseph Brown, on the other hand, who was born ten years later to a Quaker family in North Shields and would eventually become mayor of Sunderland, served his time with a Quaker practitioner in Manchester.[50]

The apprenticeship gave future military surgeons a basic acquaintance with patient-care, the preparation of medicine, and the most common surgical operations. It was not usually, however, the sum of their studies. Like many of their contemporaries who went straight into civilian practice, a large proportion of military surgeons spent a further one or more years at the burgeoning medical schools in London, Edinburgh, and Dublin, attending lectures on different medical sciences and walking the hospital wards, before applying to join either the army or navy. Admittedly, navy surgeons appointed before 1800 do not seem to have done so in such great numbers as their army counterparts, but thereafter it became commonplace.[51]

[49] *DNB*, *sub* Clark; Sir James McGrigor, *The Scalpel and the Sword: The Autobiography of the Father of Army Medicine*, ed. Mary McGrigor (Dalkeith, 2000), 28.

[50] Guys Hospital, Pupils Register, *sub* Outram, 1806: lists name of master; Lisa Rosner, *The Most Beautiful Man in Existence: The Scandalous Life of Alexander Lesassier* (Philadelphia, 1999), 16 (*re* Brown in Manchester). Ackroyd *et al.*, *Advancing with the Army*, ch. 3, sec. 3: cost of apprenticeship.

[51] Information relating to army surgeons is contained on their service record. Information about navy surgeons has been recovered through painstaking research in the surviving pupils' registers and class lists of the London hospitals, the Edinburgh and Dublin faculties of medicine, and the Dublin Royal College of Surgeons.

Recruits to both services seem to have particularly favoured the course in practical medicine given at Edinburgh by James Gregory (1753–1821), who took over the faculty chair in 1790.[52] In London, in contrast, there was a notable difference in preference. While the long-serving St George's surgeon, Sir Everard Home (1756–1832), was popular with members of either cohort, the two most-frequented lecturers were only patronized by one or the other. Future army surgeons sat in particular at the feet of the surgeon Sir Astley Cooper (1768–1841), who lectured at St Thomas's from 1791 to 1825. Future naval surgeons, on the other hand, were peculiarly the disciples of his rival at the London hospital, Sir William Blizard (1743–1835), who had founded the medical school there in 1780.[53] Sir George Magrath (1775–1857), surgeon of the *Victory* before Beatty, and Sir Henry Parkin (1779–1849), an inspector of hospitals, were just two of the leading naval surgeons of the era who passed through his hands.[54]

Irrespective of the choice, the cost to the family of sending a son to medical school was again appreciable. Board and lodging in London could seldom be had for less than 8*s*. 6*d*. per week, while most six-month courses would cost 20 guineas. When account is taken of the cost of instruments, books, clothes, and entertainment, the average medical student could expect to spend £200 a year, much the same as a young gentleman at Oxford or Cambridge.[55] Bell's assertion, then, that army and navy surgeons belonged to families who had left them to fend for themselves is completely fallacious. Their parents had clearly marked them out for a medical career, invested heavily in their training, and presumably sanctioned or even intended their entry into the service. If their failure to return home is to be attributed in some way to their being disadvantaged, then the reason more likely lies in their geographical origins than in their social or educational background.

The population of the British Isles in 1800 was unevenly distributed between the three kingdoms, if not as unevenly as today. According to the census of 1811, 57 per cent lived in England and Wales, 33 per cent in Ireland, and only 10 per cent in Scotland. There is no reason to believe that the geographical background of the nation's medical practitioners did not mirror this distribution: indeed, an even greater proportion were probably

---

[52] Gregory belonged to an Edinburgh medical dynasty. He was the author of an important textbook on the practice of medicine.

[53] For these three teachers, see Lawrence, *Charitable Knowledge*, *passim*.

[54] Information based on pupils' registers.

[55] Ackroyd *et al.*, *Advancing with the Army*, ch. 3, sec. 4.

English. Entrants to the medical services of the armed forces, however, came predominantly from the Celtic fringe, especially Scotland, which was over-represented among army surgeons by three to one. Most of the Scots and Irish, too, came from small towns or the countryside, where the possibility of building up a substantial medical clientele would have been small in what contemporaries acknowledged was an overcrowded profession, especially if there were already an established practitioner in the field who was not a relation.[56] In such circumstances entering the army and navy made sense: despite the dangers, it offered a more lucrative career than going home or trying to set up in some foreign town with no family support, especially once it began to look as if the war would last for ever.

The choice between the army and navy must have depended largely on family connections, whether friends or relations were officers or had influence in one service rather than another. Peter Wilson joined the navy, it can be assumed, because his father had a friend in the Admiralty who helped his son get his first appointment as assistant surgeon on the *Naiad*.[57] Probably a family was also more likely to direct a son towards the navy when they lived close to the sea or had a seafaring tradition. Where the surgeon had made the choice off his own bat, then his preference was probably determined by people whom he encountered during his education. Peter Cullen's decision to enter the navy was closely connected with the fact that he served his three-year apprenticeship with the Perthshire practitioner Daniel Wingate, who himself had been a navy surgeon.[58] Lecturers in the medical schools may also have encouraged their pupils down a particular service road. It may not simply be coincidental that Astley Cooper and Blizard seem to have had distinct clienteles among future military surgeons. The St Thomas's surgeon definitely urged his students in early 1809 to volunteer for army service and go to the aid of the hard-pressed medical officers struggling to cope with the sick and wounded being landed in droves on the south coast after the debacle at Corunna.[59] Blizard, similarly, had a soft spot for the navy. The 1798 edition of his *Brief Explanation of the Nature of Wounds, More Particularly*

---

[56] Our knowledge of the place of origin of army surgeons is virtually complete, since the detail is usually contained on their service record: see ibid., ch. 2, sec. 1 (esp. tables 2.1a–d). Information about navy surgeons, on the other hand, has been gleaned from a variety of sources, such as class registers and thesis frontispieces. Although the origins of only a quarter are known, there is a close fit with the army data.   [57] Lambert, *Wilson*, 21.

[58] 'Memoirs of Peter Cullen', 45–6.

[59] WL, RAMC 536/4: William Dent to mother, 17 Feb. 1809. Dent duly volunteered and went on to become an army surgeon.

those Received from Firearms, was dedicated to the scholars of the Greenwich maritime school, an institution attached to the hospital which offered free education to sailors' orphans. Perhaps Astley Cooper and Blizard acted throughout the wars as talent scouts for the respective services.

It would be wrong, too, to assume that naval service was unattractive, that it was a *pis-aller* for the unfortunate young practitioner whose prospects at home were limited. The dangers were real, but the rampant patriotism of the period might draw a young doctor into the senior service, as might a desire to see the world at someone else's expense. The material drawbacks of years afloat, moreover, were not quite as dire as Trotter pretended in his *Medicina Nautica*. Even if the basic pay before 1805 was poor, it was supplemented throughout the wars by various 'extras'. To begin with, every surgeon received a supplementary lump sum, known as Queen Anne's Free Gift, which varied from £16 to £62 per annum dependent on the size of the ship and whether the country was at peace or war. In addition, before drugs were issued free by the Admiralty the surgeon received 2*d.* a year from each man on board from his annual contribution to the Chatham Chest, and a further £5 per annum for every 100 men treated for venereal disease. This was intended to cover the cost of medicines, but on large ships could be a serious boost to income.[60] Moreover, before 1805 medical officers lucky enough to be based on shore had the opportunity to moonlight by building up a civilian practice. Finally, as the officers and crew were entitled to share the sale value of any enemy vessels captured at sea, on a sliding scale according to rank, the surgeon and his mates could look forward to a modest amount of prize money.[61] In consequence, income at any time in the conflict could easily be double the basic pay. In 1803–4 Thomas Longmore was on the *Atalante*, a brig with 110 hands, sailing with the Channel Fleet. His official annual pay came to £65. 3*s.* 6*d.*, but a letter from his brother Sam of 12 April 1804 shows that he collected overall £118. 4*s.* 3*d.* We know, too, from his surviving account book that he earned a further £20–£30 from the sale of prizes, while an exchange of letters with his mother reveals that he was also involved in the illegal import of brandy seized in the Channel from English vessels caught smuggling. Unknown to his upright father, he was cheating the excise by bottling small

[60] Details given in *Steel's Navy List.* The Chatham Chest was a naval charitable foundation supported by a charge of 6*d.* per month on the wages of every man in the navy.

[61] Ibid. (1796), 50: the surgeon shared an eighth of the prize money with the lieutenants and quartermaster of marines, the lieutenants, ensigns, and quartermaster of any land forces, the secretaries of the admiral or commodores, the bosuns, gunners, purser, carpenter, master's mates, pilots, and chaplains. Obviously, it paid to be on a small ship without marines or army personnel.

quantities of the spirit and shipping it to different addresses in London hidden in the middle of parcels of food and clothing.[62] As in all wars, there were opportunities in the naval service for the astute and the less than scrupulous.

THE NAVY AS A CAREER

Having insisted that entrants to the service were of poor quality, most contemporary commentators then bemoaned the fact that surgeons only hung around long enough to gain a training on the job. The navy, they maintained, was just too unattractive to retain doctors for any length of time. According to Charles Dunne, even the improvement in pay and conditions from the beginning of 1805 were a limited incentive to stay, given the contempt and disrespect with which naval medical officers were treated, the lack of good and improving conversation, and the tyrannical disposition of the commanders: 'It is only the servile sycophant that can change his disposition at the nod of his master, and that is found a fit tool for corruption and iniquity, and who has neither public spirit, nor the good of his majesty's service at heart, that will ever succeed to promotion in the navy, particularly under the direction of the present newly organized Transport Board.'[63] Unquestioning obedience to orders was the *sine qua non* of a successful career in the navy. By definition this was not the mark of the educated and the upright, so the navy, it was claimed, haemorrhaged talent.

As with other contemporary assertions about the naval medical service, this was a gross exaggeration. It may well have been the case that many mates and assistants resigned after a few years because they found the life unacceptable or lacked the ability, but the large majority of those who qualified as full surgeon made the navy their career and only left as a result of being invalided out, placed on half-pay, or eventually retired. As late as 1835 there were still some 700 surgeons on the active list who had received their warrant during the wars. Indeed, there were thirty medical officers still in the service who had joined before 1793, the most senior being Thomas Seeds, appointed on 14 October 1777.[64] Admittedly, virtually all were on half-pay in 1835, but they were in theory all available for further duty. And some, however old,

---

[62] WL, RAMC Longmore Papers, L19/82: Sam to T. Longmore, 12 Ap. 1802; ibid., L82: account book, *sub* 1803–5; ibid., L19/64: Mrs Longmore to Thomas—one of many letters *re* brandy smuggling.   [63] Dunne, *Chirurgical Candidate*, 71.
[64] TNA, ADM 104/12–14: surgeons for service in order of seniority, 1774–1815. These registers were the starting-point for our naval prosopography: see above, Preface, n. 3.

continued to seek re-employment long after they had been stood down. Seeds was superseded on 9 May 1801 after seventeen years service, but he was still requesting a new appointment in 1823 at the age of 67! He only finally declared himself unfit for service in 1839, shortly before he died in January 1841, by which time he was paralysed.[65]

Some surgeons, too, who escaped being placed permanently or for long periods on half-pay, when their ships were wrecked or decommissioned through old age or the coming of peace, clocked up a prodigious number of years in the service. The longest-serving medical officer who entered during the wars seems to have been a surgeon called William Gladstone (1774–1858), who hailed from the East End of London and was baptized at the Bull Lane Independent Church, Stepney. Gladstone might not have had the staying-power of his more famous namesake or lived as long, but he was almost constantly in the navy's employment from the time he was warranted as an assistant surgeon in 1794 until he finally retired with the *ex officio* rank of deputy inspector of hospitals in 1840 with a pension of £1. 4s. 3d. per day. By then he had forty-five years, two months, two weeks, and two days of service to his credit. Fourteen of those years had been spent afloat in a number of ships, notably the 100-gun *Royal George*. The last thirty-one had been spent on shore, first from 1809 as surgeon to the Royal Naval Asylum, a new orphans' school for young children based in the Queen's House at Greenwich; then, from 1823, as deputy physician to Greenwich Hospital under William Beatty, the subject of this study.[66]

A medical officer's career path was much the same, whatever the level of his competence was judged to be when he first appeared before the Board and the College of Surgeons. The first appointment would invariably be to a small vessel, at best a brig or sloop. Burnett was exceptional in first being posted as surgeon's mate on the 74-gun *Edgar* shortly after leaving Montrose to study in Edinburgh.[67] If the officer stayed alive or fit, he would then gradually work his way up the fleet, until, like Gladstone, he ended up as surgeon of a ship of the line. From there, he would either be placed on permanent half-pay or, in a limited number of cases, be given a hospital post. Only a handful of entrants during the war could expect to rise to the rank of physician or inspector of the

---

[65] TNA, ADM 104/12, fo. 19: service record.

[66] Ibid., fo. 51: service record; *IGI*, under William Gladstone; *Navy List*, 1809–40: *sub* Greenwich Hospital.

[67] *Lancet* (July–Dec. 1850), 558. The *Edgar* was at anchor off Leith with the North Sea squadron and presumably lacked a surgeon's mate.

fleet and hospitals. As few surgeons survived more than fifteen years at sea, given the rigours of the life and the rundown of the service after 1815, most were likely to be thrown into civilian life in their early middle age. The typical naval surgeon on active duty was no different from the majority of the officers and men with whom he served: he was a man in his twenties and thirties.

Moving up the naval ladder was slow and uncertain. Although promotion to a larger ship must have been connected with evidence of ability to some degree, especially once physicians of the fleet could recommend surgeons for advancement, it was also the result of influence. As with promotion generally in the navy, it helped to have an *entrée* to the Admiralty. A surgeon whose family and friends knew members of the Board would be far better placed for a successful career than one who did not. Best placed of all, however, was the surgeon who served under a successful captain. To this extent Dunne was correct: the best way for a young surgeon to progress in the service was to keep on the right side of his commanding officer, who would then request that they transfer together. If the captain was going nowhere, then second best was to attract the attention of a commander in the fleet whose prospects were better.

Nelson, for one, stuck with a surgeon he could trust for as long as his conduct was becoming. Michael Jefferson was surgeon on the *Agamemnon*, the first ship of the line Nelson commanded, from 1793 to 1796. They must have struck up a good relationship, because Jefferson was one of the doctors the then commodore consulted back in London in the winter of 1797–8 over the pain he was suffering after the recent amputation of his arm.[68] When Nelson sailed to join St Vincent in the Mediterranean the following year on the *Vanguard*, he insisted that Jefferson accompany him. When the surgeon successfully treated a wounded Nelson, who had believed he was on the point of death, at the Battle of the Nile, Jefferson duly reaped his reward by being posted ashore to run the new naval hospital at Malta. Unfortunately, he then blotted his copybook, probably through excessive drinking, and was relieved of his command, thereby forfeiting his patron's support. In the spring of 1804 Jefferson seems to have tried to use Emma Hamilton to get himself transferred to the *Victory*, but the lobbying of the Admiral's inamorata was to no avail. Nelson had a new surgeon in whom he had confidence, and whom he would soon promote to the Gibraltar station—George Magrath:

With respect to Mr. Jefferson, I can say nor do anything. The Surgeon of the Victory is a very able, excellent man, and the Ship is kept in the most perfect state of

---

[68] Nelson was wounded while effecting a landing on Tenerife in the summer of 1797.

health; and, I would not, if I could—but thank [God] I cannot—do such an unjust act, as to remove him. He is my own asking for; and, I have every reason to be perfectly content. Mr Jefferson got on, by my help; and by his own misconduct, he got out of a good employ, and has seen another person, at Malta Hospital, put over his head. He must now begin again; and act with much more attention and sobriety than he has done, to ever get forward again: but time may do much; and, I shall rejoice to hear of his reformation.[69]

Thomas Longmore's lacklustre career emphasizes the importance of the right kind of patronage. The Blackfriars merchant's son spent only the eight years 1799 to 1807 in the service, the last two in a state of declining health which finally forced him to resign and forfeit any prospect of half-pay. By the end he had risen to be surgeon of a ship of the line, but his progress had been slow. Initially, in January 1799, he had been appointed surgeon of the tiny gun-vessel *Contest*, which broke up when it ran aground off the Texel in Holland the following September. He was then ordered by Andrew Mitchell, vice-admiral of the Blue, to transfer to another gun-brig, the *Pelter*, on which he served for about a year.[70] He transferred for a second time in October 1800 to a larger ship, the *Atalante*, a sloop of 110 men, which was employed in the Home Fleet, patrolling the Channel and sweeping the Bay of Biscay for vessels trying to run the blockade. There he stayed for the next five years, until he finally was made surgeon of the *Lion*, a 64-gun ship of the line, on 17 February 1806.[71] The *Lion*, however, was bound for the East Indies on an eight-to-ten year voyage, which Longmore was unwilling to undertake. As he explained in a letter home: '[T]he thought of being separated from my family . . . was insupportable.'[72] He used the state of his health, therefore, as an excuse not to sail with his ship, and went on half-pay, only to find the next year that the navy had had enough of his malingering. In spring 1807 he was ordered to join the 38-gun *Minerva* at Plymouth within six days or his name would be expunged from the navy list. When he refused once more, he was duly dropped from the books.[73]

Throughout his years in the service Longmore's surviving correspondence demonstrates that he strove continually to move up the ladder. None of the three ships on which he found himself before his appointment to the *Lion*

[69] Nelson to Lady Hamilton, 14 Mar. 1804, off Toulon: Nicolas, *Dispatches*, v. 439.
[70] WL, RAMC Longmore Papers, L6/2, 4: warrants; L19/5: Longmore to mother 16 Sept. 1799.
[71] Ibid., L6/5, 6, 9: various warrants; ibid., L19/9, 18–98: James Johnstone (of the Sick and Hurt Board) to Longmore, 22 Feb. 1800; Longmore's family letters, 5 Nov. 1800–13 Aug. 1805.
[72] Ibid., L19/104: Longmore to his mother, 10 Mar. 1806.
[73] Ibid., L6/no number: fragment of letter *re* his movements 1806–7.

were to his satisfaction. His messmate on the *Contest* was a semi-drunk; the *Pelter* was an ill-disciplined brothel; while the *Atalante's* commander, Captain Griffiths, was a rigid disciplinarian who allowed his surgeon few opportunities to go ashore when they were cruising off the south coast. To boot, the *Atalante's* accommodation was cramped, the ship leaked and sailed like a hulk, and the company was appalling. 'Shut up with beings, who cannot raise their ideas of pleasure and enjoyment, above those things they have in common with the brutes', only his books, his 'silent yet sweet companions', made life bearable.[74] What Longmore wanted above all was to transfer to a frigate, a larger and faster ship where the prospects of taking valuable prizes would be so much greater. Longmore expected, too, that his sojourn on the *Atalante* would be short, in that his family had contacts. To begin with, he counted on the good offices of a family friend, Mr Walter English (presumably a merchant neighbour), who had the ear of one of the commissioners of the Board, the Edinburgh MD James Johnstone (1730–1802). Then, after Johnstone died, he placed his hopes in the newly appointed treasurer to the navy, the local MP for Southwark, who was beholden to Longmore senior for his election. Neither, though, came up trumps, although English may have been responsible for getting Longmore off the *Pelter*.[75] Nor could Longmore capitalize on his mother's friendship with Mrs Bligh, wife of the former captain of the ill-fated *Bounty*.[76] According to Longmore's brother Sam, William Bligh was the key which would turn the lock in the promotion door. There was not a captain in the navy with whom Bligh was not acquainted and who would not want to serve him. 'It is in his power to do everything there is . . . [T]here is not a man more respected at the Admiralty.'[77] Bligh, furthermore, was still in active service at the turn of the century, sailing with the Channel Fleet: he was the ideal officer to cultivate.

The connection, however, proved another busted flush, despite Mrs Bligh's willingness to act as intermediary, even to the extent of her visiting the Board on Longmore's account. Although in 1802 the surgeon dined on several occasions on Bligh's ship, the 74-gun *Irresistable*, the captain did not take to

[74] Ibid., L19/65: Longmore to mother, 10 Nov. 1802. Also L19/1, 17, 21: letters, 26 June 1799, 13 Aug. 1800, 19 Nov. 1800.

[75] Many of Longmore's letters refer to English and Johnstone throughout his stay in the navy. He heard of Johnstone's death in a letter from his brother, Sam, of 2 Mar. 1802: ibid., L19/40. His mother broached the possibility of using the good offices of the Southwark MP in a letter of 16 July 1802: L19/56.

[76] Bligh's notoriety as a disciplinarian is a modern fiction. He was extremely well regarded as a seaman in his day, especially by Nelson.

[77] WL, RAMC Longmore Papers, L19/40: Sam Longmore to Thomas, 2 Mar. 1802.

him. Bligh may well have helped to keep Longmore on board the *Atalante* after the Peace of Amiens, but he did little more. When, after a short period on half-pay, he got a new command in the spring of 1804—the 74-gun *Warrior*—Bligh made it quite clear to his wife that he would not take her friend's son as his surgeon. The best he would do, according to Longmore's mother, would be to help the surgeon transfer. '[H]e firmly promised he would see you and hear your own sentiments with respect to being removed and if it was your particular wish he had a friend at the Admiralty now and he was sure he could get you removed.'[78] Yet Bligh can have played little part in Longmore's eventual promotion to the *Lion* in 1806. Presumably, somebody facilitated his transfer from the *Atalante*, but by then Bligh was governor of New South Wales.

Arguably, Longmore's stalled career was principally the result of the captains with whom he sailed. His first commander on the *Atalante*, Captain Griffiths, was ill as well as a disciplinarian. He was interested in negotiating his own removal from the service, not in assisting the promotion of his subordinates. Thanks to his friend at the Admiralty, Sir Thomas Troubridge, he was 'suppressed' in June 1802 and replaced by a Captain Masefield. But Masefield does not appear to have been a dynamic commander either.[79] In consequence, unable to rise on the coat-tails of his captains, and unable to find another captain willing to take him on, Longmore was forced to rely on the influence of civilians whose voices would have been quickly lost among the cacophony of petitioners assailing the Board every day.

Longmore's progress through the service, of course, only faltered. He did in the end become the surgeon of a ship of the line, and had he been willing to go to the East Indies he might have enjoyed a long and successful career, as long as he did not die of fever. This would suggest that all but the incompetent and very unlucky were likely to rise to be the chief medical officer on one of the navy's 130–150 battleships in the fullness of time. Patronage and influence primarily determined the speed of travel. Moreover, in that every surgeon except the exceedingly fortunate, like Gladstone, was destined to be placed on permanent or semi-permanent half-pay in middle age when the war finally came to an end, all were ultimately moving in the same direction, even if none had any idea how soon that end might come, and perhaps had joined in the expectation that the conflict would last for ever.

[78] WL, RAMC Longmore Papers, L19/83: mother to Longmore, 25 May 1804. Longmore dined with Bligh on board ship for the first time in March 1802: L19/42: letter, 2 Mar.

[79] Ibid., L19/54: Longmore to mother, 12 June 1802.

Some surgeons embraced the eventual return to civilian life with relish and established successful private practices, thereby giving the lie to Trotter's belief that the navy was a poor preparation for a civilian career. Outram, for one, made the transfer from sea to land with effortless ease. Paid off as early as 1806, he rushed up to Edinburgh to study for a medical degree and then, on graduation, put up his plate in London, where he practised with great élan for thirty years until made an inspector of fleets and hospitals in 1841. Burnett, similarly, who had already attended that university before entering the service, returned to his alma mater once released in 1816, then established himself in practice in Chichester until recalled in 1822.[80] Others in this group, in contrast, such as Porter, who settled at Bristol, do not seem to have bothered to obtain further qualifications, assuming that their fifteen-to-twenty years service in the navy would guarantee them a reasonable living. To improve their chances they usually set themselves up in coastal towns, notably Portsmouth and Plymouth, where they were sure to find clients among the many retired naval officers and their families. A few even followed Peter Wilson's lead, the surgeon who settled in New Zealand, and emigrated to the colonies.

A significant proportion of surgeons, however, do not seem to have made a serious go at becoming successful civilian practitioners, which would indicate that Trotter was not totally wide of the mark. Instead, they went into semi-retirement and returned to the small towns and villages in which they were probably raised, perhaps worn out by years of arduous service afloat rather than scared that they lacked the social skills to set up in foreign territory.[81] Given that even surgeons who were placed on half-pay after only a couple of years would receive an annuity of nearly £100 per annum, this was a perfectly sensible decision, all the more so in that they often had only themselves to maintain. The navy offered medical officers few opportunities to find a wife while they were on active service afloat. Although they would have occasionally enjoyed the pleasure of mixed company when invited to balls and dinners in the ports where they briefly docked, theirs was much more a man's world than the army. By the time they were permanently based on half-pay,

---

[80] *DNB, sub nom.* Outram took his MD in 1809. Burnett did not take a medical degree until 1825, when he graduated at Aberdeen.

[81] At least 40 of the cohort of 430 naval surgeons in our prosopography died in Scotland, but only five resided in a large town—all in Aberdeen. Place of retirement is frequently recorded on the service record and can be traced through the half-pay registers in the Admiralty papers. Although we do not always know for certain that navy surgeons who retired to small towns in Ireland and Scotland were actually born there, it seems the logical conclusion. What else but family ties and childhood memories could have enticed them to move to the back of beyond?

many must have become confirmed bachelors, who were happy to return home and set themselves up as local celebrities, who had sailed the seas and fought the French.

In this regard, the histories of army and navy surgeons significantly diverged. Army surgeons, too, found themselves placed on half-pay in large numbers after 1815, but they were much more willing to invest in a civilian qualification—a university degree or a licence from one of the royal colleges of surgery—and carve themselves out a lucrative practice.[82] Surgeons who left the army in middle age and retired were usually those who had come into land or money, such as John Robb (1776–1845) of Ayr, who inherited the family's banking business and merchant house in 1821.[83] Normally, only those who quit the service in old age with a high rank gave up medical practice immediately. The large majority became civilian doctors, many establishing themselves in London, Edinburgh, or Dublin and the smart English resorts, regardless of their place of origin. Thus, William Gibney (1794–1872), who was the son of a small landowner in County Meath and entered the army in 1812, never returned to the land of his birth when he was placed on half-pay in 1818, but moved to the burgeoning spa town of Cheltenham. There he practised for over forty years and served as physician to the new hospital before dying, suitably, at Bath.[84]

As a result, few navy surgeons left large fortunes. Several army doctors were the equivalent of modern-day multi-millionaires when they died, especially those who had had a civilian practice in London.[85] Charles Este (1779–1864), whose clergyman father was one of Nelson's friends and who himself was briefly one of the Admiral's secretaries before Trafalgar, managed to amass a fortune of £60,000 (some £3.6 million today). Surgeon initially to the Foot and then the Life Guards, he was able to combine a twenty-year career in the army spanning several decades with a lucrative civilian practice in the

---

[82] Ackroyd *et al.*, *Advancing with the Army*, ch. 3, sec. 7, and ch. 5, *passim*.

[83] Robb senior was an Indian merchant: Ayrshire Sasines 1819/14209. Robb was acting inspector of hospitals at Cape Town when he heard the good news: see WL, RAMC 830, no foliation: family letters of his colleague, the army surgeon, John Murray: letter 11 Dec. 1821.

[84] William Gibney, *Recollections of an Old Army Doctor*. (London, 1896).

[85] Brockliss *et al.*, *Advancing with the Army*, ch. 6, sec. 1: information known about 202 of the 454 cohort. After 1858 wealth at death is recorded in the registers in First Avenue House. Before this, estate valuations can be found in the Inland Revenue series at the TNA and in the probate archives of the Scottish Record Office. Because of the destruction of the Dublin national archives, details about surgeons who died in Ireland are much harder to track down.

capital.[86] Inevitably, navy surgeons, given that so many returned home and lived off half-pay, were seldom so affluent. Most were certainly comfortable. Half possessed effects, cash, and investments worth £1,000 or more, and many in addition owned houses and landed property. But only a handful were rich—the 5–6 per cent who left at least £20,000—and none were plutocrats.[87] Two of the wealthiest were Daniel Quarrier (d. 1843) and Robert Dobie (d. 1873), who joined the service in 1796 and 1806 respectively and left £30,000 apiece. Unfortunately, little is known about their professional lives except that one died in Gosport and the other in London. Even their background and training is obscure, although Dobie definitely attended the University of Edinburgh before joining the service and listened to Gregory on the practice of medicine.[88]

Even the handful of surgeons who went on to the rank of physician and inspector were not particularly wealthy. Deputy Inspector Sir James Prior (?1790–1869), who died at Norfolk Crescent, Hyde Park, left a respectable £25,000. But Inspector-General Sir William Rae (1786–1873), who joined the navy in 1808 and spent forty years in the service before retiring to Newton Abbot, Devon, left only £3,000.[89] A lifetime's service was not necessarily the route to untold riches. In the case of the long-serving medical officers, though, many took with them into retirement a less tangible benefit: the honour of state recognition. In the eighteenth and early nineteenth centuries no naval medical officer who began his career as a humble surgeon was knighted for his service in the armed forces. Gilbert Blane became a knight baronet in 1812, but he was primarily a London hospital and society physician, who had looked after the Prince Regent for many years. However, from the 1830s, with the accession to the throne of a former naval officer, William IV, who had been on active service during the War of American Independence, the leading figures in the naval medical service began to be duly honoured.

---

[86] Este was forced to resign his first commission in 1803 for personal reasons. Before re-entering the service he served with Nelson in the Mediterranean in 1804, but was left behind in London when the admiral rejoined the *Victory*: E. H. D. Este, letter to M. Moss, 13 Mar. 2003; V. G. Plarr, *Lives of the Fellows of the Royal College of Surgeons of London*, revised by Sir D'Arcy Power (Bristol, 1930), 380–1; First Avenue House, Wills and Administration, Calendar, 1864, *sub* Este.

[87] Based on information about some 200 of the cohort of 430. Some 70% of army surgeons left more than £1,000.

[88] IR 26/1653, fo. 357; First Avenue House, Wills and Administrations, Calendar, 1873, *sub* Dobie.

[89] First Avenue House, Wills and Administrations, Calendar, *sub ann. et nom.* Lives: see *DNB*, *sub nom.*

In all, fourteen of the surgeons who had been warranted during the French war eventually received a knighthood, and all but one, the society and courtier physician Sir James Clark, received the honour whilst still in the navy as a reward for their services to the nation. This was a small but significant number. Their elevation was testimony to the value that the state now attributed to their calling in an age when every aspect of public health was firmly on the political agenda.[90] Two of the group—Sir John Richardson (1787–1865) and Prior—were honoured in particular for their contribution to the achievements of the naval expeditions to the Arctic under Sir John Franklin. Richardson went out in the first expedition as a naturalist as well as a surgeon.[91] The rest, bar Clark, were knighted for their general contribution to the navy's well-being. The first thus recognized were dubbed in 1831, when the new king awarded knighthoods to three serving naval medical officers: two appeared on William's coronation honours list of 25 May, thereby signalling the monarch's particular approbation; the third was knighted on 16 September. The last of the trio was the Irishman, George Magrath, who had served on the *Victory* under Nelson, and had then been William IV's personal physician as lord high admiral before he ascended the throne. The first two, elevated together, were the new director of the naval medical service, William Burnett, and the physician to Greenwich Hospital, William Beatty, who had been at the side of the king's friend, Nelson, as he lay dying. Nothing better indicates the significant position which the subject of this biography rose to occupy in the service than the fact that he was one of the pair of first genuinely naval medical knights.

---

[90] The first Central Board of Public Health, followed by local boards, was established in 1831 to deal with the cholera epidemic of 1831–2. F. B. Smith, *The People's Health, 1830–1910* (London, 1979).

[91] John McIlraith, *Life of Sir John Richardson* (London, 1868), pp. 58–124. Richardson, who joined the service in 1809, had been placed on half-pay in 1815, then went to take his MD in Edinburgh. He found it difficult to establish a practice in Leith, so applied to join the Franklin expedition.

2

Origins and Early Career

AN ULSTER SCOTS FAMILY

William Beatty was born in Londonderry in April 1773, where his father, James, was an official in the Irish Revenue Service like his father before him. Coming from Ireland and from a family with long service to the Crown, he was typical of many young men who were to provide the backbone of the professional officer cadre during the French wars. The Beattys, like many families in the North of Ireland, were originally Presbyterians, who in all probability had fled from Scotland after the restoration of the monarchy in 1660 to escape religious persecution. There was already a substantial ex-patriot Scottish Protestant community which had emigrated to the north during the Plantation at the beginning of the seventeenth century, settling on land forfeited by native Irish landowners following the bloody rebellion at the end of Queen Elizabeth's reign. There is no record of where William Beatty, the progenitor of his namesake's family, came from nor what his occupation was. All that is known is that he died in Cookstown, County Tyrone, in 1685. He was no doubt attracted to Cookstown by its thriving Presbyterian community. A church had been established at Derryloran in 1649, and its minister, the Revd John Mackenzie, who was ordained in 1673, would get to know the Beatty family well.[1]

In 1685 King Charles II was succeeded by his brother James II, who made no secret of his sympathy for the Church of Rome and his ambition to right the wrongs, as he saw it, done to the Catholics in Ireland. Early in 1687 he appointed Richard Talbot, the earl of Tyrconnel, lord deputy of Ireland, who

[1] PRONI, T.307: 1666 Hearth Money Roll, County Tyrone; NLI, MS 32,509: Philip Crossle, 'Beatty Genealogical Notes' including transcript of Armagh will of William Beatty, dated 4 Oct. 1685; Crossle 'Beatty Family' *Mid-Ulster Mail*, Cookstown, 13 Dec. 1919; Beatty Family at http://homepages.rootsweb.com/~bp2000/summaries 3.ntm (Jan. 2005); Peter Roebuck (ed.), *Plantation to Partition* (Belfast, 1981).

Map 1. Ireland in the Eighteenth Century.

vigorously set about replacing Protestants with Catholics in senior positions in the law and administrations. On 5 November 1688 the Protestant William of Orange, who was married to King James's daughter Mary, landed in England with a Dutch army to defend the right of his wife to the throne. The kingdom backed William and, just before Christmas, James fled to France. William and Mary were declared king and queen in February, and in the following month James landed in Ireland with a strong French force. The Protestants in the north were prepared for just such an eventuality. On 3 December a letter had been found in the street at Comber in County Down, warning that a massacre of Protestants was planned in six days time. On learning this news Mackenzie summoned his congregation, including the 17-year-old son of William Beatty of Cookstown, another William, and led them to the comparative safety of the city of Londonderry. They arrived just in time. The earl of Antrim had been instructed by Tyrconnel to take the city with troops loyal to King James. The citizens were uncertain as to what they should do, but the matter was settled for them when, on 7 December, thirteen apprentice boys closed the gates against Lord Antrim's army.[2]

---

[2] Ian McBride, *The Siege of Derry in Ulster Protestant Mythology* (Dublin, 1997), 16.

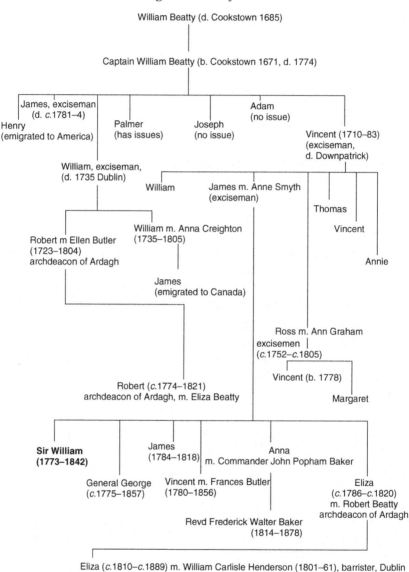

King William sent a shipload of weapons and ammunition so that the Protestants could defend themselves. Fearful for their lives, Protestants from the surrounding countryside flocked to the city, swelling its population by some 30,000, the majority of whom, like Beatty, were Presbyterians. The pacifist governor of the city, Lieutenant-Colonel Robert Lundy, who advised accommodation with James, was overthrown and replaced by the Episcopalians Major Henry Baker and the Revd George Walker. Despite the fact that he was a Presbyterian, Mackenzie became chaplain in Walker's regiment, and Beatty was amongst the first to volunteer. In March King James landed at Kinsale and held a parliament in Dublin, which passed an act of attainder directed at Protestants. The following month William and Mary were crowned in London, confirming the Protestant descent of the royal family and the opposition of the kingdom to the common enemy, Catholic France. The citizens of Londonderry declared emphatically for the new king and queen. On 18 April James led an assault on the city, which was greeted with what was to become the battlecry of Ulster Protestants: 'No Surrender.'[3] For fifteen weeks the loyal Protestant defenders held out. William Beatty, who was quickly promoted captain even though he was so young, fought heroically. His mother died during the siege, requesting to be buried in Londonderry, and he himself, worn out with fighting, succumbed to an infection and was forced to leave the city on 30 June. Mackenzie recalled that 'he had been at all the encounters and skirmishes with the enemy before, and ever behaved himself with great integrity and valour'.[4] He sought protection from the Presbyterian magnate Viscount Massereene in Moneymore, County Londonderry.

Beatty soon recovered and rejoined the Williamite army. King William landed at Carrickfergus on 14 June 1690, and brought James to battle, not far from Drogheda on the River Boyne on 1 July. Beatty was in the thick of the fighting, according to a report in the *Londonderry Journal* carrying two standards.[5] After King William's victory he remained with the army, distinguishing himself once again at the Battle of Aughrim. James fled into permanent exile in France. Captain William Beatty, now a military hero, returned to Moneymore to become a tenant farmer on the Massereene estate. His exploits, especially during the siege, were always in the background of the early life of his great-grandson, our naval surgeon in Londonderry. The effect would have been that, amongst the Protestant community, everyone would

    [3] Patrick Macrory, *The Siege of Derry* (Oxford, 1988), 210–318.

    [4] John Mackenzie, *Narrative of the Siege of Londonderry* (London, 1690; repr. Belfast, 1861), 52. This was published in response to the Revd George Walker, *True Account of the Siege of Londonderry* (London, 1689) which omitted reference to the part played by the Presbyterians, including Captain William Beatty; NLI, Crossle, 'Beatty Genealogical Notes', transcript of Armagh will of Margaret Beatty of Cookstown, dated Londonderry, 8 July, 1689.

    [5] *Londonderry Journal*, 4 Feb. 1774. According to information passed down within the Beatty family, six of William's brothers fought alongside him.

have known of the deeds of his illustrious forebear.[6] Evidence suggests that some time in the early 1690s the gallant captain switched his religious allegiance from the Presbyterians and joined the Church of Ireland. This was a judicious decision.[7]

At first both Episcopalians and Presbyterians had reaped the rewards of victory, but in 1704 the imposition of the Test Act excluded all those who were not members of the Episcopal Church of Ireland, the established church, from public office. Critically, since Presbyterians could own land, unlike Catholics, they could vote in elections and hold some minor government appointments, but not any office which required them to subscribe to the Act of Uniformity and produce evidence that they had received communion in the Church of Ireland. A response by both Presbyterians and Catholics alike to discrimination was to follow Captain Beatty's lead and convert 'prudentially' to the Episcopal Church. There is evidence that the Beatty family were just such 'prudential' converts, willing to reassert their Presbyterian credentials when opportunity arose.[8] Although joining the Church of Ireland must have been irritating when in Scotland the Presbyterian Church of Scotland was the established church, doctrinally the Church of Ireland was austere and low church, with a strong Evangelical wing, so crossing over could not have been too difficult. Disappointed that the Calvinist King William did not support them, many Ulster Scots left for the more tolerant American colonies. Amongst these emigrants was Captain William Beatty's eldest son, Henry.

Viscount Massereene relinquished control of Moneymore to the Episcopalian Thomas Dawson of Castle Dawson whose only daughter married Admiral Sir William Rowley of Tendring Hall in Suffolk. On Dawson's death in 1729 the lease passed to Rowley. The admiral's father was a servant at the courts of William and Mary and later Queen Anne.[9] For families such as the Beattys, advancement in eighteenth-century Ireland depended on the patronage of such well-connected landed families, particularly if they wished to secure appointments in government service. This in turn required them to be members of the Church of Ireland.

Captain Beatty had at least six more sons. Almost nothing is known about them except for James, William, and Vincent, who all became officers in the

---

[6] McBride, *Siege*, 39.

[7] NLI, Crossle, 'Beatty Genealogical Notes': William Beatty's name appears as a lessee of the tithes of the parish of Lissan, county Tyrone, granted 22 July 1696, and in a 1709 lawsuit to recover the grant.

[8] Information supplied by Thomas McMahon, Clones, based on his research in the Barrett Leonard Estate Papers.   [9] *Burke's Peerage and Baronetage* (London, 1938).

Revenue Service. This was the largest and best-organized of all the branches of government service.[10] Entry was by no means straightforward. Candidates had to be sponsored by gentlemen from their county, swear fealty to the Crown, be communicants of the established church, show an aptitude for arithmetic, serve a pupilage, and be examined.[11] Examination was rigorous, including written tests in arithmetic and bookkeeping, and practical exercises in the use of the various gauging instruments. Once they had qualified there was no guarantee of an appointment, and the author of *The Royal Gauger*, the bible of the service, recommended that every candidate should find a patron.[12] It seems likely that Admiral Rowley did duty for the Beatty boys. James and William entered the Revenue Service in Newry. James had to travel regularly to Dublin and, reportedly, he dismounted and kissed the ground every time he crossed the River Boyne to thank God for the Protestant victory.[13] William was eventually promoted to be a cashier in the office of the collector of customs in Dublin, where he died in 1735. His son Robert probably attended Trinity College Dublin, as he was ordained into the Church of Ireland, later becoming vicar-general and then archdeacon of Ardagh in County Longford.[14]

In 1735 Vincent, the youngest son, was appointed a gauger in the Irish Revenue Service at Downpatrick in County Down, almost certainly as a result of Admiral Rowley's influence. He had property in County Down and his barrister son, Clotworthy, was to sit as member of the Irish parliament for Downpatrick on the eve of the Union of the Irish and Westminster parliaments. Vincent Beatty could only have been appointed with the support of the county's great landowner, the 1st Viscount Hillsborough, father of the 1st marquess of Downshire, who would have believed that the Beatty family with its famous patriarch could be politically useful to him.

The Irish Revenue, as elsewhere in the United Kingdom, was organized by excise districts, which were subdivided into walks that were the responsibility of gaugers. Twice a week the gauger had to travel round his walk and record in his entry book how much of any product, on which duty was payable, had been made. This was arduous work, and there was constant supervision. Although the official salary was modest, some £60 a year, it could

[10] John Brewer, *The Sinews of Power* (London, 1989), 101–2.
[11] Charles Leadbetter, *The Royal Gauger*, 3rd edn. (London, 1750), pp. xii–xiii and 212–13.
[12] Ibid. 214.
[13] John Graham, *Derriana* (Londonderry, 1823; repr. Toronto, 1851), 125–6.
[14] He died in 1804: Cotton, *Fasti Ecclesiae Hibernicae*, vol. 3 (1849), 103. His son, Robert, also became archdeacon of Ardagh and married our naval surgeon's sister: see below, Ch. 5, p. 170.

be doubled or even trebled by fees and allowances, but given the level of scrutiny, there was almost no opportunity for corruption.[15] Moreover, officials in the Revenue had to be men of some substance, as they were obliged to provide sureties of £200 for any money they owed the Crown at their death, or when they resigned or in the event of fraud or defalcation.[16] By 1751 Vincent Beatty leased a house in English Street, one of Downpatrick's most fashionable residential areas. He held the tenancy of a farm on the Hillsborough estate, and owned at least one house in the town, which he let out. This suggests that he had done well for himself by investing in property through purchases and leases.[17]

Vincent is known to have had at least seven children. Two of his sons followed him into the Revenue Service, suggesting that they were well educated and shared his loyalty to the Crown. Ross was stationed at Clones in County Cavan, and James, who was probably born in the 1740s, became a gauger in Londonderry. The patronage of the Rowley family must once again have played a part in James's appointment. Londonderry was in the pocket of the Hills of Brook Hall, who were cousins of the Rowleys and descended from the 1st Viscount Massereene. Sir Hugh Hill was not only prominent in the city's affairs, succeeding his father as its member of parliament and serving as mayor in 1772; he was also collector of the excise for the district. Just like other landowners, he was active in finding appointments for qualified candidates in the Revenue Service, not just in his own collection but elsewhere in Ireland too. He was well placed to do so, as his cousin John Beresford was a commissioner and for many years president of the Revenue Board in Dublin. As mayor of Londonderry, Hugh Hill revived the 'ancient custom' of commemorating the breaking of the siege in 1689.[18] He had probably met the venerable Captain William Beatty, who still lived nearby at Dungiven. He could not but have known of James Beatty's descent from the hero. There is no record of when James and his wife, Anne Smyth, arrived at the Waterside in Londonderry, but it must have been before the birth of their first son, our William, in April 1773.

After the destructive siege, Londonderry did not recover until the middle of the eighteenth century, when it prospered with the growth in the Atlantic trades. As a port it enjoyed a particular advantage, as it was the nearest

---

[15] Leslie Clarkson and Elizabeth Crawford, *Ways to Wealth: The Cust Family of Eighteenth Century Armagh* (Belfast, 1985).   [16] Leadbetter, *Royal Gauger*, 213.

[17] NAI, Crossle, 'Beatty Genealogical Notes', v. 6: Transcript of Down will of Vincent Beatty: made 3 Mar. 1781; proved 19 Jun. 1783; PRONI, Down Freeholders' Lists: D/654/A3/1A.

[18] McBride, *Siege*, 35.

significant landfall to North America.[19] By the time James Beatty took up his walk in the Waterside, however, the port was beginning to decline. In 1773 there could not perhaps have been a less auspicious time or even place in the British Isles for William Beatty to come into the world. The north of Ireland had been in the grip of recession for four years, and both Protestants and Catholics were leaving the country in their thousands to establish a new life in North America. A large number of those who were quitting were linen weavers, many of whom were also tenant farmers.[20] It was estimated that by the time William was 2 years old a quarter-of-a-million Ulstermen had emigrated to North America. The outbreak of the War of American Independence in 1775 had a devastating effect on the port, abruptly halting further emigration. The sympathies of much of Ulster were at first with the Americans, because of their shared attitudes to religion. After France joined the war in 1778, and following John Paul Jones's daring assault on Belfast Lough when he seized the Royal Navy sloop *Drake*, allegiances changed.

The war only served to exacerbate Ulster economic difficulties: rents went unpaid, manufacturers were forced out of business, and the Revenue declined. Presbyterians and Catholics, excluded from political and government office, became even more discontented. There was some measure of relief in 1778, allowing Presbyterians once again to enjoy the civil rights they had possessed before the introduction of the Test Acts. This did nothing, though, to relieve the tense political situation and demands for the legislative independence of the Irish parliament. Matters came to a head in 1782, when the government was finally forced to yield, granting full legislative independence to the Irish parliament and a measure of Catholic emancipation. These partial measures did not assuage the sense of grievance. As a government official with Presbyterian antecedents and relatives, James Beatty would have found himself with divided loyalties. After the Peace of Versailles in 1783, Londonderry's trade with America resumed. The biggest traffic was 'the most valuable of all products the human race', with between 4,000–5,000 people taking passage every year.[21] In this busy port, with those about to leave Ireland for good always waiting for their ships to sail, and seafarers from different parts of Europe and the eastern seaboard of North America thronging the wharves, James Beatty and his wife brought up their growing family of four sons and two daughters, William, George, James, Vincent, Anna, and Eliza.

[19] George Vaughan Sampson, *County Londonderry* (Dublin, 1801), 284.
[20] Jonathan Bardon, *A History of Ulster* (Belfast, 1992), 210.   [21] Ibid. 367.

EDUCATION AND TRAINING

The boys almost certainly went to school at Foyle Academy, but its school roll for the period does not survive.[22] William would have received the sort of classical education common at the time, which consisted of a grounding in Latin and Greek, mathematics, natural history, physics, and perhaps some moral philosophy and navigation. He would have probably left school at the age of 13 or 14. The temper of the family home would have been one of loyal service to the Crown, which demanded commitment and a certain degree of sacrifice. Gaugers had to work long hours, riding their walks and writing up their entry books.[23] Loyalty brought some benefits, a position in the local community, and above all 'connection' with the Protestant ascendancy, whose patronage was vital if sons wished to enter government service. In the more settled times following the Peace of Versailles trade in Londonderry revived, and William Beatty might have decided to become a merchant or manufacturer. One of his mother's brothers, William Smyth, was a merchant in the city, and his own brother James was to make this his chosen career.

Why our William chose medicine and a naval career is unknown. The most likely explanation is that, at the time he left school, another of his mother's brothers, the naval surgeon George Smyth, settled in Londonderry on half-pay. Smyth had joined the navy in 1778 and served during the American War.[24] He almost certainly tapped into his brother-in-law's patronage network to secure an appointment. The Rowleys were one of the most exceptional families in Nelson's navy. Sir William, the admiral, died in 1768, but his son Joshua rose to the rank of vice-admiral, and was created a baronet in 1786 for his distinguished service. Two of his sons, Bartholomew and Charles, also attained flag rank, and Charles earned a baronetcy in his own right. Josias, the son of Clotworthy, Sir William's third son and sometime MP for Downpatrick, became an admiral as well and got a baronetcy too.[25] With such powerful backing, Smyth would have had no difficulty in getting into the navy and advancing in his career. When he finally left the service in September 1806 Smyth set up in practice as a surgeon in nearby Buncrana.

---

[22] PRONI, SCH/1298/1/1.   [23] Brewer, *Sinews*, 109.

[24] TNA, ADM 11/40, fo. 58.

[25] *Burke's Peerage* and *DNB*, *sub* Rowley family and individual members.

Presumably William Beatty was apprenticed to his uncle and destined for service at sea or with the East India Company. But even if the teenage William Beatty was just inspired by his uncle's example and not apprenticed to him, there were doctors practising in County Londonderry who took apprentices destined for careers in the armed services. At least nineteen young surgeons who were apprenticed in the county joined the army or navy during the French wars, suggesting that it was a popular choice of career for bright students who wished to move away. Londonderry's strong connection with the navy medical service is illustrated by the fact that three surgeons who practised in the port during the early 1820s were half-pay officers: James Burnside, John Monteith, and Cornelius Kelly. A fourth, William Henderson, died there in retirement in 1846. Apart from the ministry and the law, where prospects were limited, medicine was one of the few professional careers open to able young men of limited means who wished to better themselves. There are almost no details of the apprenticeships of naval surgeons, but they are recorded for those in the army. In Londonderry Dr Cudbert and Dr Hamilton trained two each, and almost certainly candidates for the navy as well. Samuel Leatham, who took apprentices in the city, actually advertised himself as an army surgeon, more than hinting that his pupils were destined for a career in the services.[26]

Not many of those who served a medical apprenticeship in Ireland could find employment there. Although the population was large and growing, household incomes were low, and the only way doctors could earn sufficient income was by dispensing medicines as an apothecary in addition to practising their craft. Only three of the doctors who took apprentices in Londonderry advertised themselves just as surgeons. It was not easy to dispense medicines, as the Dublin Corporation of Apothecaries used its charter to limit such practice to its own members, and gaining entry was difficult without patronage.[27] To improve their prospects of employment elsewhere, most apprentices who could afford to do so took university classes. If they were well-connected members of the Church of Ireland they went to Trinity College Dublin, where they could tap into a network of patronage which dominated Irish medicine. Presbyterians, and almost certainly some Catholics, went to Scottish universities or to one of the London teaching hospitals. The ten army doctors

[26] Databases of doctors who served in the army and navy during the French wars, held by Prof. Brockliss, University of Oxford.

[27] *Report from the Select Committee on Medical Education*, 1834, part ii, q. 4902, quoted in Irvine Loudon, *Medical Care and the General Practitioner, 1750–1850* (Oxford, 1986), 44.

who came from County Londonderry took such classes before entering the service. Hugh McLintock spent two years in Edinburgh before he joined in 1812, whereas David Broun studied for two years in Glasgow and London before he joined in 1814. Unfortunately, unlike the army, the navy did not record this information or, if it did, it has not been preserved. There is compelling evidence from Beatty's precise dissection of Nelson's body to trace the course of the bullet which killed him that he attended anatomy classes for at least one or two years. Beatty's outstanding success in his examination before the Company of Surgeons in 1795 confirms this assumption, and suggests too that he had witnessed operations, if not assisted at them (see below). He must also have assisted in embalming a person of quality, otherwise he would not have known how to preserve Nelson's body during the long voyage home from Trafalgar, and make it presentable if it was to be exposed to public view. Beatty's letters at the time suggest that he knew precisely what he was doing. Where he studied, however, is unknown. Before 1800 class lists do not survive for the University of Glasgow, the most likely place. Another possibility is that he moved to London. There he possibly attended Dr Fox's classes at the United Borough Hospitals, south of the Thames. This may explain how he came to be a close friend of his exact naval contemporary, Sir Benjamin Fonseca Outram, who seems to have studied at the Borough before January 1794, when he entered the service.[28] The advantage of London was that it was near the seat of power and patronage. It was not unusual for boys as young as 16 or 17 years old to attend medical classes and walk the wards.

The years of William's apprenticeship in Ulster were marked by conflict between the Protestant and Catholic communities. In County Armagh there was open sectarian warfare in the 1780s between rival gangs of tenant farmers, the Protestant 'Peep O'Day Boys' and the Catholic Defenders. In December 1788 there were elaborate celebrations to mark the centenary of the closing of the gates of Londonderry by the apprentice boys. By the time of the centenary of the raising of the siege in August 1789, the political landscape had been transformed by the outbreak of the French Revolution, which fatally divided Ulster between those who wished for reform and those who wanted to continue to affirm the Protestant Ascendancy. Two years later, in

---

[28] Original *DNB*, *sub* Outram (not recorded in the Oxford *DNB*). Beatty claimed to have studied with Outram (though where he does not say) in the dedication he wrote on Outram's copy of the *Authentic Narrative of the Death of Lord Nelson* (London, 1825): now in the National Maritime Museum.

October 1791, the United Irishmen organization was formed in Belfast to champion the cause of reform, particularly Catholic emancipation, and, as might be expected, found strong support in Londonderry. The United Irishmen based much of their appeal on ideas of equality which were central to the revolution in France.

Beatty was presumably raised in the Church of Ireland and belonged to the section of the Ulster community most loyal to the establishment. His mother, however, seems to have come from a Presbyterian background, for his uncle, George Smyth, was buried in the Presbyterian cemetery at Old Glendermott along with his cousin Vincent Beatty, son of Uncle Ross.[29] It is quite possible that Beatty's political loyalties were torn, like those of many of his contemporaries, even though his father was a servant of the Crown. This, then, would have only been a further incentive to follow a career in the navy. In pursuit of this goal he must have left Londonderry in 1789 or 1790, to take medical classes and walk the wards. His uncle would have recommended classes in subjects such as anatomy, chemistry and materia medica. He would also have told him to witness as many 'capital' operations as he could. Beatty's inclination for a naval medical career may have been galvanized by the diplomatic dispute that developed between Britain and Russia in 1791, instigated by Russia's occupation of the former Turkish Black Sea fortress of Ochakov.[30] William Pitt mobilized the fleet against Russia, offering Beatty an excellent opportunity to join the service.

On 5 May 1791 Beatty was examined before the London Company of Surgeons, and qualified as second mate of a third-rate.[31] No record of his examination in physic has survived. Five days later, at the age of 18, he was warranted as second mate to the veteran surgeon John Wardrop of the 64-gun *Dictator*, which was preparing for sea at Sheerness.[32] Beatty's initial experience of naval life may have resembled that of Joseph Emerson, who joined Nelson's 64-gun *Agamemnon* as second mate in 1793:

Our birth, (the mate's) is a neat one—neatly paper'd—we always have two mould Candles (which are allow'd us) burning on the table, cover'd with a green cloth, & two neat metal candlesticks . . . We have a roast leg of Mutton, a plumb-pudding,

[29] Londonderry Public Library, M. and D. Todd, 'Register of Gravestone Inscriptions in Old Glendermott Burial Ground, Church Road, Londonderry'.

[30] Paul Webb, 'Sea Power in the Ochakov Affair of 1791', *International History Review*, 2 (1980), 13–33.

[31] Royal College of Surgeons of England, Examination Books, 1745–1800, p. 65. Beatty's name was recorded as Batty, a common variation of Beattie in Scotland and northern England.

[32] TNA, ADM 35/510; ADM 51/249.

& beef-steak-pye for dinner...I sling my hammock over my chest in the back pit—& sleep very comfortably....The surgeon is a sensible, easy man, & all gentleman. He is very communicative & has much professional merit. I am happy that I can learn something from him.[33]

The Ochakov dispute was resolved through negotiation, and the *Dictator* was decommissioned. Beatty's first taste of naval medicine must have confirmed his choice of career though, for he accepted a warrant as second mate of the 32-gun *Iphigenia*, commanded by the Scotsman, Captain Patrick Sinclair, in September 1791.[34] Beatty would serve with the frigate, which operated out of Milford Haven, for more than a year, gaining knowledge of his craft from her experienced surgeon James Fea, who was a licentiate of the Company of Surgeons and had served during the American War.[35]

WAR WITH FRANCE: WEST INDIES

Revolutionary France declared war on Britain on 1 February 1793, and on that day Beatty achieved his first promotion, moving with Fea as his first mate into the 32-gun frigate *Hermione*, captain John Hills.[36] He was accompanied by his younger brother George, who enlisted as a volunteer, probably with the aim of securing a commission in the Marines. George's ambition may have been for a military career, but army, unlike marine, commissions had to be purchased and probably were beyond the modest means of the family. Both men would enjoy remarkably successful careers in the armed forces during the ensuing two decades of war, and find their lives intertwined with that of Nelson, the hero of the age.

William Pitt's ministry planned to cripple France by destroying the maritime-colonial foundation of her power in the West Indies. West Indian commerce comprised roughly two-fifths of French foreign trade, two-thirds of French oceanic shipping, and may have employed as many as a fifth of French registered seamen.[37] The upheaval of the revolution had radically destabilized France's colonies, provoking power struggles between the metropolitan

---

[33] Joy Lody, 'Treasure in a Parish Chest', *Nelson Dispatch*, 6 (1999), 434–5.

[34] TNA, ADM 35/880, ADM 36/11520 and http://www.stirnet.com/HTML/genie/british/ss4as/sinclair05.htm (Jan. 2005).   [35] TNA, ADM 51/476.

[36] TNA, ADM 35/747, ADM 36/12011.

[37] Michael Duffy, *Soldiers, Sugar and Seapower: The British Expeditions to the West Indies and the War Against Revolutionary France* (Oxford, 1987), 4–37.

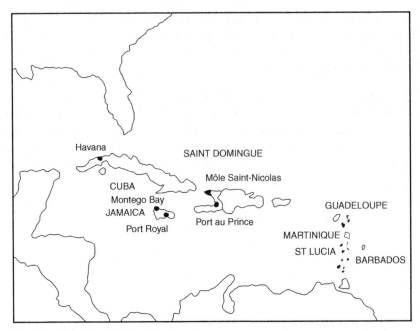

Map 2. The West Indies Theatre.

revolutionaries and the old white planter elite, and within the colonies
themselves, where revolutionary ideals of liberty and equality encouraged the
political aspirations of the poorer whites classes, mulattos, and slaves. Threatened by chaotic civil war and slave uprisings, and the loss of power and
privilege, anti-revolutionary French proprietors launched overtures to the
British government, pledging to accept its protection if it would restore their
predominance. In early April 1793 an accord was reached with emissaries from
Saint-Domingue, France's wealthiest colony, which produced approximately
two-fifths of the world's sugar and more than half of its coffee.[38] In June, while
a great expeditionary force for the West Indies was being prepared, Pitt's
ministry authorized the governor of Jamaica to invade the island if sufficient
assistance from the counter-revolutionaries appeared probable.

In the spring of 1793 the *Hermione* escorted a convoy to the West Indies,
where it joined the squadron of Commodore John Ford. Ford's squadron
played a major role in the invasion of Saint-Domingue, designed to take
advantage of anti-revolutionary support. In September 1793 the ports of

[38] David Geggus, *Slavery, War and Revolution: The British Occupation of Saint Domingue*
(Oxford, 1982), 1–114.

Jérémie and Môle Saint-Nicolas were occupied by detachments of soldiers landed by Ford, aided by a diversion to the Bay des Flamands in the south by the *Hermione* and several other frigates, which captured ten French merchantmen. The bloodless seizure of the powerful naval base of Môle Saint-Nicolas was a particularly important coup.[39] In the port, on 5 December 1793, Ford appointed Beatty acting surgeon of the armed schooner *Flying Fish* under the command of Lieutenant James Prevost, replacing Ian Duncanson, who had died in Port Royal Hospital in September.[40] Well prepared by more than two years' experience as a mate, Beatty assumed responsibility for the welfare of her crew of thirty seamen. During the remaining part of the month the *Flying Fish* conveyed deputations of French royalists, who wished to negotiate joining the British, to and from Môle Saint-Nicolas.

In early 1794 the British mounted a major offensive against the French West Indian colonies with the arrival of a fleet under Sir John Jervis, later Earl St Vincent, and an army of 7,000 commanded by Lieutenant-General Charles Grey. In March Martinique was captured, followed by St-Lucia and Guadeloupe in April. In May the arrival of naval and military reinforcements at Saint-Domingue allowed the British to extend their footholds. Ford had established a close blockade of the capital Port-au-Prince, and the *Flying Fish* cruised off the approaches, intercepting five French ships attempting to enter or leave during the month. At times the blockading ships penetrated so far into the port as to engage the enemy forts. In addition, the schooner functioned as a supply ship, transporting provisions and stores from Port Royal. Ford's squadron also effectively supported the army ashore. On 4 May the *Hermione* and the *Flying Fish* helped to repulse a French assault upon Fort Le Cul in Léogane to the west of Port-au-Prince, by standing along the shore and firing upon the enemy, who were routed and pursued by a British counter-attack.[41]

In late May Ford sailed from Môle Saint-Nicolas, carrying Major-General John White and 1,465 British troops to capture Port-au-Prince. Success depended upon the capture of Fort Bizoton, which was 3 miles to the southwest of the town, and dominated the littoral. On 1 June Ford deployed his two most powerful ships of the line and a frigate to engage the fort, while others, including the *Flying Fish*, dispersed any republican French troops who concentrated to dispute the landing. These ships cleared the shore for the assault troops, who were completely disembarked by late afternoon. A fortuitous

[39] TNA, ADM 52/3158.   [40] TNA, ADM 35/672, ADM/12012.
[41] TNA, ADM 52/3035.

thunderstorm compelled all firing to cease at about 6 p.m. Captain Daniel of the 41st Regiment exploited the pause to launch a daring bayonet assault with his sixty men, taking the fort by storm. He was reinforced by the main body under Major Spencer, so that at daybreak the *Flying Fish*'s master, Francis Banks, could record, 'saw ye British flag hoist at Fort Besicton, our troops in Possession'. The next stage of the operation proceeded smoothly, with the landing of troops to the north of the port, covered by the cannon-fire of two frigates. They seized the perimeter defences at Salines. On 4 June, after the remaining French positions had been abandoned, Port-au-Prince capitulated. The conquest of such a significant naval base was achieved with minor losses: Ford's ships suffered only fifteen casualties, while nine soldiers were killed and three wounded. Approximately forty-five French ships were taken in the harbour, twenty-two carrying rich cargoes of sugar, coffee, cocoa, and indigo.[42]

EPIDEMIC

It was not long after extensive military operations were mounted on shore that the army and navy were decimated by disease, which at times crippled their efforts. Many troops and sailors had departed from Britain already debilitated by typhus, dysentery, and relapsing fever, contracted in cramped, unhygienic base camps, and spread on board equally unhealthy troopships. Once they arrived in the Caribbean they became vulnerable to yellow fever, malaria, and other tropical diseases. Yellow fever, the endemic scourge of the West Indies station, had probably first been introduced from Africa during the 1640s. During 1793–8 the Caribbean and the northern coasts of America were afflicted by a 'pandemic' of the disease, caused by the wartime movements of refugees and the influx of a large number of susceptible European combatants. In the West Indies the severity of the outbreak may have been aggravated by the unusually high temperatures and rainfall of these years, which encouraged the breeding of the disease's transmitter, the domestic mosquito *Aedes aegypti*. The mosquito reproduced in sources of clean water such as springs, wells, and barrels, and it was this close proximity to soldiers and seamen that made it such a great threat. The unusually high mortality rate may also have been the result of the arrival of a particularly virulent strain from Boullam in West Africa in March 1793.[43]

[42] TNA, ADM 52/3035. W. M. James, *The Naval History of Great Britain* (London, 2002), i. 225–7.   [43] Geggus, *Slavery*, 347–72; Duffy, *Soldiers*, 326–61.

Typically, an attack of yellow fever begins with weakness, sudden headache, burning fever, inflammation of the eyes, and back-pain. A high pulse declines with the development of compulsive vomiting. Jaundice and delirium are common. Perhaps the two most horrific symptoms are the vomiting of partly digested blood, and generalized haemorrhage in the final stages. Attacks last for approximately two weeks, and if the sufferer survives, he or she will then be immune. William Turnbull, an experienced naval surgeon who wrote a cogent summary of contemporary medical theory and practice, provided a contemporary description of the disease feared by seamen as the 'Black Vomit' or 'Yellow Jack':

What peculiarly marks this description of fever is the suddenness of its attack and the rapid progress of the symptoms of debility. The redness of the face very speedily yields to a yellow tinge; the increased action, to fainting on the slightest motion; the eyes become a pure yellow colour, which is quickly diffused over the whole of the skin. The vomiting, at first frequent and violent, soon diminishes; and the pure bile at first evacuated becomes tinged with blood. Haemorrhages arise from the mouth, ears, anus and urethra. Towards the close of life the blood from the anus has a black, gritty sediment, and is extremely offensive. Indeed, every part of the body is affected with strong marks of putrescency. Large petechiae are discovered throughout the skin, consisting of red or livid patches. Their first appearance is either during the comatose state, or a few hours previous to death; and of all the symptoms, they are the most universally fatal.[44]

Unfortunately, contemporary medical science had no clear understanding of the nature or transmission of the virus, beyond its prevalence in tropical coastal areas, and of the threat it posed to new, non-immune arrivals. Doctors possessed no effective means of prevention or treatment. The most widely accepted medical opinion mistakenly identified 'marsh miasmata' or harmful vapour emanating from damp or swampy soil, rather than mosquitoes, as the source of infection. Robert Kerr, surgeon of the 74-gun *Elizabeth* during the American War, whose ship's company was attacked by yellow fever off St-Lucia in 1779, wrote that its cause, 'seemed evidently to have been the marsh miasma since all those who went ashore at the watering place were first seized'.[45] The swiftness with which yellow fever struck, its agonizing symptoms, high rate of mortality, and the seeming hopelessness of any cure, caused severe demoralization among soldiers and sailors. Many turned to alcohol from a mistaken belief in its ability to prevent fever, or as a temporary

[44] William Turnbull, *The Naval Surgeon* (London, 1806), 167.
[45] W. Watson, 'Two British Naval Surgeons of the French Wars', *Medical History*, 13 (1969), 218.

escape from fear of infection and the sufferings of the ill comrades who surrounded them. Naval surgeons did recognize proximity to the land as a primary source of infection, however, by observation that soldiers, and seamen serving ashore or collecting wood or water were most vulnerable. This led to the sensible recommendation to avoid anchoring in river-mouths or too close to the shore.

The ferocity of the yellow fever epidemic was truly horrific, especially among the recent arrivals from Europe. The army suffered the most appalling losses: about 2,800 of Grey's 7,000 men died from the disease. The navy too was ravaged. Some of the most graphic accounts of the epidemic have been documented by naval surgeons. In June 1793 the Scottish surgeon's mate Peter Cullen had joined Ford's command at Port Royal in the 74-gun *Hannibal*. Soon after her arrival, Cullen reported evacuating 100 sick to the hospital, the great majority being yellow fever cases, whom he visited twice a day.[46] Cooper Willyams, chaplain of Jervis's flagship the *Boyne*, reported the deaths of forty-six masters and 1,100 seamen in the transport fleet.[47] A thorough account of the epidemic was recorded by the Irish surgeon Dr Leonard Gillespie of the *Majestic*, who served in the squadron off Guadeloupe in late 1794. He calculated that Jervis's ships had already lost one-fifth of their companies to the disease. In 1798 Gillespie was appointed physician of the Martinique hospital, where he reported the deaths of 14,000 soldiers over the next few years. Gillespie developed his medical experiences on the station, including his thoughts on the causes and treatment of yellow fever, in two studies, *Advice to Commanders of HM Fleet in the West Indies* (1798), and *Observations on the Diseases which Prevailed in HM Squadron in the Leeward Islands, 1794–96* (1800). It has been estimated that approximately 43,750 white British soldiers died of disease, largely from yellow fever, malaria, and dysentery, in the West Indies between 1793 and 1801. This number represented about half of all those deployed. Although the mortality rate in the navy was not as high, its losses were also heavy. During the same period, between 19,000–24,000 sailors aboard the fleet and transports perished.[48] Captain John Hills of the *Hermione* died of yellow fever in August 1794, and Captain Patrick Sinclair of the *Iphigenia* had perished the previous May, probably also from the disease.

During the early years of the war the Royal Navy suffered from a chronic shortage of medical officers, and the problem was particularly acute in the

[46] NMM, IGR/22, 'Diary of Peter Cullen'.
[47] Cooper Willyams, *An Account of the Campaign in the West Indies in the Year 1794* (London, 1796), 61.   [48] Duffy, *Soldiers*, 331–4.

West Indies, where casualty rates from disease were extremely high. With considerable understatement Cullen remarked that 'Medical Officers were very scarce at this time'.[49] Beatty's predecessor in the *Flying Fish* probably died from yellow fever, and the lack of surgeons opened the way for his transfer to a 28-gun frigate with a complement of 200 men soon after the fall of Port-au-Prince. On 25 June Ford warranted Beatty acting surgeon of the *Alligator*, a significant increase in trust and responsibility, which reflected the commander-in-chief's confidence in the young medical officer's ability.[50]

Yellow fever struck Port-au-Prince soon after its fall to the British. In July as many as ten to twelve civilians and twenty-five to thirty soldiers were dying each day. The disease spread to the ships in the harbour, and upon joining the *Alligator* Beatty was confronted with the outbreak of a virulent epidemic. The captain Thomas Affleck's brother and predecessor William had died, probably of yellow fever, in February. The terrible course of the epidemic can be traced in the entries in the ship's muster and pay books marked 'departed this life', 'discharged dead', and 'discharged to sick quarters'. When mustered on 28 June, two days after Beatty's arrival, only four names appeared on the sick list. During the ensuing week, while the *Alligator* escorted seven prizes to Port Royal, twenty-two seamen and marines died, with as many as five perishing in one day. Once there, large numbers of the sick were evacuated to the hospital, where many more succumbed. Before the epidemic ended in late July, approximately thirty-five members of the ship's company had died on board, and fifteen more in Port Royal Hospital. In total, the epidemic claimed approximately fifty lives or one-quarter of the *Alligator*'s entire crew.[51]

Since Beatty's medical log has not survived, it is difficult to speculate upon how he attempted to combat the disease. Most newly qualified naval surgeons who went out to the West Indies during the early years of the war had no personal experience of tropical medicine, and what training they might have received was of limited value. Since yellow fever baffled the greatest medical minds of the day, it is not surprising that naval surgeons such as Thomas Downey, who sailed to the West Indies in late 1795, privately confessed their own bewilderment: 'With respect to the treatment of the disease, I was much at a loss.'[52] Downey turned to the writings of three leading fever experts which he had brought from England or acquired in the Caribbean, and he was familiar with the remedies of a fourth. Bleeding was recommended by the military medical officers Robert Jackson, assistant inspector of hospitals, the

[49] NMM, IGR/22, 'Diary of Peter Cullen'.   [50] TNA, ADM 36/11245.
[51] TNA, ADM 35/173; ADM 36/11245.   [52] Watson, 'Two British Naval Surgeons', 223.

surgeon Dr Colin Chisholm, and Nelson's friend Dr Benjamin Moseley, and by the civilian Philadelphia physician Dr Benjamin Rush. All seem to have recognized that cinchona bark, while efficacious against malaria, had no effect upon yellow fever. Jackson and Rush claimed that cold effusions promoted recovery. Chisholm, like many army surgeons, advocated courses of mercury. Downey attempted to assess the merits of their recommended treatments, and appears to have placed most faith in calomel. He submitted a report on his observations to Trotter, who quoted it in his *Medicina Nautica*. Beatty may also have followed the practice of Gillespie, who opposed the army surgeons' reliance upon bleeding and mercurial medicines in favour of bark mixed with wine or lemon juice, demulcent drinks, and tepid baths.[53]

On 28 June Beatty had the *Alligator*'s lower deck washed, and disinfected by fumigation with tobacco smoke and cleansing with vinegar. Disinfection was routinely carried out whenever an infection occurred, reflecting the view that the epidemic was the result of effluvia from bogs and marshes which stuck to clothing, the human body, and any part of the ship. This process was repeated for three successive days after the frigate reached Port Royal and Beatty had transferred the most serious cases to hospital. Perhaps the best treatment of yellow fever, considering the ignorance of its pathology, was that advocated by the French West Indian doctors. In contrast to the often violent intervention favoured by the British, who prescribed purgatives and emetics to relieve vomiting, and 'inflammatory' drugs to induce perspiration and encourage remission of fever, as well as bleeding, the French tended to let nature take its course, and emphasized re-hydrating drinks, warm baths, and careful nursing.[54] Although naval surgeons failed in their attempts to prevent or cure yellow fever, at times they demonstrated truly heroic dedication, despite great personal risk. In 1796 Downey was invalided home because of illness and exhaustion, and was returning to England in a convoy when several of its ships were afflicted with the disease. The frigate *Daedalus* had lost her surgeon, and Downey agreed to take his place. He spent two successive days without sleep tending to the sick, before he fell ill himself. As the epidemic claimed more victims, Downey 'saw them at intervals when I had strength to be supported to their cots'.[55]

[53] Watson, 'Two British Naval Surgeons', 220–23. Gillespie, *Observations*, 60–78, 129–360.

[54] Geggus, *Slavery*, 369–71; Duffy, *Soldiers*, 358–60; Laurence Brockliss and Colin Jones, *The Medical World of Early Modern France* (Oxford, 1997), 438–9.

[55] Watson, 'Two British Naval Surgeons', 222.

Regardless of whatever cure Beatty may have tried, the epidemic only ceased once the *Alligator* had weighed anchor on 13 July, and left the source of infection behind. During the rest of the month the frigate collected merchant ships from Jamaica's ports for convoy to Havana. In an attempt to make up the serious loss of manpower caused by the disease, Affleck resorted to the navy's traditional tactics when volunteers proved scarce. He took on board merchant seamen who had been imprisoned in Montego Bay's gaol, and on 23 July he pressed thirty-five sailors from commercial vessels in the port. The next day Beatty carefully examined the new recruits and rejected thirteen as medically unfit, being vigilant to avoid introducing typhus or any other infectious disease into the ship. Beatty continued regularly to order the fumigation and disinfection of the ship with vinegar. On 28 July the escorts and convoy of more than 120 ships set sail. The treatment of the many injuries caused by accidents and the hard labour of working the ship was one of the naval surgeon's most common duties. Aid was often extended to merchantmen which did not carry surgeons. On 1 August the *Alligator* answered a distress signal and took in tow the London vessel the *Duke of Clarence*, which had lost its fore topmast, and Beatty was rowed across to tend to those hurt during the accident. The convoy reached Havana on 8 August without losing a single ship to enemy action.[56]

Fortunately for Beatty and the others who had escaped the ravages of yellow fever, the *Alligator* was then ordered to escort a great convoy of over 130 sail to England. The crew's health was excellent during the voyage, allowing Beatty to enjoy a considerable amount of leisure, a welcome relief after the anxious battle against the epidemic. The rhythm of his days perhaps resembled those of his fellow surgeon James Kerr during a similar trans-atlantic passage:

We are now at sea and our way of life settled according to custom . . . my time for rising is at seven or half after seven o'clock. Breakfast at eight. At nine I see my patients which takes half an hour or an hour. From that to eleven generally read or write in my cabin, then take a walk on deck, give the captain an account of the sick. After having stretched my limbs, seen what the admiral is doing and what the fleet . . . I come down to my cabin again and take up a book till the drum beating The Roast Beef of Old England warns me to dinner. . . . After dispatching this necessary piece of business and the grog being finished, the remainder of my time till supper is spent variously in reading, writing, card-playing, backgammon,

---

[56] TNA, ADM 51/1150; ADM 52/2715.

walking or conversation as humour leads. From supper time at 8 O'clock till bed-time is spent in chit-chat over our grog drinking.[57]

Kerr, like Downey, was a poet, addressing verses to his lost love, whom unfeeling relatives had taken from Scotland to India. During his many years at sea Beatty must have devoted much of his free time to wide reading, which helped him to acquire the cultivated literary tastes of a gentleman, as well as the fluid writing style he would demonstrate in his account of the death of Nelson. On 13 October 1794 the convoy arrived without incident at Liverpool.[58]

Beatty's career as a surgeon began in the West Indies, the navy's most dangerous station, where prolonged service carried such a grave risk. He must have been relieved to leave Port Royal behind, whose notorious graveyard, the Palissades, received the corpses of thousands of sailors during the early years of the war, the majority being victims of yellow fever. During the period from 13 October to 18 February 1795, when the *Alligator* was paid off at Portsmouth, twenty-five seamen and marines deserted, many perhaps pressed men desperate to avoid another spell of service in the West Indies. It is interesting to note the pay that Beatty earned for his strenuous duty. After deductions for the pensions fund for officers' widows, the Chatham Chest, and Greenwich Hospital, he received £35. 5s. 1d. for his approximately seven-month warrant aboard the *Flying Fish*, and £39. 8s. 6d. for nearly eight months as acting surgeon of the *Alligator*. The expense of Beatty's surgical instruments and drugs was partially offset by his 'Free Gifts', which totalled £24. 3s. 2d. for the *Flying Fish* and £26 15s. 4d. for the *Alligator*. The pay books of the *Flying Fish* also record the allowances that surgeons received to augment their meagre pay. Beatty earned an additional 15s. for a cure of venereal disease, and his 'two pences' from the Chatham Chest amounted to another £1. 13s. 3d. These supplements were not paid until July 1799, more than five years after he had left the ship.[59]

Although service in the Caribbean was extremely dangerous, it offered great opportunities for many of those officers and ratings lucky enough to survive. The wealth of its shipping made it an extremely lucrative source of prize money. As many as one in three of all prizes seized during 1797–1800 were captured in the Caribbean. According to the legislation of 1708, which set out the division of prize money, the commander-in-chief earned

[57] Watson, 'Two British Naval Surgeons', 215.
[58] TNA, ADM 51/1150; ADM 52/2715.
[59] TNA, ADM 35/672; ADM 35/173; ADM 102/851.

one-eighth, the captain one-quarter, the master and lieutenants one-eighth, the warrant officers (including the surgeon) one-eighth, the petty officers (including the surgeon's mates) one-eighth, and the seamen and marines one-quarter. The greatest fortunes were therefore reaped by admirals such as Jervis, who earned approximately £11,230 during his campaign, while his able seamen received £5. 5*s*. 11*d*.[60] As a warrant officer Beatty would have earned a substantial sum, perhaps worth several years' pay, from the captures made by the *Hermione*, *Flying Fish*, and the many rich prizes taken with Port-au-Prince. In addition to these financial rewards, Beatty benefited from the rapid rate at which surgeons died, or were invalided home from the West Indies, by the almost immediate promotion to acting surgeon, which provided valuable experience.

COURT MARTIAL

Immediately after leaving the *Alligator* in Portsmouth in February 1795, Beatty travelled to London to earn promotion to surgeon. George had followed his brother into the *Alligator* and returned to England with him. He obtained a commission as second lieutenant in the Marines in May 1795, probably through the Rowley interest, and was appointed to the *Theseus*.[61] Although still officially a mate, William had served as acting surgeon for approximately fourteen months, during which time he had gained in knowledge, skill, and confidence, especially while being responsible for the care of the *Alligator*'s crew of 200. On 19 February Beatty distinguished himself in his examination before the Company of Surgeons by winning one of the highest qualifications awarded to a candidate. This reflects the excellence of his earlier study of surgery (wherever it took place), which was improved by aptitude, application, and experience. He qualified for surgeon of a second-rate, a ship of the line carrying ninety to ninety-eight guns and a complement of over 700 men (see Ill. 3). Of a sample of 105 candidates who passed examinations in surgery during 1793–1815, only eighteen others were judged competent for appointment to ships of the first and second rate, indicating that Beatty placed among the top 20 per cent.[62] Beatty also passed a second examination in physic at Greenwich Hospital, but unfortunately the results have not survived.

---

[60] Duffy, 113.   [61] ADM 196/58, fo. 8.
[62] Royal College of Surgeons of England, Examination Books, 1745–1800, p. 116.

There was a great demand for surgeons as the navy rapidly mobilized in the early years of the war, so that Beatty's promotion was quickly followed by appointment to the 28-gun frigate *Pomona* at Sheerness on 8 March, commanded by the youthful Lord Augustus Fitzroy, who had also been born in 1773. Beatty's prospects seemed excellent. His captain was the fourth son of the wealthy and powerful duke of Grafton, a former prime minister, whose own father, Lord Augustus Fitzroy (1716–41), had been a naval officer. Establishing a good relationship with Fitzroy could have opened an influential channel of patronage. During the initial months of her commission the *Pomona* was employed in escorting convoys through the Channel and in cruising for enemy warships and commerce. On 19 July, however, an incident occurred which appeared to shatter Beatty's hopes of a successful career. During a weekly muster of the crew Fitzroy accused Beatty of contemptuous behaviour, and confined him to his cabin to await court martial. Beatty must have endured a torment of anxiety imprisoned in his tiny wooden cell, threatened with ignominious dismissal from the service, until the trial was convened on board the *Malabar* at the Nore on 4 August. The incident between Beatty and Fitzroy can be reconstructed from the detailed records of the court martial, and deserves particular attention as a rare and important insight into the young surgeon's character.[63]

The president of the court martial was Captain Matthew Squire of the *Magnificent*, second-in-command of the Royal Navy vessels in the Medway and the Nore. The twelve other captains on the panel included William Bligh, who probably would have reacted with hostility to any officer condemned for challenging his commander's authority. Once the prisoner had been brought before his judges, the intimidating formality of the proceedings commenced with a statement of the formal charge, which was 'to try Mr William Beaty Surgeon of HMS *Pomona* for disrespect and contemptuous behaviour to the Right Honble Lord Augustus Fitzroy'. The charge was elaborated upon by Fitzroy, who read out the letter he had written to Vice-Admiral Charles Buckner requesting a court martial, which described Beatty's alleged offences in detail. Fitzroy acted as prosecutor, calling eight witnesses to make his case, including first lieutenant David Cree, second lieutenant David Gilmour, the surgeon's mate James Billing, William Linton, the schoolmaster of the *Dryad*, who was on board at the time, midshipman John Willoughby, captain's clerk James Dennis, quartermaster John Acres,

---

[63] TNA, ADM 1/5333, Minutes of Proceedings at a Court Martial Held on Board HMS *Malabar* at the Nore, 4 August 1795.

sergeant of marines Francis Walton, and seaman John Brown. Beatty, who defended himself during the trial, was then allowed to cross-examine the witnesses. Finally, questions were put to the witnesses by members of the court martial to clear up any ambiguity.

According to a collation of the witnesses' testimony, on Sunday 19 July a dispute occurred between Fitzroy and Beatty, provoked by critical comments made by Fitzroy during and after the weekly muster of the ship's company. When seaman William Lancaster's name was called, Beatty's mate James Billing replied that he was ill and unable to attend muster. Fitzroy asked whether he was in his hammock. Beatty answered no, but that 'he had a very bad leg and a scorbutic Inflammation and it would be highly improper to walk upon it but was absolutely necessary'. Fitzroy then ordered that Lancaster be brought upon deck, and the following exchange occurred:

BEATTY: My Lord, I can only say that he ought not to walk on his Leg (as I stated before).
FITZROY: I saw him walking the Deck only yesterday.
BEATTY: I can only say my Lord it is improper.
FITZROY: 'Tis not improper if I order it.

Lancaster was assisted upon deck by two carpenters and the muster continued, until the seaman John McIntyre was called, who also failed to appear, apparently on account of illness. Fitzroy sent the boatswain in search of him, who reported that McIntyre was in his hammock. When questioned by Fitzroy upon his status, Beatty replied that he had examined McIntyre that morning, and prescribed the necessary medicine, but that 'if he is in his Hammock it is without my knowledge or leave, he being a Convalescent'. Fitzroy then turned to the assembled officers and declared: . . . 'there was certainly a proof that neither the Surgeon or Mate knew the state of the sick, as there was one Man reported to be able to come upon Deck who was in his Hammock, and another that was not in his Hammock, and reported not able to come upon Deck.'

Fitzroy and Beatty continued to discuss the two cases upon the quarterdeck following the muster, in increasingly acrimonious terms. Fitzroy claimed to have seen the seaman Lancaster walking on his leg earlier, and asserted 'that there appeared to be nothing more the matter with him than with his Lordship, and at this rate we may have them all in the Sick List'. Beatty responded 'that was to go to the head [the latrines in the foreword part of the ship's hull] and was a case of necessity'. Fitzroy then criticized Beatty for the number of ill he discharged to Haslar: 'he had sent more Men to the Hospital since he had been in the Ship than he had done for some months before, and that we received very few of them back.' Fitzroy cited this as further proof of Beatty's incompetence, and bluntly declared 'you don't know your duty'. Beatty retorted that 'he knew his Duty before he came into the Ship and did not come there to learn it'. Beatty requested that Fitzroy appeal to the ship's officers, whom he was confident would support him. When Fitzroy refused, he described Beatty's reaction, which terminated the altercation: 'he in a very contemptuous manner and meaning to ridicule me, pulled his Hat off, and made me a low bow, all of which happening on the Quarter Deck and in the face of the Ship's Company.' Fitzroy shouted to his officers to observe Beatty, declaring 'that he never received such a mark of contempt from any officer in his Life', and commanded that the surgeon be placed under arrest.

Much of the testimony in the trial, which would have been farcical had so much not been at stake for Beatty, concerned the description and interpretation of his bow: of the way in which he removed his hat, its depth, and how he slowly scraped his foot upon the deck. Clearly an argument between Fitzroy and Beatty had broken out over the cases of Lancaster and McIntyre, which escalated into a much more serious dispute, revealing the captain's disapproval of the way the surgeon managed the *Pomona*'s sick berth. Beatty had reacted with great indignation to Fitzroy's censure, as Linton observed: 'he seemed to elevate his voice at something that his lordship mentioned to him of his Duty.' Accusing an Ulsterman of not doing his duty may have touched a raw nerve. Acres the quartermaster and Walton the marine sergeant also reported signs of emotion. Walton observed that 'He looked very white, his countenance changed', and Acres thought the bow 'was in ridicule on Account of his face colouring'. Although virtually all of the witnesses observed that some form of quarrel had occurred, the great majority, including lieutenants Cree and Gilmour, and Willoughby the midshipman, testified that there was nothing offensive in Beatty's behaviour that morning. When a member of the court asked Cree, 'did he [Beatty] appear to conduct himself in the manner he ought to have done to his Superior Officer?', he replied, 'All the time I was present he did'. Gilmour answered Beatty's question, 'Did you see any marks of contempt or disrespect in my behaviour', with the reply, 'I did not'. Beatty's judges plainly expressed their opinion of the whole incident in their verdict: 'And the Court having proceeded maturely to consider the whole of the Evidence on the part of the prosecution were of Opinion that the charges were not proved and that they were frivolous' (see Ill. 4). Such language did not spare Fitzroy, as his fellow captains emphatically conveyed annoyance that they had should have been distracted from the important duty of fighting the war to pander to his absurd notions of injured dignity. Although acquitted, however, it is difficult not to believe that Beatty intended the bow to express his outrage at Fitzroy's slurs upon his professional reputation, and the injustice of the captain's refusal to allow an appeal to the *Pomona*'s other officers in his defence. The symbolic gesture offered one way for Beatty to show contempt for the accuser and his accusations, once he had been forbidden from vindicating himself by Fitzroy's invocation of his ultimate authority.

Although Beatty was exonerated of disrespectful conduct, an analysis of the court martial must also assess the more fundamental, implicit criticism which lay behind the formal charge. There appears to be no foundation whatsoever in the records of the *Pomona* to support Fitzroy's censure that the surgeon was in any way deficient in his duty. Fitzroy's accusation that Beatty was some-how encouraging or abetting Lancaster and others in malingering is dis-proved by Linton, who reported that the seaman 'seemed to be very lame' when summoned on deck. Rather, Beatty's plea that Lancaster be excused because attendance would be 'hurtful' to his inflamed leg demonstrates concern for his comfort and recovery. Fitzroy's charge that Beatty sent an unnecessarily large number of sick to hospital, whom he was unable to cure on board ship, is also unfounded. During the four months that Beatty had been surgeon only six crew had been discharged, by no means an excessive number in a frigate with a complement of approximately 200 men.[64]

It is important to assess what the incident reveals about Beatty's character and his relationship with Fitzroy. The surgeon's indignant reaction suggests that he took great pride in his professional reputation, and that he was independent enough to defend it against unjust condemnation, from what-ever source. It took great moral courage for Beatty, an Irish warrant officer from a modest background, to stand up to his aristocratic English captain. Clearly he was not intimidated by Fitzroy's vastly superior social and service rank, power, and influence. There may also have been something of the fire and rashness of youth in Beatty's retorts to Fitzroy and the exaggerated bow. All in all, Beatty appears as a conscientious, humane surgeon, mindful of the sailors' welfare. In contrast, Fitzroy's peremptory behaviour during the muster, with his mutterings about malingering and the unnecessary discharge of sick to

[64] TNA, ADM 51/1154.

the hospital, suggests a haughty authoritarian with little sympathy for his crew. The decision of the *Pomona*'s commissioned officers to support Beatty, rather than side with their captain, despite the power he held over them, is telling, suggesting that Fitzroy was a poor leader, commanding little natural authority or respect. Fitzroy's promotion from lieutenant in 1790 to commander in December 1792, and then to captain in March 1794, had been rapid and probably owed much to the influence of his father, the Whig grandee.

On another level, it is possible to see in Fitzroy's arrogant, high-handed treatment of Beatty the lack of respect which so infuriated naval surgeons during the period. It was not uncommon for captains to consider men such as Beatty as social inferiors, whom they would no more admit to dine at their tables than the surgeons' fellow warrant officers, the carpenter or the gunner. Surgeons very strongly felt that their professional education, training, and qualifications entitled them to a commission, which recognized their status as officers and gentlemen, and the important nature of their work. In 1831, during his campaign to convince the Admiralty formally to grant commissioned rank to the navy's surgeons, the head of the medical service Sir William Burnett, a contemporary of Beatty, looked back to this period and stated how bitterly 'the highly talented and well educated Medical Officers' resented their status, which they considered 'equally obnoxious as degrading'.[65] There was an interesting sequel to the incident aboard the *Pomona*, which appears to confirm that if there was any officer who did not know his duty or was incompetent, it was Fitzroy and not Beatty. In May 1799 Fitzroy himself faced a court martial, charged with 'disobedience of orders and misconduct' in failing to bring home a convoy of East Indiamen under his charge from St Helena. In this case Fitzroy was declared guilty by the judges, who included Captain Thomas Masterman Hardy, and removed from his command.[66]

MISFORTUNE

Fortunately for both Beatty and Fitzroy, they did not serve together for much longer. When the *Pomona* was paid off in September 1795, Beatty was posted

[65] NMM, ELL/245.

[66] TNA, ADM 1/5349. Augustus Fitzroy's younger brother William was a naval officer, who also attained the rank of post-captain at the age of 22. His career was marred by rumours of cowardice before he was dismissed the service in April 1811 for tyranny and oppression, after having ordered his ship's master to be placed in irons.

to the 38-gun frigate *Amethyst*, led by his former commanding officer on the *Alligator* Thomas Affleck. Affleck, who probably had a hand in Beatty's appointment, must have appreciated his handling of the yellow fever epidemic.[67] Beatty's immediate re-employment suggests that his reputation was undamaged by the court martial. His next period of service was to end abruptly and dramatically, however, for on 29 December 1795, approximately three months after he joined, the *Amethyst* was wrecked near Guernsey and nearly lost with all hands. The harrowing tale can be pieced together from the customary court martial held to inquire into the circumstances of the loss, convened aboard the *Orion* at Portsmouth on 8 March 1796, to which Beatty was summoned as a witness.[68]

On 28 December the *Amethyst* had been cruising in company with a squadron of other ships in the vicinity of Guernsey, when she lost sight of her comrades during the night. When the frigate's position had been calculated at 4 p.m., it was agreed that she could safely continue sailing southward until 4 a.m. next morning, before which she would have to wear (i.e. alter course from one tack to the other by turning before the wind), to avoid approaching too close to the island. At approximately 4 a.m., however, during the changing of the watch, lookouts in the maintop shouted 'oh God, there is a rock close under the Lee Bow'. Affleck, who had just come upon deck, described his attempts to avoid collision: '. . . the helm was instantly rigged, the mizzen sheet hauled aft, and in the act of coming to, found the ship strike forward, but did not bring up; it then blowing a heavy gale of wind, and the ship under her fore-sail, I judged it expedient, (from the land being close a head), to wear, and run the risk of clearing the rocks when the ship went safe out.'

Affleck judged from the force of the impact that the damage done to the ship's hull had been severe, and ordered an immediate course to be set for England. Soon after the carpenter reported 'Water to be rushing into the Coal hole in a Torrent', which rapidly flooded into the well. All the pumps were put into action, and chains of seamen were formed with buckets at the fore and main hatchways to bail out the rising water. Despite the sailors' most strenuous efforts, the water level continued to rise as the heavy wind and swell buffeted the *Amethyst*. To lighten the ship, Affleck ordered most of the anchors cut away from the bows, and all the forecastle guns and many from the main deck were thrown overboard. Three attempts were made to plug the leak by lowering sails over the bows, but each failed. It became apparent

[67] TNA, ADM 35/12; ADM 36/11301.   [68] TNA, ADM 1/5335; ADM 14/73/3832.

that the frigate would never reach England, and the pilot advised making for Alderney, which was the nearest land. At 7.30 a.m. the carpenter reported that the water was gaining so fast 'that the ship could not swim two hours longer'. When asked where the *Amethyst* could be run ashore to save the crew, the pilot reported that Bray Bay, Alderney, was about two hours away, given the ship's rate of sailing. At approximately 9.15 a.m., with more than four feet of water in the hold, the pilot navigated the ship through the channel into Bray Bay, 'in a most masterly and cool manner', where she was run aground and the single sheet anchor let go to hold her head upon the beach. All masts were cut away to stabilize the wreck, although the 'surf broke heavy over her as far aft as the main mast'. Affleck mustered the crew on the quarterdeck, where they were evacuated by boat from the shore at the ebbing of the tide. At low water the stern was dry, facilitating the operation.

It had been a near-run thing for Beatty and the other members of the crew. There can perhaps be no more terrifying experience for the sailor, than to find himself lost in the darkness, with breakers looming ahead. Many hearts aboard the *Amethyst* must have sunk when the horrified lookout cried out, 'my God, she has struck, we are all lost'. The tension and anxiety during the exhausting two-hour struggle to keep the frigate afloat during the run to Alderney must have been intense. Although the *Amethyst* was a complete wreck, there was at least one consolation in the disaster, that by the unnamed pilot's courage and skill not one member of the crew was lost. As Affleck rightly emphasized, 'we all owe our existence to the Pilot'. Unfortunately for the captain, the court martial held him personally responsible for the catastrophe, which was 'attributable to the misconduct of the said Captain Thomas Affleck'. His sentence was a harsh one: 'and [we] do adjudge him to be reduced from his present rank on the list of post captains to the bottom of the said list, and to be incapable of being again employed in H M naval service for the remainder of his life.'

Although no explanation of the court martial's verdict is included in the minutes of the trial, it is possible to gain some insight into their reasoning from their cross-examination of the *Amethyst*'s master and lieutenants. It appears that, although Affleck had determined that wearing the ship before 4 a.m. was imperative to avoid the dangerous waters around Guernsey, he had given no precise orders to any officer to carry out the manoeuvre at that time, or sooner if an increase in the ship's speed rendered it necessary. He had also given no order to be informed of any change, with the effect that the *Amethyst* had run on after losing sight of the rest of the squadron. The master, Boyle

White, who took over the watch at 4 a.m., was on the point of ordering the manoeuvre on his own responsibility when the frigate struck the rocks. The fact that Affleck himself was not upon deck at the time may have seemed particularly damning. Affleck's judges also seemed critical of his organization of the ship's watches, the lack of adequate standing orders to govern navigation, and his failure to make greater use of the master's skill and experience.

There was an evident breakdown of discipline following the wreck, while the *Amethyst's* crew was quartered at Alderney. The second lieutenant, John Guyon, reported the great difficulty in 'endeavouring to keep the people quiet, when liquor was cheap and a great deal of money among them'. By 15 February 87 crew had taken advantage of their greater freedom to desert. Many of the ship's company were discharged to the *Diamond* under the command of Sir Sydney Smith.[69]

ALCMENE

Less than three weeks after Affleck's trial Beatty was on active service again, only approximately £40 the richer for his life-threatening experience aboard the *Amethyst*.[70] Despite the loss of a patron, on 26 March he joined the 32-gun frigate *Alcmene*, captain William Brown. Brown's career had begun at the end of the American War, and he would die in 1814 as a rear-admiral and commander-in-chief of the Leeward Islands station.[71] The *Alcmene* (see Ill. 5) would be memorable as the ship upon which Beatty served the longest, a period of nearly five years from March 1796 to March 1801. For much of the time the *Alcmene* would be cruising the Atlantic approaches to Portugal, France, and Spain, attempting to intercept enemy warships and privateers, and preying upon their commerce. Frigate command of this nature was eagerly sought after by ambitious naval officers, as it offered the greatest opportunity for personal distinction by victorious ship-to-ship engagements, and self-enrichment by the capture of lucrative enemy prizes. Beatty would be fortunate to serve under enterprising commanders who made the most of their opportunities.

From March until December 1796 most of the *Alcmene's* duties involved escorting convoys, some including as many as 200 merchant ships, to and from Oporto and Lisbon, and cruising off Portugal, France, and Spain (who

[69] ADM 36/11301, Beatty, although summoned, was not amongst those called to give evidence.
[70] ADM 35/12; ADM 102/851.   [71] Old *DNB*.

had joined in the war with Britain in October 1796). On 21 August, off Cape Finisterre, the frigate captured a 14-gun French privateer, *La Rochellaise*, after a prolonged chase in which the enemy threw eight of her guns overboard before being overtaken. In early 1797 the frigate escorted convoys to Ireland. On 12 February the *Alcemene* briefly anchored off Londonderry, probably the first time that Beatty had set eyes on his home since 1791, although there was no opportunity to go ashore. On 7 March, after leaving Cork, the frigate pursued a 16-gun French privateer from Bordeaux, *Le Surveillant*, which carried over 150 men. The frigate and the chase exchanged a constant fire with their bow and stern guns before the French ship surrendered.[72]

MUTINY

At the end of March the *Alcmene* returned to Spithead from Ireland, and was refitting at the naval base when mutiny broke out in the Channel Fleet on 16 April. The sailors of each ship elected two delegates to represent their long-standing grievances to the Admiralty, demanding an increase in seamen's pay, improvements in the amount and quality of provisions, including the issue of fresh vegetables in port, and better treatment for the sick and wounded. After negotiation, most of the seamen's grievances were addressed. A second mutiny broke out at the Nore on 12 May, three days before the Channel Fleet returned to its duty. The mutineers at the Nore were joined by the North Sea Squadron, but their leaders' more radical demands alienated the moderate majority of seamen, whose ships abandoned the movement in increasing numbers. By 13 June the mutiny ended, when loyal sailors seized control of the remaining ships.[73]

The *Alcmene*'s crew did not join the mutiny, and her refit continued, but her sailors must have sympathized with its demands. On 24 April Captain Brown mustered the ship's company, and read them the royal pardon granted to the mutineers by George III and the Admiralty's pledge to redress their grievances. A period of extreme tension followed the mutinies. The Channel Fleet's success had given sailors a sense of their latent power, and had shaken many officers, who feared further challenges to their authority. There was trouble aboard the *Alcmene* on 2 July, while the frigate was escorting a convoy to Oporto. A seaman named James Davis was confined for drunkenness and

---

72 ADM 51/1164; ADM 52/2659.
73 Conrad Gill, *The Naval Mutinies of 1797* (Manchester, 1913).

disobedience of orders. A small party attempted to release him from his irons, and Brown charged George Rankin and John Anderson, who were identified as the instigators, with mutiny. On 10 July, in Lisbon, ordinary seaman George Ellis was also charged with mutinous abuse of Brown, who had broken up a fight involving the seaman.[74]

The three men were court-martialled off Cadiz on 22 and 24 July by a panel chaired by Vice-Admiral Sir Charles Thompson, second-in-command of St Vincent's Mediterranean Fleet.[75] Anderson was tried for attempting to free Davis from his imprisonment 'in a disorderly and mutinous manner', and Rankin for haranguing the ship's company 'to stir up Mutiny'. Several witnesses, including second lieutenant Richard McKillop, testified to seeing Rankin angrily addressing a group on the forecastle and shouting 'now's the time' and 'follow me boys', before a number of seamen ran below to where Davis was shackled. Immediately before they arrived, master-at-arms Henry Trimbell testified that Anderson, apparently upon his own initiative, had attempted to release Davis, but desisted when warned off. Davis was actually taken out of his irons (which had no lock) by this group of men, but they dispersed when the prisoner prudently declared that he did not wish to be released without the captain's permission. The incident ended when armed officers arrested Rankin and Anderson.

Seaman George Ellis was tried for 'making use of the most abusive, infamous and mutinous language'. He had been fighting a fellow crew member when Captain Brown grabbed him by the hair and pulled him away. According to Marine lieutenant Miles Sandys, Brown may have hit him once or twice in the face. Ellis cursed Brown and denounced his officers while he was being dragged below. He accused Brown of unjustly having him flogged after an earlier incident of disobedience of orders, which he claimed was provoked by McKillop, who had struck him. The enraged prisoner threatened to run Brown through with a sword.

In his defence, Rankin presented a certificate from the American Consulate in Lisbon confirming that he was a 33-year-old American citizen, who had been pressed into the Royal Navy approximately three months before. He pleaded for his behaviour to be excused upon the grounds of temporary insanity, caused by the combination of excessive drinking and the effect of a blow to the head he had suffered ten months ago in Boston in a fall from the main topmast. The 20-year-old Essex native Ellis offered a similar defence, in

---

[74] TNA, ADM 51/1210.   [75] TNA, ADM 1/5340.

a paper explaining that he too was subject to bouts of insanity when drunk, brought on by a childhood accident in which a nail had been driven into his head. It is perhaps surprising that Beatty, the ship's surgeon, was not called to offer a medical opinion upon these defences of insanity, because several witnesses testified to support them. Anderson also submitted a written plea to the court, in which he revealed that he was a pressed Danish sailor, who had been left behind in Lisbon by his ship after he had fallen ill. He was dragged from his lodgings at night by McKillop, taken aboard the *Alcmene*, 'and kept there against my own will'. The name of Anderson had been given him by his captors, despite repeated attempts to make them understand that his real name was Jens Christian Larsen. He begged for leniency upon the grounds of ignorance of the navy's articles of war and his previous good behaviour.

Anderson was acquitted, perhaps because he had listened to the warnings of the master-at-arms. Rankin was found guilty and sentenced to death. Ellis too was convicted and sentenced to 'receive three hundred lashes on his bare back with a cat of nine-tails, on board of or alongside such ship or ships at such time or times, and in such proportions as the Commander In Chief shall direct'. Despite apparently being an American citizen, Rankin's execution was carried out aboard the *Alcmene* the next day. Its log for 25 July records that at 9 a.m. the prisoner, 'after the usual Ceremony, was run up to the Fore Yard Arm & hung by the Neck till he was dead'. Ellis's punishment was administered in the ship's launch the following day. He would have been attended by Beatty as medical officer, and the gruesome spectacle was witnessed by boats from all the fleet's ships. Ellis had been sentenced to receive 100 lashes alongside the *Alcmene*, to be repeated alongside each of two other warships. If fully carried out, a flogging round the fleet was a virtual death sentence. The fact that Ellis survived suggests that Beatty halted the punishment, probably once the prisoner had lost consciousness.[76]

What do these incidents reveal about the condition of the *Alcmene*'s crew? Rankin was a recently arrived supernumerary from another ship and therefore an outsider, and he had conspicuously failed to win support from the vast majority of the *Alcmene*'s crew, and especially its marines, one of whom replied to his cry 'are you with us?' with 'no, you Buggar, we are not'. The failure of the bulk of the ship's company to follow Rankin, and the prisoner Davis's own refusal to be released from confinement, suggest that it accepted the justice of his punishment. Several witnesses testified to Rankin's being

[76] TNA, ADM 51/1210.

Map 3. The Bay of Biscay and The Blockade.

drunk, which further encourages the belief that this was an isolated incident, probably reflecting personal resentment over his own impressment rather than any deep-seated discontent among the crew. Brown and McKillop appear to have been strict disciplinarians, and the captain's severe response to the two incidents suggests that he was determined to assert his authority in the wake of the mutinies. The same motivation is revealed in the court martial's decision to make examples of Rankin and Ellis, which probably reflected St Vincent's firm resolve to discourage any further disorder in the fleet.

CRUISING

The remaining months of 1797 were spent operating off the coasts of Spain, France, and Portugal. On 13 August the frigate defended an American brig from attack by two North African pirate galleys. On 6 November the *Alcmene* helped to repulse an attack upon a convoy she was escorting into Gibraltar by Spanish gunboats which sallied out from Algeçiras (the adjacent enemy port to the west) across the bay. In a confused night action the frigate came to the aid of her comrade the *Andromache*, which was badly damaged in action with the gunboats and the Spanish forts.[77]

In November 1797 the Scot, George Hope, assumed command of the *Alcmene* at Gibraltar. He would later distinguish himself in command of the *Defence* at Trafalgar.[78] The *Alcmene* and the other members of her squadron were repeatedly in action during early 1798, capturing two French privateers, the 18-gun *Benjamin* and the 2-gun *Bonaparte*, off the approaches to Lisbon in January. The squadron continued to take a fair number of prizes as well, including the recapture of the English merchantman the *Camilla*, which had fallen prey to a French commerce raider. On 4 April, off Cape St Vincent, the *Alcmene* intercepted a rich Spanish prize, *El Cid*, bound for Cadiz from the River Plate. In the spring of 1798 the frigate was assigned to the Mediterranean. Much of the time Hope cruised off Spain and France, and carried the war into the enemy harbours, with several daring attempts to cut out warships and merchant vessels. In June the *Alcmene* took two more prizes, a French brig from Smyrna bound for Marseilles, and a Spanish ship from Naples headed for Barcelona. She also intercepted a French packet carrying dispatches from Toulon to Malta.[79]

Hope's ship joined Rear-Admiral Nelson in Aboukir Bay on 14 August, nearly two weeks after the Battle of the Nile. Nelson ordered the *Alcmene* to assist in the blockade of the French army in Egypt, where Bonaparte was now cut off with little hope of reinforcement or re-supply. Off Alexandria on the 22nd, she intercepted the French gunboat *La Légère* from Toulon carrying dispatches to the French general. The dispatches were captured by the courageous action of two seamen, who observed the French throwing several bags overboard. James Harding and John Taylor dived into the sea, even

---

[77] TNA, ADM 51/1164; ADM 51/1210.
[78] R. H. McKenzie, *Trafalgar Roll* (London, 1913), 180.
[79] TNA, ADM 51/4408; ADM 52/2659.

though the ship was travelling at 6 knots, and pulled them out, preserving valuable intelligence for Nelson. They were later rewarded for their initiative with £20 pensions from the City of London. In early September the frigate distributed provisions among the blockading squadron, including cattle, onions, rice, tobacco, and 5,000 lemons and a large supply of fresh fruit to prevent the development of scurvy. Hope supplied the ships of the line with 624 lemons each, while the smaller frigates were given half that number. On 21 September he succeeded in an audacious cutting-out expedition involving all the ship's boats, which seized seven supply ships from under the guns of the French fort in Damietta Bay. Eight vessels in total were taken during the operation, although three were found to be the property of owners in Tripoli and later returned. Most of the others were laden with wine and brandy for the French army, making them immensely popular as well as lucrative captures, because the alcohol was purchased for consumption by the British fleet. The *Alcmene's* ship's company must have toasted their good fortune when drinking the wine and brandy intended for their enemy, which they would be paid for capturing. For many weeks after the ship's logs recorded the issuing of '30 gallons of prize wine to the purser'.[80]

On 14 January 1799 the *Alcmene* joined Nelson at Naples to assist in the evacuation of the Neapolitan royal family, as French armies swept down the Italian peninsula. Nelson had urged King Ferdinand to declare war on France during the previous autumn and attack the newly proclaimed French republic based at Rome. Although the allied Neapolitan and Austrian army had briefly taken Rome in November, a counter-offensive had driven deep into the kingdom and threatened Naples. Nelson and the British diplomatic representative, Sir William Hamilton, planned for the secret removal of the king and queen to Sicily with treasure worth approximately £2.5 million. Great care was essential, as there was a strong sentiment in the city opposed to the king's departure, and the pro-French faction at court considered kidnapping Nelson and the Hamiltons and holding them hostage. On 20 December Nelson ordered *Alcmene's* boats, their crews armed with cutlasses, to assist in the evacuation, which was achieved via an underground passage from the palace to the shore. Nelson and the *Vanguard* departed for Palermo on the 22nd, where he was joined by the *Alcmene* on 5 January 1799.[81] It is possible that Beatty first became acquainted with Nelson and Lady Emma Hamilton during the evacuation.

80 TNA, ADM 51/4408.   81 Ibid.

Captain Henry Digby replaced George Hope at Gibraltar on 8 March 1799. Digby had already distinguished himself as a bold and resourceful frigate captain, who had captured fifty prizes while in command of the *Aurora* during 1797–8.[82] His extraordinary success continued aboard the *Alcmene*. Digby normally sold his prizes quickly, without waiting for the decisions of the Admiralty court, and paid out the money immediately, making him a popular commander. Digby's popularity was not only due to his success with prizes, for his standing orders governing life aboard the *Alcmene* reveal a sincere commitment to the health and welfare of his men. Regulations placed great emphasis upon a healthy diet, which included regular supplies of fresh vegetables, and the hygienic preparation of food through inspections of the galley and individual messes. Officers were instructed to see that excellent standards of cleanliness were maintained, and that the ship's company was well clothed. Digby's enlightened, humane attitude is demonstrated by the important role he assigned to the ship's medical officer, who was encouraged to exercise initiative, and recommend anything which might lead to improvements in the crew's diet and general health.[83]

Even before the end of the month, Digby snapped up two Spanish vessels off Cadiz carrying silk and wine from the River Plate. On 4 April the *Alcmene* captured a 14-gun French privateer soon after it had sailed from Malaga. The next month, off Cape Finisterre, the frigate took two Spanish ships: an 18-gun privateer after a chase involving the frequent exchange of gunfire, and a 4-gun vessel laden with cocoa. In June Digby received intelligence of several large French privateers preying upon British commerce off the coast of Portugal, and sailed in search of them. On 22 June he gave chase to a ship sighted boarding an American merchantman. The dogged pursuit carried on through the night, 'using every possible exertion'. Both warships rounded the island of Corvo (in the Azores) next morning. When the wind failed, the enemy had recourse to her oars, and 'preserved its distance by towing and sweeping to the westward'. The arduous chase continued during the 24th and 25th, when both ships resorted to towing in the light breeze and frequent calms. They passed a convoy from Brazil of more than forty sail escorted by two brigs, which might otherwise have been attacked by the enemy. At 6 a.m. on 26 June Digby reported that the wind from the north strengthened, allowing him to gain on the chase, when 'a running fight commencing, she struck at 7 . . . having suffered in her hull, sails and rigging'. After five days of

---

[82] Minterne: List of prizes captured by the *Aurora*.
[83] Minterne: *Alcmene* Order Book, 'The Surgeon'.

exhausting pursuit the *Alcmene*'s crew had distinguished themselves by capturing the powerful 28-gun Bordeaux privateer *Le Courageux*, which carried 253 men, eliminating a grave threat to British commerce. The French ship had been out for twenty-three days, laying in wait for the convoy.[84]

On 18 July Digby achieved a daring coup, responding to intelligence provided by a Jersey privateer named the *Phoenix*, which reported two Spanish ships anchored in Vivero. At sunset, taking advantage of surprise and the failing light, the *Alcmene* sailed into the port and ran between the two vessels, which were lying about two cable-lengths apart. Lieutenants Charles Warren and William Oliver boarded them 'in spirited and masterly manner'. The *Alcmene* and her prizes escaped, despite the fire of two Spanish forts, concealed by the smoke from the frigate's guns and the growing darkness. Digby had taken two valuable prizes, *La Felicidad*, pierced for twenty-two guns, and the brig *El Bisarro*, both loaded with naval stores destined for the arsenal at Ferrol.[85] On 16 September the *Alcmene* further reduced the danger to British merchant shipping with the capture of a 6-gun French privateer, *Les Deux Amis*, which had sailed from France for Saint-Domingue.[86]

Early on the morning of 17 October, while cruising off the Atlantic approaches to Spain, the *Alcmene* joined two 38-gun British frigates, the *Naiad* and the *Ethalion*, which were in pursuit of two Spanish frigates, the *Thetis* and *Santa Brigida*, both mounting thirty-four guns. The British force was strengthened by the arrival of a fourth frigate, the 32-gun *Triton*. At 7 a.m. the Spanish ships separated to increase their chances of escape. The senior British officer, Captain William Pierrepont of the *Naiad*, signalled for the fastest frigate, the *Ethalion*, to follow the leading Spaniard, the *Thetis*. The *Ethalion* passed the *Santa Brigida*, firing a broadside into her, and engaged the *Thetis* at 11.30 a.m. in a running battle which lasted approximately an hour, before the Spaniard surrendered.

The three other British frigates chased the *Santa Brigida* throughout the day and night, the *Alcmene* jettisoning 18 tons of water to increase the ship's speed. Early on the morning of the 18th Digby ordered the ship to be towed when the wind dropped. The *Santa Brigida* turned south and rounded Cape Finisterre, the Spanish captain, Don Antonio Pillou, hoping to lose his pursuers among its shoals, which he knew well. He nearly succeeded, for at

[84] Henry Digby to Earl St Vincent, 6 July, 1799, *NC* (1799), 342.
[85] Digby to St Vincent, 30 July 1799, *NC* (1800), 72.
[86] Digby to Lord Keith, 22 Sept. 1799, *NC* (1800), 140.

about 5 a.m. the leading British ship, the *Triton*, which was making 7 knots, struck a reef at Monte Lora. One of her officers 'thought we were done for', but although taking on water, the damaged ship extricated herself and resumed the chase. Soon after the *Alcmene* opened fire upon the *Santa Brigida* with her bow chasers, and Pillou replied with his broadside. At approximately 7.30 a.m. the British frigates closed in on the *Santa Brigida*, which was engaged from the leeward by Digby, who, 'with an officer-like presence of mind . . . cut off the entrance of Port de Vidre'. The *Santa Brigida* struck her colours just before 8 a.m. The British were left in a dangerous position, lying among the shoals off Muros, but their withdrawal was assisted by a fortuitous wind from the shore. Four large ships from Vigo made a half-hearted attempt to rescue the *Santa Brigida*, but abandoned it in the face of the squadron's resolution. The *Alcmene* bore the brunt of the fighting, suffering one seaman killed and one petty officer and nine seamen wounded. One marine was wounded aboard the *Triton* from the sliding of a carronade, while the *Santa Brigida* lost two killed and eight wounded.[87]

The officers and crews of the four British frigates were astounded to discover that the *Santa Brigida* and the *Thetis* were register ships from Vera Cruz carrying approximately £661,206 in bullion, as well as valuable cargoes of cocoa, sugar, cochineal, drugs, arnotto (a reddish-orange vegetable dye), and indigo. Beautiful works of art were also hidden aboard the ships. On the *Santa Brigida* the boarding party discovered gold sacramental plates and a gold crucifix buried in a bag of cochineal. After the bullion's sale to the Bank of England and the deduction of various fees, approximately £652,000 of prize money was distributed. Although the two frigates were not purchased by the navy, the sale of their stores, masts, and rigging may have fetched an additional £20,000. The seizure of the two prizes was one of the most spectacular and lucrative captures made during the entire war, realizing every sailor's dream of Spanish treasure. On 28 and 29 October the bullion of the *Santa Brigida* and the *Thetis* was transported from the dockyards of Plymouth to the dungeons of the citadel in an extraordinary procession. It was led by troopers of the Surrey Dragoons with a trumpeter sounding a charge, and a band of fifes and drums playing 'Rule Britannia' and 'God Save the King.' The booty followed in sixty-three wagons organized into nine divisions, with seamen mounted on the first, centre, and last wagons flying

[87] TNA, ADM 51/1318; ADM 52/2651; ADM 52/2652; William Pierrepont to Lord Bridport, commander of the Channel Fleet, 19 Oct. 1799, *NC* (1800), 144; Dispatches from James Young to Bridport, 24 Oct. 1799, *NC* (1799), 200 and (1800), 142; account by *Triton* officer, *NC* (1799), 542.

British flags over the Spanish. Behind it marched armed marines and seamen with another band performing 'Britons Strike Home'. More dragoons and trumpeters formed the rear of the cavalcade, which was escorted on both flanks by parties of armed midshipmen, sailors, and marines. According to a witness: 'Thousands of spectators, assembled on the occasion, testified their satisfaction, by repeated cheers, at seeing so much treasure, once the property of the enemy of old England, soon to be in the pockets of her jolly tars and marines.' The remaining money was transported to the citadel on 31 October, while the rich cargoes of the frigates were landed at the customs and excise docks.[88]

According to the very unequal customary division of the prize money, each of the four frigate captains received a share of £40,730, the lieutenants £5,091 and the midshipmen £791. The common seaman received £182 each. Beatty and the other warrant officers each earned £2,468 from the capture of the treasure ships, which represented more than forty times his annual pay.[89] The prize money was paid very quickly, finding its way into the pockets of the lucky captors in early January 1800. After the great hardship, stress, and anxiety of his service aboard the *Pomona* and the *Amethyst*, Beatty was rewarded by this and the *Alcmene*'s many other successes. During Digby's tenure of command alone, the frigate captured or shared in the capture of approximately sixteen prizes, in addition to the ships taken by his predecessors.[90] Some idea of the proceeds from the other prizes is indicated by the 10.6 Spanish dollars paid to each seaman for the *El Cid*.[91] How Beatty disposed of much of the money reveals a generous nature and concern for the future welfare of his sisters. A note later found in the pocket of a coat owned by his sister Anna's husband, Commander John Popham Baker, states that it was during his service in the *Alcmene* that Beatty 'laid the foundation of independence and was immediately liberal and affectionate to his sisters'.[92]

After a major refit, in early 1800 Digby resumed his very successful cruising off the Atlantic coasts of France and Spain. In late January, off the Isle of Rhé, he intercepted a Bordeaux merchant ship carrying wine and oil.

[88] *NC* (1799), 543.

[89] *NC* (1800), 79. The translation of historical money values into current ones is extremely difficult, but in 1999 the value of the prizes was estimated as being worth the equivalent of approximately £120 million, making Beatty's share roughly £454,000: J. R. Hill, *The Prizes of War: The Naval Prize System in the Napoleonic Wars, 1793–1815* (Stroud, 1998), 16, 176–8.

[90] Minterne: List of prizes captured by the *Alcmene*.   [91] TNA, ADM 52/2651.

[92] S. D. Clippingdale, 'Sir William Beatty', *Journal of the Royal Naval Medical Service* (Oct., 1916), 459.

In February the *Alcmene* and *Doris* recaptured the Liverpool letter of marque *Mercury*, which had been transporting a cargo of silk to London. The *Mercury* had taken a 12-gun French privateer, but several of her own crew had assisted the French prisoners to seize control of the British ship, who intended to sail her into L'Orient. Fortunately *Alcmene* and *Doris* had rescued the *Mercury* and liberated her crew. In March, off the Straits of Gibraltar, Digby recaptured a Liverpool vessel laden with silk. In May *Alcmene* joined St Vincent's fleet maintaining a tenacious blockade upon Brest. On the 5th the frigate stood into the harbour to assess the strength of the enemy fleet. On 7 May the *Alcmene* struck the Black Rocks, a victim of the hazards of close blockade. She narrowly escaped being wrecked, and was fortunate to get off with only the loss of her rudder. The frigate limped home to Plymouth to undergo extensive repairs. It was July before the *Alcmene* rejoined the Channel Fleet, and in contrast to the freedom, excitement, and profit of her earlier service the frigate spent most of the remaining months of 1800 sharing the hardship, risk, and monotony of the Channel Fleet's blockade, which was doggedly maintained however harsh the weather. During this time Beatty's most important duty, in addition to treating the many injuries caused by keeping the ship at sea in all conditions, involved the prevention and treatment of scurvy, illustrated by the regular supplies of lemon juice issued to the ship's company.[93]

Digby left the *Alcmene* at Torbay in March 1801, and was appointed to the 36-gun frigate *Resistance* in May. He must have been very satisfied with Beatty's performance of his duties, for he took the surgeon with him into his new commission. Digby's appreciation of Beatty was illustrated by a controversy which ended in the conviction of the *Resistance*'s Lieutenant Henry Lutwidge for manslaughter. Lutwidge had struck a drunken seaman named James Fagan over the head with a boat-tiller, who died the following day. Beatty, who knew nothing of the blow, had certified the death as the result of apoplexy and suffocation brought about by intoxication. In exonerating Beatty from any blame in the affair, Digby wrote that the surgeon had served for eleven years, including the last three with him, and declared that his humane and attentive care of the sick had ever been acknowledged.[94]

Beatty served with Digby until January 1802.[95] The most memorable aspect of this commission involved escorting a convoy to Quebec, Beatty's

[93] TNA, ADM 51/1318; ADM 51/1361; ADM 52/2652.
[94] Minterne: Papers Relating to the Trial of Lt Henry Lutwidge.
[95] ADM 35/1442; ADM 36/14715.

only voyage to North American waters. Digby's good fortune did not entirely desert him even on this seemingly mundane duty. On 22 August, off Newfoundland, the *Resistance* captured a French privateer, the 8-gun *Elizabeth* from Cayenne.[96]

The preliminaries of the Peace of Amiens with France, Spain and Holland were signed in October 1801, and Beatty left the *Resistance* a few months later to enjoy his first prolonged break after approximately eleven years of demanding continuous duty afloat. During that time he had served upon nine different ships: a schooner, seven frigates, and a ship of the line. He had been employed in the varied climates of the Channel, the Caribbean, the North Sea, the Mediterranean, and the North Atlantic. His wide experience included combined operations, commerce raiding, cutting-out expeditions, convoy escort, and blockade duty. Beatty had survived a yellow fever epidemic, an unjust court martial, shipwreck, and an attempted mutiny, to earn a considerable sum of prize money aboard the *Alcmene*. The capture of the *Santa Brigida* was also significant as the surgeon's baptism of fire, the first time that he was called upon to treat casualties in battle.

George Beatty's career had also prospered during these years. While serving as first marine lieutenant of the *Blenheim* in the Mediterranean, he had participated in the abortive nighttime attack upon Santa Cruz de Tenerife on 25 July 1797, where Nelson had lost his right arm. He was then posted to the *Theseus*, and fought at the Battle of the Nile. George continued to serve in the eastern Mediterranean with Sir Sydney Smith and was wounded at the siege of Acre. The exact nature of his wound is unknown, but a review before the Royal College of Surgeons in 1801 refused to give him a pension on the grounds that it 'was found not Equal in prejudice to the habit of Body with the Loss of a Limb'.[97]

However diverse and arduous William Beatty's record appears, a study of the careers of 430 other surgeons who served with him during these years suggests that their experiences were very similar, except of course for his court martial and his extraordinary good fortune in sharing in the capture of such a valuable prize. All in all, Beatty's practice as a surgeon reflects the reality that the vast majority of mortalities suffered by the navy during the French wars were caused by disease and accident, accounting for approximately 84,400, or 81 per cent of total losses. Foundering, wreck, fire, and explosion caused 12,680 deaths, or 12 per cent, while only a very small minority of deaths,

[96] ADM 51/1385.   [97] ADM 196/58, fo. 8.

6,540, or 6 per cent, were attributable to direct enemy action.[98] As these statistics demonstrate, the most constant and fundamental responsibilities of the naval surgeon were the maintenance of health, the treatment of injury, and the prevention and cure of disease. When Beatty was re-employed he would serve with Viscount Nelson in the Mediterranean. His experience as a surgeon in Nelson's fleet during 1804–5 would emphasize the important strategic implications of improvements in the Royal Navy's health through advances in diet, hygiene, and organization implemented during the preceding decade.

[98] Lloyd and Coulter, *Medicine and the Navy*, iii. 182.

3

The Mediterranean and Trafalgar

A BRIEF PEACE AND THE RENEWAL OF WAR

In March 1802 the Peace of Amiens ended a decade of exhausting conflict. While many in government, and in political and diplomatic circles, distrusted France's first consul, Napoleon Bonaparte, and expected the resumption of war, the rapid demobilization of the fleet meant that many naval surgeons were left without employment, and faced an uncertain future. Not all were eligible for half-pay. Beatty had not received another warrant after leaving the *Resistance* in January 1802. By this time he had served long enough to be among the fortunate 320 surgeons who received half-pay. The 100 most senior, including his uncle George Smyth, received 3 shillings per day, while Beatty and the others were paid at the rate of 2s. 6d.[1] Little is known of his life during the brief cessation of hostilities. At the age of 29 Beatty contemplated the same career choices as his comrades who had entered the medical corps early in the war and considered setting themselves up in private practice. Those who were ambitious of embarking upon careers in civilian medicine as surgeons or surgeon-apothecaries sought to improve their chances of success by enrolling in university courses or learning the latest surgical techniques at teaching hospitals. Those aspiring to careers as physicians sought university degrees.

These routes were illustrated by two of Beatty's colleagues who later served at Trafalgar. Forbes McBean Chevers, who received his first surgeon's warrant in May 1795, enrolled for a medical degree at the University of Edinburgh during 1802–4. William Shoveller, whose career as a surgeon began in September 1794, walked the wards of St George's Hospital in London with Everard Home during 1802. It is possible that Beatty, in order to prepare himself for private practice, studied at Guy's Hospital, where he

[1] TNA, ADM 25/143.

became acquainted with its chief physician William Babington, and encountered, perhaps for the first time, his naval contemporary Benjamin Outram.[2] Beatty may also have visited his family in Londonderry during 1802–3. He must have been exhausted by the physical and mental stress of more than ten years of duty at sea, during which time he had enjoyed only one brief period of leisure, a two-month wait for appointment to the *Resistance* in the spring of 1801. It was perhaps during a visit home in 1802 or 1803 that he made provision for his sisters from the prize money he had earned aboard the *Alcmene*.

Those who doubted Bonaparte's sincerity proved to be correct, and Britain declared war on the consulate in May 1803. With the recommissioning of the fleet, the Admiralty struggled to find adequate numbers of medical officers, who were discouraged from service by its failure to address their long-standing dissatisfaction over their pay, the expense of drugs and instruments, and rank. The grave shortage of qualified surgeons during the yellow fever epidemics in the West Indies in 1795 had compelled the Admiralty to address some of these concerns to promote recruitment. In 1796 it offered surgeons an increase in pay of £1 a month, the free issue of part of the medical chest, and some improvement in the eligibility for half-pay. This still left the navy surgeons inferior to their army counterparts in income and status, and in 1797 a number petitioned for equality. Morale was further damaged when they were excluded from the 1802 increases in naval pay, while in 1804 army surgeons enjoyed an augmented salary. It was in the recruitment of mates that the Admiralty experienced the most acute crisis, however, when the army clearly offered so much more to the aspiring medical officer. Denying surgeon's mates the relative security of half-pay meant that there was little incentive for those who had found other employment to give it up and return to the navy once war resumed. William Burnett, himself a naval surgeon during this time, reflected: 'I can from my own knowledge positively state that it was wholly impractical to procure Assistant Surgeons in sufficient number for the Service during the period.'[3] The failure to attract and retain the services of well-educated, well-trained, and zealous mates threatened dangerous consequences, both immediate, in the chronic shortage of assistants

---

[2] Prosopographical database (Preface, n.3); KCL: FP1/1, Index of Pupils and Dressers, Guy's and St Thomas's Hospitals 1723–1819; FP3/1: Guy's Hospital Entry Books, 1778–1813; NMM, HIS/6. Both Babington and Outram would assist Beatty's career at a later date: see below, Ch. 5, pp. 160, 171, 174. He may already have met Outram in 1790–1: see above, Ch. 2, p. 45. Unfortunately Beatty does not appear in the Guy's list of pupils.   [3] NMM, ELL/245.

to support surgeons in their work, and in the near future, when there would be no pool of candidates for promotion, as the size of the navy continued to grow rapidly and as disease, ill heath, accident, and age reduced the number of surgeons fit for service.

The analysis of a sample of surgeons indicates that, with the renewal of war, the navy retained the loyalty of the majority, despite their dissatisfaction over conditions of service. Beatty accepted a warrant to the 74-gun *Spencer* in early July 1803, the appointment to a line-of-battle ship with a crew of 590 men reflecting his experience and seniority.[4] Chevers and Shoveller also answered the Admiralty's recall. It is interesting to assess their motives. Many surgeons probably returned to the navy because there had been insufficient time to complete the transition to civilian medicine and establish themselves in practice. Officers such as Beatty, who had profited from prize money, may have been minded to take advantage of the opportunity to augment their savings as an investment in the future development of their medical careers. There were perhaps other more important and less pragmatic reasons. Beatty and his colleagues may have enjoyed the camaraderie of a seafaring life, despite its hardship and risk, which was the only adult existence that most of them had known. Beatty and other humane, conscientious surgeons experienced great personal reward in their care of the navy's officers and men. Shoveller and Chevers also made careers of the medical corps, serving as surgeons for thirty and twenty-seven years respectively, before both retired on pensions of 15s. a day.[5] Beatty and his comrades must also have been inspired by patriotic devotion to the nation, which was menaced with invasion from the spring of 1803, as Bonaparte concentrated an army in Boulogne and planned to wrest command of the Channel from the Royal Navy to stage a crossing.

Beatty joined the *Spencer* at Plymouth on 3 July 1803. Her commander, Robert Stopford, the son of the Irish aristocrat Lord Courtown, was a very experienced officer, who began his career in the War of American Independence and had been promoted captain in 1790. He had served in home waters and the West Indies before the Peace of Amiens. The ship carried the flag of Rear-Admiral J. R. Dacres, and was assigned to Vice-Admiral William Cornwallis in the Channel, who deployed her in the blockade of French naval forces in Brest, and in the Spanish port of Ferrol, where a squadron of ships of

[4] TNA, ADM 35/1805; ADM 36/16353.
[5] Database of naval surgeons who served during the French wars, held by Prof. Brockliss, University of Oxford.

the line had been trapped at the declaration of war. The *Spencer* spent the next year in the anxious, arduous watch of the French battle fleet to prevent its support of any invasion. She maintained her station despite being battered by the severe winter storms, including one recorded by her log off Ushant on 28 January 1804: '3.13 am very hard Gales & a high Sea, found the Ship labour very much & ship a great deal of Water... At 6.30 am... split the Fore-sail in setting it, at noon very hard gales and cloudy with a heavy Sea.' In early June 1804 the *Spencer* fell victim to one of the major perils of close blockade, striking rocks off Ferrol. The impact punched such a great hole in the ship's hull that she leaked 2 feet of water per hour. The damage made an immediate return to Plymouth imperative, where the *Spencer* received extensive repairs. In August 1804 the *Spencer* joined Lord Nelson, commander-in-chief of the fleet in the Mediterranean, who was entrusted with the blockade of the French fleet at Toulon and the protection of Malta, Sicily, and Britain's strategic interests in the Levant.[6] In December 1804 Spain's declaration of war on Britain dramatically increased the naval forces available to Napoleon (who had crowned himself emperor of the French in May) to realize his invasion plan.

WITH NELSON IN THE MEDITERRANEAN

The survival of a number of important but neglected sources, including fifteen volumes of papers relating to the health, victualling, and logistics of Nelson's Mediterranean Fleet, Stopford's Order Book for the *Spencer*, and Beatty's medical log for the *Victory*, provide fascinating insight into how the commander-in-chief, his physicians of the fleet, and individual surgeons such as Beatty co-operated to achieve unprecedented levels of health and high morale during 1803–5. In a medical report dated 19 September 1803, Dr John Snipe, the first physician appointed to the fleet, outlined how this would be achieved in a statement of the fundamental principles of naval medicine, which reflected the work of medical reformers such as Lind, Blane, Trotter, and the fever specialist Robert Robertson (1741/2–1829), whose recommendations had been confirmed by the experience of a decade of war. Snipe emphasized strict attention to sailors' hygiene; clothing adequate to all seasons; clean, dry, well-ventilated ships with suitable accommodation for the

[6] TNA, ADM 51/1454.

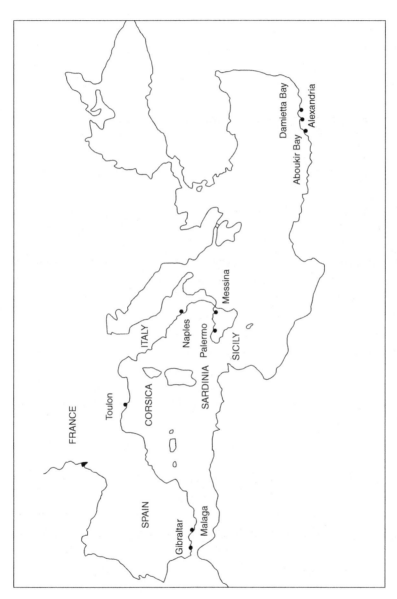

Map 4. The Mediterranean Theatre.

sick; 'and as Nourishing a Diet as situation and local circumstances will permit, composed of fresh Meat, and succulent Vegetables'. Snipe recognized that the success of these advances depended upon a close partnership with the navy's executive officers, at every level of the chain of command from admiral to midshipman, who understood and supported them: 'Nearly the Whole of this is Hing'd on the improved mode of Discipline, which at this moment enables the British Fleet to Ride Triumphant on the Seas, and bid Defiance to the hostile Bands of our combined Foes.'[7]

The Mediterranean Fleet was fortunate in serving under such a humane commander-in-chief as Nelson, who appreciated the critical importance of health in maintaining operational efficiency. Much of Nelson's solicitude for the welfare of his crews was inspired by his own heroic struggles with disease and wounds, which had caused him great pain and had at times threatened death or the termination of his career. Nelson had contracted malaria, scurvy, yellow fever or tropical sprue, and dysentery while serving in India, the West Indies, and Central America.[8] He had shared the agony of epidemics, and had witnessed how they could cripple naval and military campaigns. Nelson had suffered wounds in action, which included the loss of sight in his right eye at Calvi, a blow to the abdomen at the Battle of St Vincent, the loss of his right arm at Tenerife, and concussion at the Battle of the Nile.[9] From the assumption of his command in the Mediterranean, he demonstrated a determination to do everything possible to safeguard the health and fitness of his crews. In August 1803, when seeking advice from Dr Andrew Baird, the inspector of hospitals and friend of St Vincent, he declared that 'the health of our seamen is invaluable, and to purchase that, no expense ought to be spared'.[10]

HYGIENE AND SHIPBOARD CONDITIONS

By discipline, Snipe was referring to a series of developments first introduced during the Seven Years War, including the divisional system, and the growing practice for captains such as Digby and Stopford to formulate order books to govern the management of their ships. Ship's companies, which could be as

[7] WL, Nelson Papers, MSS 3680: Dr John Snipe, 19 Sept. 1803.
[8] A.-M. E. Hills, 'Nelson's Illnesses', *Journal of the Royal Naval Medical Service*, 86 (2000), 72–80.
[9] L. P. Le Quesne, 'Nelson and His Surgeons', ibid. 85–88.
[10] Nelson to Dr Andrew Baird, Aug. 1803, Nicolas, *Dispatches*, vii. p. ccxv.

great as 850 men in first-rates such as the *Victory*, were separated into
manageable divisions. These were assigned to lieutenants, midshipmen, and
petty officers, who became responsible for individual seamen's hygiene and
the cleanliness and repair of their clothes. Encouraged by Blane, in 1796
St Vincent had first ordered the general issue of soap to the Mediterranean
Fleet for the personal use of sailors and for the washing of their clothes.
Nelson's surgeons repeatedly requested Snipe for adequate amounts, and he
purchased it locally when supplies from England were delayed.[11] Order
books supported attempts for greater hygiene and cleanliness aboard ship by
defining practice and specifying penalties for those who failed the inspections.
Stopford and Beatty were clearly keen to maintain the highest possible
standards of hygiene aboard the *Spencer*. On 14 October 1803 able seaman
William Willey was punished with twelve lashes of the cat for the heinous
crime of pissing in the cockpit.[12]

Regular references to the washing, mending, and airing of clothes, bedding,
and hammocks in the *Spencer*'s logs testify to a well-organized sanitary
regime. These initiatives were essential to combat the spread of infectious
diseases such as typhus, encouraged by the overcrowding on contemporary
warships, a problem which was most acute in the line-of-battle ships. The
routine washing of the ship's decks was another important measure for
maintaining cleanliness aboard, yet it was recognized that water contributed
to the problem of dampness, which promoted rheumatism, tuberculosis, and
respiratory infections. Care had to be taken in order to promote rapid drying.
Lind and Blane advised scouring with hot sand or dry rubbing instead of
using water.[13] Dampness and foul air were related problems in ships whose
holds were rarely cleaned or disinfected. Water from rain or leaks accumu-
lated in the bilges and was contaminated by decaying matter, causing stifling
odours. Ports, scuttles, and hatchways often had to be closed for prolonged
periods during rain or high seas, and again the problems were more severe in
two- and three-deck ships such as the *Spencer* and the *Victory*. Contemporary
medical belief in the miasmatic origin of disease, although misguided, had a
beneficial effect by inspiring efforts to encourage the circulation of fresh dry
air, which reduced the risk of airborne infection from micro-organisms.[14]

---

[11] TNA, ADM 1/407: Snipe to Nelson, 7 Dec. 1803.　　[12] TNA, ADM 51/1454.

[13] Gilbert Blane, *Select Dissertations* (1822), in Christopher Lloyd (ed.), *The Health of Seamen:
Selections from the works of Dr. James Lind, Sir Gilbert Blane, and Dr. Thomas Trotter* (London,
1965), 180–88.

[14] Arnold Zuckerman, 'Disease and Ventilation in the Royal Navy: The Woodenship Years',
Eighteenth-Century Life, 11 (1987), 77–89.

Ventilation was assisted by the use of windsails, cylinder-shaped canvas tubes which directed air from the upper decks down the hatchways and into the lower regions of the ship. Portable stoves were utilized to combat humidity, as illustrated by their employment to dry out the *Spencer*'s lower deck on 21 January 1804 after a spell of squally weather.[15] Nelson's general orders reflected an awareness of the health problems created by dampness and an unwholesome atmosphere. Restrictions were imposed upon the washing of the fleet's middle and lower decks with water, while stoves and efficient ventilation were advocated to combat humidity and increase the flow of clean, dry air.[16]

DIET

Nelson's charismatic, inspiring personal leadership has long been recognized, but less well known is his achievement as a far-sighted, meticulous, and efficient organizer, which was equally important in contributing to his success. These qualities are strikingly illustrated by his constant struggle to ensure that his ships' companies received a balanced and nutritious diet of fresh meat, fruit, and vegetables. The basic weekly ration of food issued to Nelson's ships is set out in the records of the Mediterranean Fleet's agent-victualler, Richard Ford, which was 7 pounds of hard tack, 4 pounds of salt beef, 2 pounds of salt pork, 2 pints of peas, 8 ounces of butter, 12 ounces of cheese, and half-a-pint of vinegar per man. Because Nelson, Ford, and his assistants were so determined and zealous in procuring supplies of fresh provisions from North Africa, Sardinia, Italy, and other Mediterranean sources, the fleet rarely had to rely solely upon its preserved victuals. The magnitude of their achievement is illustrated by Ford's returns from February 1804 to April 1805, which indicate that the 6,000–8,000 strong fleet consumed about 1 million pounds of fresh beef, and approximately £47,000 was spent upon fresh fruit and vegetables. Between October 1804 and January 1805 the fleet received approximately 62,400 oranges and 35,700 lemons. Nelson had great faith in the nutritional and medicinal value of onions, which were antiscorbutic, and 34,051 pounds were procured during the same period. The *Spencer*'s log records the reception of supplies of cabbage,

---

[15] TNA, ADM 51/1454.
[16] TNA, ADM 1/411: Leonard Gillespie's Report, 14 Aug. 1805, fo. 337.

turnips, and leeks. The fleet also consumed 200,000 gallons of good Mediterranean wine, and 40,000 gallons of brandy.[17] Nelson's ships paid regular wooding and watering visits to Palma Bay, Sardinia, and to the Maddalena Islands off its northern tip, where extensive private provisions markets developed, which allowed ships' messes and individuals to purchase their own supplies of fresh meat, fruit, and vegetables. Marine lieutenant Marmaduke Wybourn described a visit to Pula Bay in April 1805, when 'hundreds of Natives flocked down bringing quantities of provisions, Animals, Vegetables, Fruit etc., which of course met with a most welcome reception'.[18]

There were occasional problems with provisions which had to be condemned, either because they or their containers were of inferior quality. Barrels and casks were sometimes damaged in transit or from incorrect stowage. Surveys of the *Victory's* stores in August 1803 revealed rancid and maggoty cheese and butter. In January 1805 372 pounds of rice had to be destroyed because of rats 'eating holes in the head of the Cask'. The pests also caused the destruction of salt pork, oatmeal, and pease. In February 2,542 pounds of bread were discovered to be 'maggotty, weevilly, and unfit for Men to Eat'.[19] These were exceptions, however, and in some cases reflected the length of time that provisions had been stored. Nelson was extraordinarily vigilant to guarantee that all provisions were of the highest quality. In October 1804 he instructed the fleet's masters to go on board supply ships arriving from Malta and 'take a most strict and careful survey on the pork, tongues, pease, and wheat', to guarantee that the casks and bushels were complete and of the highest standard. Nelson ordered the officers to randomly select pieces of meat from the casks and boil them to make certain that they did not shrink, and the same test was applied to the pease. The wheat was also rigorously examined. He recommended that Ford supervise the inspection.[20]

Nelson encouraged the fleet's pursers to exercise initiative in purchasing large quantities of provisions when advantageous opportunity allowed, but he also scrutinized their returns for irregularities indicating either fraud or negligence.[21] Nelson was particularly concerned that pursers did not fail in their duty to provide fresh fruit and vegetables whenever possible, as they had

---

[17] WL, MSS 3677: Stores on *HMS Victory* 1803–05; MSS 3678: Provisions in the Squadron.

[18] Anne Petrides and Jonathan Down (eds.), *Sea Soldier: An Officer of Marines with Duncan, Nelson, Collingwood and Cockburn. The Letters and Journals of Major T. Marmaduke Wybourn, RM, 1797–1813* (Tunbridge Wells, 2000), 71.

[19] WL, MSS 3677: Stores on *HMS Victory* 1803–05.

[20] Nelson to Masters, 22 Oct. 1804, Nicolas, *Dispatches*, vi. 251.

[21] Nelson to Respective Captains, 10 Oct. 1805, ibid. vii. 102–5.

been instructed. He reprimanded those who were appropriating onions purchased on account of government for medicinal purposes for their own benefit, and placing them in the seamen's soup instead of the vegetables which they were obliged to furnish themselves. On 30 December 1803 Nelson forbade the practice in a general order, repeating 'my positive directions that the Pursers are obliged to purchase vegetables for the Ships' soup'.[22] In May 1804 he wrote to Captain George Ryves of the *Gibraltar* querying an 'extraordinary charge' of £100 for onions, cabbage, leeks, and pumpkins, which should have been met by the purser.[23] In addition to concern for a wholesome diet, Nelson also considered the seamen's preferences, as food occupied such a central place in shipboard life, ritual, and comfort, offering another example of his great emphasis upon maintaining high morale. In June 1804 he warned the Victualling Office that his sailors would grumble over the replacement of cheese with rice.[24]

Spain's declaration of war in December 1804 deprived Nelson of a major market of victuals for the fleet. He and Ford, however, redoubled their efforts to sustain their excellent standards. Nelson was always careful to anticipate disruptions caused by changes in the Mediterranean political and strategic situation. In June 1804 he warned a friend not to worry when it appeared that French intervention in Naples would cut off that source of supply: 'we shall do very well. I have always looked too far forward, ever to be really distressed.'[25] Excellent evidence of Nelson's foresight is provided by his rapid identification of an alternative source for oranges and lemons, articles essential to the fleet's health for its use in the prevention and treatment of scurvy. In June 1804 Dr Snipe and John Gray, surgeon of the Malta Hospital, visited Sicily, then under British protection, to assess the prospect of purchasing lemons, 'collecting on the spot every information relative to this valuable antiscorbutic'. There they discovered that Britain could 'procure it at a better quality, and on more advantageous terms' than ever before. Snipe informed Nelson that 'if the person employed to see it squeezed, strictly does his Duty, it will be of a very superior quality to any I ever saw issued to his Majesty's Fleets'. Snipe entered into negotiations with John Broadbent, 'a very intelligent Merchant of Messina', who agreed to supply the lemons, which were already exported from Sicily to Hamburg, St Petersburg, and

---

[22] Nelson to Respective Captains, Memorandum, 30 Dec. 1803, ibid. vii. p. ccxvii.
[23] Nelson to Captain George Ryves, 19 May 1804, ibid. vi. 25.
[24] Nelson to Victualling Office, 18 June 1804, ibid. 74.
[25] Nelson to Captain Pultney Malcom, 18 June 1804, ibid.

other northern ports. Broadbent reported that 'the best season for gathering the former Article is the months of October or November when the Fruit is intended for long voyages'. The lemons was generally transported double wrapped in light paper, or in sound casks filled with seawater.[26]

On 12 June Snipe contracted for 30,000 gallons of the juice itself, 10,000 gallons for the Mediterranean Fleet and 20,000 gallons for home consumption, at 1 shilling a gallon (casks included), to be delivered for transport to Malta before 31 December.[27] The price was eight times less expensive than that demanded for inferior juice in England, leading Nelson to point out to the Admiralty the 'immense sums' which might be saved in future purchases. George Saunders, the dispenser of the Malta Naval Hospital, supervised the squeezing of the fruit, with the authority to reject any he considered to be unfit. Saunders also superintended the preservation of the juice, which was mixed with one-tenth part brandy and stored in pipes of chestnut. In January 1805, when replying to Nelson's request on behalf of the Admiralty for an additional 30,000 gallons, Broadbent reported that there had been a delayed, poor harvest, which ripened at the end of December, and produced only one-third of the normal yield. To cover the extra cost this entailed, and expenses unforeseen in the original contract, Broadbent requested an additional 6d. a gallon, which was approved by Nelson and the Sick and Hurt Board, after Snipe had revisited Messina to see for himself, and reported that the merchant 'saved no expense nor attention to make the Lemon Juice of the first quality'.[28]

CLOTHING

Nelson devoted the same scrupulous care to ensure that his seamen were adequately clothed, again probably responding to the advice of Snipe. In September 1803, when reflecting upon incidences of influenza, other fevers, and rheumatism, Snipe maintained that 'much of this deplorable Waste of Men to the Service was occasioned by the Want of proper warm Clothing'. He urged the Admiralty to provide free uniforms, including trousers and flannel inside waistcoats, an expense it would be repaid many times, because

[26] WL, MSS 3677: Snipe, Broadbent, Saunders, and Nelson correspondence 1804–05.
[27] WL, MSS 3678: Contract between John Snipe, John Gray and John Broadbent.
[28] WL, MSS 3677: Snipe, Broadbent, Saunders, and Nelson correspondence 1804–05; MSS 3681, Sick and Hurt Board to Nelson, 29 May, 1805.

'it would prevent many from being sent to the Hospital, a number of which either Die, or are Invalided'. Snipe also advised the issue of warm stockings and strong shoes, arguing that they would reduce the problem of ulcers, rope burns, rheumatism, and other injuries to sailors' feet and legs, encouraged by the practice of going barefoot and wearing short trousers in wet and cold conditions.[29] The *Victory's* captain, Thomas Hardy, was also anxious to see his people warmly clothed for the winter, and warned Nelson that slop frocks and trousers received from the *Diligent* supply ship in early August 1804 were 'of a very inferior quality'. Hardy much preferred the frocks and trousers which Nelson had designed and ordered from Nathanial Taylor, the Malta storekeeper, who had supplied 5,000 of each in June 1804. Hardy resembled a protective, thrifty matron fussing over her children when he wrote to Nelson: 'I beg leave to observe to your Lordship, that the Maltese cotton washes and wears remarkably well.'[30] Not only were Taylor's clothes of superior manufacture, but they were cheaper. Nelson championed Hardy's complaints to the Admiralty: 'instead of being made of good Russia duck as was formerly supplied . . . the frocks at 4s. 8d. each, and the trowsers at 4s. per pair . . . are made of coarse wrapper-stuff, and the price increased—the frocks two-pence each, and the trowsers three-pence per pair.' Nelson, again anxious about morale, warned that compelling his sailors to pay for such stuff 'will no doubt occasion murmur and discontent'. With great indignation, he declared that the contractor who furnished the clothes 'ought to be hanged'.[31] Nelson forwarded Hardy's letter, along with samples of the clothes sent from England with those available at Malta for comparison. Hardy had his way, and ordered 395 Maltese cotton frocks and 857 pairs of Russian duck trousers for the *Victory's* crew on 14 September.

In 1804 Nelson again demonstrated an admirable solicitude for the health of his seamen by insisting that they receive thick Guernsey jackets to supplement their woollen slops, which would protect them from contracting fevers and rheumatism during the approaching winter. In November he was delighted by the delivery of the coats, which previously had usually been limited to fleets serving on cold-weather stations. Nelson praised the quality of the material, but was concerned 'that they are considerably too narrow and short to be tucked into the Men's trowsers'. He recommended that they should be made ten inches to a foot longer, 'as they shrink very considerably

[29] WL, MSS 3680: Snipe to Nelson, 9 Sept. 1803.
[30] WL, MSS 3677: Hardy to Nelson, 11 Aug. 1804.
[31] Nelson to William Marsden, 12 Aug. 1804, Nicolas, *Dispatches*, vi. 154.

in washing'. A greater length was essential, for when the able seamen were out on the yards working the sails the short jackets were pulled out of their trousers, and this 'exposes them to great danger of taking cold in their loins'. With the necessary alteration, Nelson declared that the Guernsey jackets 'certainly would be the best and most valuable slops that ever were introduced into the Service, and be the means of saving many a good Seaman's life'. Sharing Hardy's almost mother-like concern for the sailors under his command, Nelson advised: 'Perhaps the Guernsey jacket, in its present state, might answer the largest of the boys.'[32]

HOSPITAL MANAGEMENT AND PREVENTATIVE MEDICINE

All aspects of Nelson's administration of naval affairs in the Mediterranean revealed the same priority he granted to preserving the health of his seamen and promoting their recovery when ill. Nelson was eager for the re-establishment of a naval hospital at Malta to strengthen the fleet's medical resources, after the previous one had closed in 1802. In late 1803 he dispatched the indefatigable Snipe to survey possible sites in Valetta. In the meantime, Snipe arranged for the temporary occupation of an army regimental hospital. Following Snipe's recommendation, Nelson urged the Admiralty to select the villa of Count Bichi, built in 1700 and overlooking the harbour, which should be expanded. He seconded the physician's recommendation for sufficient space to encourage patients' recuperation: 'the additional building to the said Palace mentioned by Doctor Snipe is absolutely necessary, for the convenience and comfort of a Naval Hospital, and that a certain space of ground attached to the said building is also indispensably necessary for a garden, a place for the convalescent Seamen and Marines to enjoy a little exercise and fresh air.'[33] Snipe planned to cultivate the garden to produce an 'abundance of Vegetables for the use of the Sick', and advised that 'if Lemon and Orange Trees were planted the Fleet on this Station might be amply supplied with those Antiscorbutic Fruit'.[34] Nelson urged Dr Baird to support the choice of the site: 'take care we have the ground with the house; for, with the ground, it is the most healthy and eligible situation in Valette

---

[32] Nelson to Navy Commissioners, 20 Nov. 1804, ibid. vi. 276.
[33] Nelson to Marsden, 10 May 1804, ibid. vi. 8.
[34] TNA, ADM 1/407: Snipe to Nelson, 9 Dec. 1803.

Harbour.'[35] The new hospital would provide for the care of 150 sailors and marines. The able and experienced Dr Leonard Gillespie was intended as the first physician for the new hospital. In January 1805, however, he succeeded Snipe as physician of the fleet. Snipe's health had been undermined by his tireless service in the Mediterranean, and he was transferred to a position ashore at the Plymouth Naval Hospital, where he became second physician.

Nelson took his responsibility as commander-in-chief to supervise the management of the Malta and Gibraltar naval hospitals very seriously, as indicated by the contracts entered into by Snipe for their management and provisioning, which stressed hygiene, a nutritious diet, and high levels of staffing, with one nurse to every ten patients.[36] Recovering patients on a full diet would receive 1 pint of broth, 1 pound of mutton, 1 pound of fresh vegetables, and fresh fruit daily. Nelson kept in close personal touch with the running of the hospitals, ordering frequent surveys of their victuals, stores, and dispensaries. He warned the first governor he appointed to the Malta Hospital, Lieutenant William Pemberton, to pay 'very strict and particular attention to the Cleanliness and Comfort of the Patients'.[37] The great trouble he took to see that convalescent seamen and marines received every possible comfort is illustrated by an order to John Gray, the surgeon of the Malta Hospital, 'to supply the necessary Quantity of Milk to the Patients in their Tea Morning and Evening', the additional expense of which would be settled between Snipe and the victualler, William Higgins.[38] Nelson demanded exemplary standards of ability, efficiency, and duty from staff assigned to the hospitals, and quickly removed those who fell short. In the summer of 1804 he dismissed the purser who acted as agent for the Malta Hospital, and welcomed the sacking of a dishonest dispenser from Gibraltar, 'a character so dangerous, not only to the individual, but also to the Public Service'. Making an example of the latter would be a warning to any who considered advancing himself by 'sacrificing the upright and honest man'.[39]

Nelson always demonstrated particular humanity towards the wounded, no doubt inspired by sympathy from one who had felt their pain and distress. Following a successful action against enemy ships in July 1804, he ordered casualties to be transferred to the fleet's flagships, where they would receive

[35] Nelson to Baird, 30 May 1804, Nicolas, *Dispatches*, vi. 41.
[36] WL, MSS 3681: Contract for Victualling Naval Hospital at Gibraltar; Contract for Victualling Naval Hospital at Malta.
[37] TNA, ADM 1/407: Nelson to Pemberton, 21 Dec. 1803.
[38] WL, MSS 3681: John Gray to Nelson, 22 Feb. 1804.
[39] WL, MSS 3681; Nelson to Sick and Hurt Board, 7 Aug. 1804, Nicolas, *Dispatches*, vi. 143.

the best treatment. Nelson commended their sacrifice by describing wounds as the 'marks of honour', and declared, 'our grateful Country is not unmindful of the sufferings of her gallant defenders'. Nelson instructed the wounded men's captains and surgeons to provide them with certificates, which they would require to claim pensions, and he promised to recommend casualties to the generosity of the Patriotic Fund at Lloyd's, a private charity set up to reward valour and assist injured officers and seamen and their families. These orders were repeated in early October 1805, when a battle with the Combined Fleet appeared imminent.[40] A small number of the chronically ill, who had little hope of recovery, were invalided home after health surveys conducted by the physician of the fleet and several surgeons and captains. In late 1804 two members of the *Spencer*'s crew were invalided after recommendation by Beatty and Stopford: Lieutenant John Bell, who suffered from an ear infection which caused deafness and vertigo, and landsman Charles Dougherty, who suffered from severe epilepsy.[41]

In addition to concern for diet, hygiene, and warm clothing, other important preventative measures were employed to preserve the health of the Mediterranean Fleet. Dr Edward Jenner had developed a reliable vaccination against smallpox in 1798, and its adoption by the navy was encouraged by many of its physicians, surgeons, and serving officers. The first mass vaccination in the Mediterranean Fleet probably occurred at Gibraltar in the summer of 1800, and the practice became general thereafter, which effectively contained the disease.[42] Snipe sought to protect the fleet's seamen who went ashore on wooding and watering parties at the Maddalena Islands and other places from infection by tropical fevers such as malaria. In November 1803 he prescribed a dose of Peruvian bark (which contained quinine) mixed with spirits or wine and water for all seamen going ashore on these duties, which would be given both before their departure and after their return. Nelson's general order authorizing the practice is recorded in Stopford's order book.[43] In October 1804 Beatty carefully followed this precaution when the *Spencer* was taking on fuel and water for the fleet at Agincourt Sound (now known as the Maddalena Anchorage, which lies at the northern tip of Sardinia). Over five days he prescribed more than 7 gallons of spirits and 2 gallons of wine mixed with

[40] Nelson to Captain Ross Donnelly, 12 July 1804, ibid. vi. 109; Nelson to Respective Captains, 10 Oct. 1805, ibid. vii. 106. [41] WL, MSS 3376: Health Surveys.

[42] R. Morriss, 'Practicality and Prejudice: The Blockade Strategy and Naval Medicine During the French Revolutionary War', in P. van der Merwe (ed.), *Science and the French and British Navies, 1700–1850* (London, 2003), 83–5.

[43] WL, MSS 3680: Snipe to Nelson, 1803/11/07; NMM, STO/7: Nelson to Respective Captains, 12 Dec. 1803.

bark for the 272 men who were employed ashore.[44] Snipe reflected the accepted belief that impure air was the source of infection, and rather ingeniously attributed its spread to ships whose crews had not gone ashore to noxious effluvia contained in green wood, leading to the recommendation that all wood should be smoked before being brought aboard. He also urged that only the purest water be taken from the head of the springs, and that contamination be prevented by careful maintenance of the casks.

Those sailors who served with Nelson were convinced of his sincere concern for their welfare by his labour to give them the best possible provisioning, clothing, and care when ill or wounded. Nelson's humanity, which helps to explain the power of his leadership and the devotion he inspired, emerged as another influential contributor to the fleet's health, for in addition to these material elements, he also recognized the critical significance of promoting happiness and high morale. Sailors who were satisfied with their lot and trusted their officers would fight much more enthusiastically for king and country. The benefits of encouraging contentment, confidence, and optimism went far beyond operational efficiency and fighting spirit, however, for the navy's medical officers had long recognized a link between psychology and illness, as William Turnbull observed in 1805: 'It has been very properly suggested by a number of writers on seamen's diseases, on account of the known effect of melancholy, and of a discontented temper, in producing scurvy and other maladies, that every means should be employed and encouraged to promote gaiety and good humour.'[45] Nelson and his physicians Snipe and Gillespie appreciated the danger, hence the admiral's insistence upon keeping the men continuously employed. Nelson informed his friend Dr Moseley that, 'by changing the cruising ground' in the western Mediterranean, rather than maintaining a monotonous close blockade of Toulon, he had 'not allowed the sameness of prospect to satiate the mind'.[46] Gillespie recorded that Nelson's positive efforts to dispel ennui, depression, or dissatisfaction by enriching shipboard life were even more important in sustaining his men's mental as well as physical well-being: 'The promoting cheerfulness amongst the men was encouraged by music, dancing and theatrical amusements; the example of which was given by the Commander-in-Chief in the *Victory*, and may with reason be reckoned amongst the causes of the preservation of the health of the men.'[47]

[44] WL, MSS 3677: Account of Wine and Spirit Supplied to *Spencer*'s Surgeon.
[45] William Turnbull, *The Naval Surgeon* (London, 1806), 48.
[46] Nelson to Moseley, 11 Mar. 1804, Nicolas, *Dispatches*, v. 438.
[47] TNA, ADM 1/411: Leonard Gillespie's Report, 14 Aug. 1805, fo. 337.

HMS *VICTORY*

As commander-in-chief, Nelson was responsible for the appointment of medical officers to fill vacancies in the ships and hospitals under his command, and his decisions were normally confirmed by the Sick and Hurt Board. One of Snipe's final duties had been to assist Nelson in the selection of a new surgeon for the *Victory* to succeed George Magrath, whom Nelson appointed surgeon of the hospital at Gibraltar in December 1804. Nelson had the greatest respect for the Irish surgeon. He consulted Magrath about his own illnesses, 'whom I admire for his great abilities every day I live', and commended him as 'by far the most able medical man I have ever seen'.[48]

Medical appointments within the fleet were influenced by a number of considerations. The selection of a surgeon was often the prerogative of the admiral if the vessel were a flagship, or of the captain in other cases, when the officers had a strong preference of their own. Thus, in October 1805, when Nelson insisted upon Collingwood shifting his flag into the *Royal Sovereign*, he enquired: 'If you have any particular attachment to your Surgeon in the *Dreadnought*, he must of course go with you.'[49] Nelson had moved Dr Matthias Felix into the *Royal Sovereign*, but when Collingwood wished to retain Richard Lloyd, Nelson replied: 'it is very reasonable and proper that your Surgeon should go with you.' Patronage clearly played a role in some appointments. Nelson denied any special interest on behalf of Dr Felix, whom he had appointed because he was the most senior surgeon in the fleet, but he listened to the patronage requests made by friends and colleagues. When Nelson's friend Vice-Admiral Robert Deans requested a place for his midshipman son, he promised to lose no opportunity to make him a lieutenant: 'Nothing gives me greater pleasure than being useful to the sons of brother Officers, and much more so to the sons of old and respected messmates.' Nelson also agreed to Deans's request to promote assistant surgeon David Gray of the *Achilles*: 'if I can get hold of the French Fleet, you may rely that Mr Gray shall be made a Surgeon; however, I have put him on my list, and if I go home, I shall leave him as a legacy to Sir Richard Bickerton.'[50]

The exact circumstances of Beatty's appointment to the *Victory* in December 1804 are unknown. The decision was made by Nelson, who

[48] Nelson to Lady Hamilton, 27 May 1804, ibid. vi. 36.
[49] Nelson to Collingwood, 3 Oct. 1805, ibid. vii. 66.
[50] Nelson to Deans, 16 Apr. 1805, ibid. vi. 405.

warranted him, probably in consultation with Snipe, Magrath, and Hardy.[51] There is no evidence of any intervention by a patron on Beatty's behalf, suggesting that his selection over all the other surgeons in the fleet—several of whom, like Felix, were senior to him in service—was based on merit. Nelson and Hardy, who placed such great emphasis upon the health and welfare of the fleet and of the *Victory*'s crew, would have been determined to appoint the best available surgeon to the flagship. The fleet's surgeons submitted weekly reports to Snipe on the medical conditions of their ships' companies, and referred any patients they were unable to treat to him. Snipe therefore had an excellent opportunity to assess the medical abilities of the fleet's surgeons, and there is little doubt that Nelson would have consulted his opinion. Snipe must have spoken strongly in Beatty's favour. Magrath and Beatty became friends during this time, and given Nelson's great respect for Magrath, it is also probable that he would ask his current surgeon about a successor. Magrath, a fellow Ulsterman, would hardly wish to forfeit the admiral's regard, and if he recommended Beatty, as is very likely, it must have been from confidence in his skill. Stopford too would have given a good opinion of Beatty. When informed by Nelson of his surgeon's promotion, Stopford declared, 'I should be wanting in justice towards Mr Beatty . . . if I did not acknowledge that his conduct has merited my entire approbation'. Although regretting his loss, Stopford nonetheless rejoiced in Beatty's 'removal into a Ship bearing your Lordship's flag, a situation in which he can but feel much pride and gratification'.[52] During the five months that the *Spencer* had served with the fleet, it is possible that Nelson and Hardy became familiar with her surgeon, if they had not already met Beatty during his earlier service in the Mediterranean with the *Alcmene*. Beatty's personal qualities may also have influenced his appointment. Given Nelson's very sociable temperament, it is unlikely that he would have appointed an officer to the flagship who would not contribute to its harmony. Nelson, too, may have remembered Beatty's brother George, the marine officer who had fought with him when he lost his arm.

The excellent health enjoyed by Nelson's fleet is also explained by his evident respect for the fleet's medical officers, and his recognition of the importance of their work, which encouraged them to strive to deserve his good opinion. Nelson's appreciation of the navy's surgeons is emphasized

[51] TNA, ADM 6/64: A List of the Commissions, Warrants . . . Granted by Lord Nelson . . . Between 17 Aug. 1804 and 4 March 1805.
[52] NMM, CRK/12/85, Stopford to Nelson, 27 Dec. 1804.

by his powerful endorsement of their petitions for improved pay and status, which were being reviewed by the Sick and Hurt Board during 1804. Taking Magrath as an exemplar, Nelson declared to Dr Andrew Baird: 'But we must lose such men from our Service, if the Army goes on in encouraging Medical men, whilst we do nothing. I am sure much ought to be done for our Naval Surgeons, or how can we expect to keep valuable men? I look to you not only to propose it, but to enforce it, to Lord St Vincent, who must be anxious to preserve such a valuable set of men to the Navy.'[53] To solve the problem of recruitment at the resumption of war, the Admiralty introduced reforms in January 1805, which addressed medical officers' dissatisfaction with their pay, eligibility for half-pay, and status.[54] When news of the Order in Council reached the Mediterranean in April, Nelson received the following letter:

We the Physician and Surgeons of the Fleet under your Lordship's Command, impressed with the most grateful sense of the favours lately conferred on the Medical Corps of the Navy...should deem ourselves guilty of ingratitude...did we not embrace the earliest opportunity of returning you our most grateful acknowledgements in return for the very prompt and favourable recommendation...and we are very well satisfied that we owe in a great measure to your Lordship's efficacious recommendation...the speedy adoption of the present Medical Establishment... which holds out so many additional inducements to Professional Men of experience to serve in His Majesty's Navy.[55]

The letter was written by Snipe's replacement, Gillespie, and was signed by the surgeons of the fleet's line-of-battle ships, including Beatty. In coming together to thank Nelson, the fleet's medical officers demonstrated a strong sense of *esprit de corps*, which he had done much to foster. They resembled a medical 'band of brothers', united in their determination to serve their commander-in-chief and patron to the best of their abilities. Gillespie and Beatty, serving on the same ship, were particularly close, all the more so in that the new physician of the fleet was a native of Armagh.

Those interested in naval medicine in the age of sail are very fortunate in the survival of the *Victory* at Portsmouth. The places where Beatty lived and worked aboard her may be visited, and fascinatingly evoke the life of a contemporary naval surgeon. Beatty examined and treated the sick in a wing berth on the starboard side of the upper gun deck beneath the forecastle.

---

[53] Nelson to Baird, 30 May 1804, Nicolas, *Dispatches*, vi. 41.   [54] *NC* (1805), 212.
[55] BL, Add MSS 34929, fo. 132: Gillespie to Nelson, 15 Apr. 1805.

Nelson occupied the stern section of the deck, which comprised his dining and sleeping quarters. The sick berth contained a skylight, which let in the daylight (something Trotter considered essential for the diagnosis of patients) and assisted ventilation. There was an internal toilet called a roundhouse, as well as easy access to the heads. The sick berth was segregated from the rest of the deck by moveable canvas bulkheads stretched upon wooden frames. There were several cots covered with hospital bedding for convalescents, which could be surrounded by curtains, as well as benches, basins, and tubs for bathing, and barrels of water for drinking and washing. Vinegar was available for disinfection. The sick berth possessed its own stove and cooking utensils for the preparation of oatmeal porridge, mutton broth, and other food for the sick. The purser maintained a separate fund for the necessaries for the sick, which were frequently supplemented by milk, eggs, wine, and other delicacies thanks to the generosity of Nelson, Hardy, and other officers.

When Magrath left the flagship, three of the fleet's surgeons surveyed the medicines and equipment which Beatty inherited, providing a rare insight into their actual contents in an operational man-of-war. The sick berth contained twenty-two beds with sheets, blankets, pillows, and nightcaps, two urinals, three bedpans, and fourteen spitting-pots. Beatty had 70 pounds of soap for the cleansing of patients or new recruits, and fumigant powder, mostly nitre, for disinfection. Pestles, mortars, measuring-glasses, and syringes were used for the preparation and delivery of prescriptions, testifying to Beatty's status as physician and apothecary as well as surgeon. The skill that this required is emphasized by the extensive contents of the medicine chests, which contained over 150 drugs.[56] Before the 1805 reforms surgeons had to purchase many drugs at their own expense. Magrath received gratuitous supplies of opium, calomel, vitriols, rhubarb, senna, jalop, cantharides, and Peruvian bark, but had been required to provide 140 drugs himself. These would now be purchased on Beatty's behalf.[57] The sick berth was fitted with a simple dispensary for the prescription of some medicines, and Beatty had a portable chest for treating officers in their cabins. Befitting an officer who was solicitous about his health, Nelson carried his own personal medicine chest aboard the *Victory*. The permanent dispensary was located below the waterline in the relative safety of the aft orlop deck, where Beatty occupied a small adjoining cabin. Beatty's two assistant surgeons, as they were now

[56] W. E. Court, '18th Century Drugs for the Royal Navy', *Pharmaceutical History*, 17 (1987), 2–6.
[57] WL, 3680: Remains of Gratuitous Medicines on Board HMS *Victory* 30 Dec. 1804, An Inventory of Private Medicines on Board HMS *Victory*.

called, Neil Smith and William Westenburg, messed in the nearby cockpit with the midshipmen and master's mates.

As physician of the fleet, Gillespie was admitted into 'the honour of forming one of the suite and family of L. Nelson', whom he admired for his 'noble frankness of manner' and 'freedom from formality and pomp'.[58] Beatty too appreciated Nelson's open, friendly charm and natural dignity, in sharp contrast to the deportment of his former commander Lord Augustus Fitzroy. Beatty's observations upon Nelson's daily habits published in his *Authentic Narrative* are clearly derived from personal contact, indicating that he was a frequent guest at the admiral's table, where Nelson 'was alike affable and attentive to everyone'.[59] Beatty's detailed assessments of Nelson's health, and the impact upon it of his diet, exercise, and working routines, reveal intimate knowledge, and suggest that the admiral had consulted him professionally. Particularly interesting is Beatty's belief that Nelson's sight would have failed entirely had he lived for several more years. Several of the *Victory*'s officers also consulted Beatty, including Captain Hardy and Lieutenant John Pascoe, whom the surgeon recommended for leave to recover from severe rheumatism in August 1805.[60] Gillespie retired after the *Victory*'s return to Spithead in August, and Nelson sailed to confront the enemy without a new physician, which increased his reliance upon Beatty as the only medical officer to whom he could turn for immediate advice upon medical matters within the fleet, and about his own health.

In contrast to the exciting chases and cutting-out operations of Beatty's earlier cruises under enterprising frigate captains such as Digby, blockade duty in the ships of the line *Spencer* and *Victory*—what Edward Codrington of the *Orion* described as being 'in the team'—must have seemed dull by comparison.[61] In addition, there was very little opportunity to accumulate prize money, let alone the tidy sums that Beatty had acquired with the *Alcmene*. A volume recording prizes captured by the *Victory* during Beatty's time aboard lists only one, a Spanish tartan taken on 29 June 1805 in the sight of several other ships, thus reducing the share payable to the ship's crew. Her cargo was sold for £9,958. 9s. 12d., and once the sum had been divided among all the captors, Beatty received £8. 7s. 11d., paid in July 1806.[62]

---

[58] Gillespie to sister, 7 Jan. 1805, *Chambers's Journal*, 14 (1945), 231.
[59] William Beatty, *Authentic Narrative of the Death of Lord Nelson* (London, 1807), 80.
[60] TNA, ADM 1/411: Beatty to Hardy, 18 Aug. 1805, fos. 330, 350.
[61] Jane Bourchier, *Memoir of the Late Admiral Sir Edward Codrington* (London, 1873), i. 44.
[62] TNA, ADM 238/12.

The privilege of serving aboard the flagship and enjoying the society of Nelson may have compensated, however.

Beatty's colleague and friend Gillespie was a rather thrifty character, who rejoiced in his comfortable salary of £465 a year, which he could save and 'still live in a princely style free from any expense' thanks to Nelson's hospitality, with whom he took all his meals.[63] Although Beatty could look forward to little in prize money, under the new 1805 pay regulations as a surgeon who had served for more than ten years he received approximately £250 per annum. Beatty assisted Gillespie in the examination of surgeon's mates, who would be promoted acting surgeon by Nelson to fill vacancies in a fleet that often had to wait months for new medical officers to be sent from home. In December 1804 they examined Beatty's first mate Richard Webster, 'touching his Abilities in the Practice of Physic and Surgery', and certified him as 'perfectly capable of serving as Surgeon in any of His Majesty's Ships of the third rate', confirming his suitability for advancement.[64]

Beatty's medical log, which he began to compile on a daily basis from 29 December 1804, provides illuminating insight into the nature of his work and the medical condition of the *Victory*'s crew. Beatty and Hardy co-operated closely to attain high standards of hygiene and cleanliness. The importance of strict discipline in encouraging both has been emphasized by the example of the *Spencer*, and on the *Victory* it also played an important role in reducing the damaging effects of intemperance upon her crew's health. Beatty and virtually all other medical officers constantly condemned the navy's excessive allowances of alcohol. They associated it with destruction of the digestive system and liver, and with the development of scurvy and malignant fevers.[65] Intoxication was a major cause of the many accidental injuries, such as falls from above, below, and overboard, which surgeons treated. Hardy's humane care for his men has already been emphasized, but there was a sterner side to his paternalism, illustrated by the number and severity of punishments for breaches of discipline. He appears to have made a determined effort to control drunkenness, which was a cause of 135, or approximately 60 per cent, of the 225 floggings carried out while Beatty was surgeon. The average penalty for intoxication was thirty-six lashes, with sentences of forty-eight and even sixty lashes inflicted upon persistent

---

[63] Gillespie to sister, 7 Jan. 1805, *Chambers's Journal*, 14 (1945), 231.
[64] WL, MSS 3377.   [65] Blane, *Select Dissertations*, in Lloyd, 191.

offenders.[66] Dressing the wounds of those punished for drunkenness must have made the navy's attitude towards alcohol seem even more illogical to surgeons.

A sick berth containing twenty-two beds may seem very small for a ship which carried approximately 820 men, yet such was the state of the *Victory's* health that all of the beds were rarely needed (see Ill.1). Daily numbers on the sick list averaged between ten to fifteen during Beatty's tenure as surgeon. Thus, on 21 April 1805, when the fleet was cruising off Sardinia, the *Victory's* sick berth had only ten occupants, and since four were classified as the victims of wounds or accidents, only six were suffering from illness or disease. There was one case of flux (probably dysentery or gastritis), one of venereal disease, two cases of ulcers (probably infected wounds or sores on the legs), and two seamen were classified under 'other complaints', which tended not to be serious. The overall health of the Mediterranean Fleet from August 1803 to August 1805 can be accurately estimated from the nearly uninterrupted weekly medical returns of the sick submitted to Nelson by Snipe and Gillespie, and from the monthly returns of the Gibraltar and Malta hospitals. During the first quarter of 1805 the average number on the sick list was approximately 206, divided into the following categories: fever 12, flux 9, scurvy 4, ulcers 43, wounds and accidents 38, rheumatism 15, pulmonary inflammation 15, venereal 7, and other complaints 63. Many of those injured by accident would be suffering from hernias, a chronic problem caused by the immense physical strain of shipboard labour. Gillespie considered rheumatism and consumption (tuberculosis) to be the two most serious illnesses in the fleet, responsible for the greatest number of invalids or mortalities. Many victims of disease tended to be among the older, more vulnerable men, in a fleet where the average age of the seamen was below 30. Most on the sick list were not seriously ill, however, because only about fifteen altogether were actually confined to bed at any one time. The majority were cured aboard ship by their surgeons themselves, or in consultation with the physician, for on average eighty-one were discharged to duty each week.[67]

High standards of hygiene limited the incidence of typhus and other infectious diseases. The fleet's new recruits received a thorough medical survey by its ships' surgeons before being accepted, and were washed and issued clean clothes to prevent the introduction of infection. Beatty, for example, examined and certified a marine recruit as fit for duty on the *Victory*

---

[66] TNA, ADM 101/125/1; ADM 51/4514.   [67] WL, MSS 3680.

on 15 April 1805.[68] French and Spanish prisoners incarcerated on a ship of the fleet were segregated to prevent them contaminating their captors. The prescription of Peruvian bark may have helped the wooding and watering parties in resisting malaria. The efficacy of vaccination in limiting smallpox is illustrated by the report of just one occurrence of four cases on board the *Hydra* in April 1805.[69] The excellence of the fleet's provisioning explains the low incidence of scurvy, although there were occasionally minor outbreaks. Soon after the resumption of war in 1803 Nelson experienced difficulty in securing adequate quantities of lemons from Naples, and had to request supplies from England.[70] In May 1804, in response to a letter from Captain Robert Barlow of the *Triumph* reporting thirty-seven cases of scurvy, Nelson relayed advice from Snipe: 'that it is necessary, in order to remove an inveterate scurvy, to give each man so afflicted six ounces of lemon juice, and two ounces of sugar, daily, in addition to the present quantity issued by the Purser, for the space of twelve days.'[71] Nelson's reply suggests that all the fleet's crews normally received preventative doses of lemon juice as well as frequent supplies of fresh fruit and vegetables. There was a potentially serious outbreak of scurvy during the winter of 1804–5, after Spain's entry into the war had temporarily disrupted the provision of fresh supplies. This probably inflated the average number on the sick list in early 1805 quoted above, but Gillespie reported how citrus fruit had halted the epidemic's development: 'Several of the Ships' Companies appear to be slightly affected with Scurvy Indicating the want of Fresh Meat and Vegetables, it is probable that this disposition would have been much more manifest had it not been for the Supply of Lemons and Oranges lately furnished, the use of which has been attended with the most salutary effects.'[72] Beatty pre-empted any crisis on the *Victory* with the aid of 504 pounds of lemon juice which he received while she was provisioning at Agincourt Sound on 19 January.[73] Nelson's development of Sicily as a source of lemon juice guaranteed future supplies.

Nelson and his medical staff were extraordinarily vigilant in guarding against any infection being contracted by contact with the land or other ships. The gravest threat was posed by the outbreak of a virulent epidemic of yellow fever in southern Spain during late 1804 and early 1805. The disease reached

---

[68] BL, Add MSS 34,929, fo. 51: Beatty to Nelson, 15 Apr. 1805.
[69] WL, MSS 3680: Sick Return, 7 Apr. 1805.
[70] TNA, ADM 1/407, Nelson to Nepean, 12 July 1803.
[71] Nelson to Barlow, 15 May, 1804, Nicolas, *Dispatches*, vi. 19.
[72] WL, MSS 3680, Gillespie, 24 Feb. 1805.   [73] TNA, ADM 51/4514.

Gibraltar and killed many among the garrison and civilian population. Nelson, Gillespie, and Beatty had all seen what yellow fever could do and were determined to keep the fleet out of its reach. The commander-in-chief warned his captains: ... 'the greatest precaution is necessary to prevent the Fever now raging at Spain and at Gibraltar from getting into the Fleet, Ships are particularly desired not to board on any account vessels coming from Gibraltar, Cadiz, Malaga, Alicante, Carthegena or any place where the fever has been.'[74] Even those who had been in contact with ships from these ports were forbidden from coming aboard the fleet.

TRAFALGAR

In early 1805 Napoleon developed an invasion plan, which involved the concentration of France and Spain's combined battle fleets at Martinique, from whence they would sail to Boulogne to cover the projected descent upon Britain during June or July. The commander of the Toulon Fleet, Vice-Admiral Pierre de Villeneuve, escaped the British blockade on 30 March, and freed the Spanish squadron at Cadiz under Vice-Admiral Don Frederico Gravina. The Combined Fleet reached Martinique on 16 May, but Rear-Admiral Missiessy, who had been waiting with the Rochefort Squadron, had already returned to Europe. Once Nelson received certain intelligence that Villeneuve's destination was the West Indies, he sailed in pursuit, and reached Georgetown, Barbados, on 4 June. When Villeneuve learned of Nelson's arrival he gave up waiting for the Brest Fleet, which could not elude its blockade, and departed for Ferrol. Nelson had warned the Admiralty of Villeneuve's course, and he was intercepted off the port by a fleet under Sir Robert Calder on 22 July. Villeneuve lost two ships in an indecisive engagement and withdrew to Vigo. Soon after he ventured north to Ferrol. Believing that he lacked sufficient strength to break the British blockade of Brest and liberate its fleet, however, the French admiral abandoned Napoleon's invasion plan and retreated south, reaching Cadiz on 21 August. Vice-Admiral Cuthbert Collingwood assumed command of the fleet blockading Cadiz, and Nelson returned to England in the *Victory* to recover from the damage to his health suffered by the unrelieved stress of more than two years' duty in the Mediterranean.

[74] NMM, STO/5: Nelson to Captains, 14 Oct. 1804.

The fitness of Nelson's fleet had been largely unimpaired during its epic return voyage to the West Indies of over 6,000 miles, despite the fact that it had stayed only nine days, and therefore had little opportunity to rest or resupply. The excellence of its earlier provisioning is emphasized by the *Victory*'s logs, which for the first time revealed a sustained reliance upon salt beef and pork. Nelson informed the queen of Naples that his ships 'received not the smallest refreshment, or even a cup of water'.[75] Despite this, he proudly proclaimed to Sir Alexander John Ball: 'We have lost neither Officer nor man by sickness since we left the Mediterranean', and he reported to William Marsden, secretary to the Admiralty: 'The squadron is in the most perfect health, except some symptoms of scurvy.'[76] Nelson's assessment is confirmed by Gillespie's 4 August 1805 report that 214 men were on the sick list, a number not much greater than the fleet's average over the previous two years, despite its great exertions. There had been a minor outbreak of scurvy, but the regular issue of lemon juice had restricted its development to only twenty-three cases. In addition to most of the sick, Gillespie reported that 276 other seamen and marines on four ships (but none on the *Victory*), also displayed some scorbutic symptoms, who 'stand in need of the salutary aid of vegetables and fresh meat in order to re-establish a vigorous state of health'. Only seven of the sick list, however, were ill enough to be confined to the fleet's sick berths. Nelson arranged for supplies of fresh fruit, vegetables, beef, and water to be waiting for the fleet at Tetuan (on the north African Coast opposite Gibraltar), where it took on provisions on 23 July. By mid-August Gillespie reported that 'the number of scorbutics in the Fleet is considerably diminished'.[77]

The medical condition of the *Victory*'s officers and men had been uniformly good during the cruise to the West Indies. When Beatty closed his medical log in January 1806 he gave the following account of losses from accident, disease, and invaliding up to the Battle of Trafalgar on 21 October: 'The *Victory*'s casualties from the 29th December 1804 till the day of Battle amounted only to five deaths, and two hospital cases. Of the fatal cases, 1 died of fever, 3 of consumption, and one from injury of the Spine, the hospital cases were consumption, and were sent to the Gibraltar Hospital in July 1805.'[78] These are truly remarkable statistics, the loss of only five out of

[75] Nelson to Queen of Naples, 21 July 1805, Nicolas, *Dispatches*, vi. 480.
[76] Nelson to Ball, 21 July, 1805, Nelson to Marsden, 20 July, 1805, ibid. 479, 474.
[77] TNA, ADM 1/411, fos. 335–9: Gillespie's Report, 14 Aug. 1805.
[78] TNA, ADM 101/125/1.

approximately 850 men, or less than 1 per cent of the *Victory*'s complement over a period of ten months, testifying to Beatty's skill as a surgeon. In describing the effective preventative measures which preserved the men's health, especially from catarrhal coughs and rheumatic fevers over the winter, Beatty emphasized Hardy's support:... 'and [this] is attributable solely to Captain Hardy's attention to their subordination, temperance, warm clothing, and cleanliness, together with the measures daily adopted to obviate the effects of moisture, and to accomplish the thorough ventilation of every part of the ship.'[79]

Gillespie gave up his position as physician of the fleet when the *Victory* anchored at Spithead on 18 August 1805. When submitting his final medical returns to Nelson, he reported the deaths of 110 seamen and marines and the hospitalization of 141 over the previous two years. Numbers on the sick list had averaged approximately 190. Many of those admitted to hospital recovered and returned to duty. These are exceptionally low figures for a fleet whose average strength was approximately ten–twelve ships of the line and two–three frigates carrying 6,000–8,000 men. The totals are even more impressive when it is remembered that most of the ships had been continuously at sea for nearly the entire period, and had just returned from the gruelling chase of Villeneuve's fleet. Despite the great rigours of the Mediterranean Fleet's services, only about 1.5 per cent of its strength had been lost from disease, accident, or enemy action, and an average of only approximately 2.7 per cent were on the sick list at any one time. There could be no more striking evidence of the efficient collaboration of the fleet's commander-in-chief, physicians, surgeons, and sea officers to safeguard its health.[80]

In early August 1805 Britain formed a coalition with Austria and Russia against Napoleon. Confronted with the threat in central Europe, Napoleon abandoned the invasion of Britain and later that month marched the Grande Armée eastwards to prevent the concentration of his new enemies. On 28 September Nelson, in the *Victory*, arrived off Cadiz and resumed command of the blockading fleet, which reinforcements increased to thirty-three ships of the line. Napoleon had ordered Villeneuve's fleet, and the several thousand soldiers it carried, to support the French army's operations in southern Italy. When Villeneuve learned that the British fleet had been weakened by the detachment of six ships to take on water and provisions at

---

[79] Beatty, *Authentic Narrative*, 20.
[80] TNA, ADM 1/411, f. 335: Gillespie's Report, 4 Aug. 1805.

Gibraltar, he sailed for the Mediterranean on 20 October. He was also stung into action by suspicion of his imminent ignominious dismissal. News of the Combined Fleet's movement was relayed to Nelson by his frigates, which remained in touch with the enemy throughout the night, while he manoeuvred to retain the weather-gage (i.e to hold the windward position vis-à-vis the French and Spanish ships), and the initiative to attack.

Villeneuve's fleet of thirty-three warships had formed line of battle during the night, and after dawn on 21 October was sighted by the British, approximately 20 miles off Cape Trafalgar. It was about 10 miles to the east and steering for the Straits of Gibraltar. Nelson had personally explained his intended plan of attack to his ship captains, and had also circulated it in written form to ensure that all clearly understood his objectives. He sought to concentrate overwhelming force against the enemy's centre and rear, which would be destroyed before its van could come to its aid. Nelson adjusted his tactics for an assault in two rather than three divisions, because his fleet of twenty-seven ships of the line was smaller than at first envisaged. He also judged that there would be insufficient time for a decisive outcome if the attack were delayed to allow his ships to form into line abreast, given the distance between the two fleets and the light airs. Villeneuve had ordered his fleet to wear, directing it back towards Cadiz, which further convinced Nelson of the need to strike immediately. The attack was therefore delivered in two columns sailing roughly in line ahead, the windward division of fourteen ships led by Collingwood, and the leeward of twelve by Nelson. The *Africa*, whose captain was Beatty's former commander and friend Henry Digby, had been separated from the rest of the fleet during the night. She was about 6 miles to the north, and would join the battle by engaging the enemy van.[81] Anticipating the great physical strain of the battle, many British captains ensured that their crews were prepared to endure it by a meal. The *Victory*'s able seaman John Brown recorded that the ship's company was piped to dinner at noon, and Edward Codrington of the *Orion* also gave his crew dinner so that 'we were all strong, fresh, hearty, and in high spirits'.[82]

Although virtually all officers aboard the flagship and the British fleet welcomed the prospect of battle and the opportunity to win the glory and honour of victory, the attitude of the fleet's surgeons was much more ambivalent. They were compassionate individuals inspired by great concern

[81] For studies of the campaign and Battle of Trafalgar see Julian Corbett, *The Campaign of Trafalgar* (London, 1919); Oliver Warner, *Nelson's Battles* (London, 1965); John Terraine, *Trafalgar* (London, 1976).   [82] Bourchier, *Codrington Memoir*, 75.

for the men under their charge—what Snipe called 'the most Sacred duty of every Medical Character'. They would be called upon to treat the appalling wounds inflicted upon their friends and shipmates by naval combat. Gillespie probably spoke for Beatty, and many of his fellow medical officers, when he contrasted his reaction to that of the rest of his comrades on board the *Victory* when battle appeared imminent in January 1805:

For my own part I behold with great coolness the enthusiasm of all around me in anticipating the laurels to be gained in the expected battle. I regard such things as necessary evils in which every man is bound to do his duty to the utmost of his power, and not as a matter of any great degree of exultation. The humane and reflecting mind cannot but be struck with the carnage of warfare, and if to remedy the disaster towards our fellow creatures encountered in it be the duty of a Christian, I may with reason be satisfied with the part which it is my lot to act in this drama.[83]

The war at sea against France had raged for more than ten years, and Beatty had served for virtually the entire period. He had been in action several times, yet had only been called upon to treat casualties in battle once, during the capture of the *Santa Brigida*, a brief and one-sided engagement in which the Spanish frigate had been overwhelmed by three adversaries. Beatty's first mate, the Scot Neil Smith, had entered the service after the Peace of Amiens, receiving both his diploma and naval qualification from the Royal College of Surgeons in July 1803, indicating a high degree of proficiency. No record of second mate William Westenburg's examination for mate or assistant has been found before January 1807, when he failed, suggesting that he had been warranted acting mate by Nelson sometime before Trafalgar, and was of limited ability.[84] Neither had experience of battle. There is nothing to suggest that Beatty's career had been atypical when most naval service involved blockade, escort duty, or cruising against enemy commerce. Combat against the enemy was comparatively rare, but a conflict between two great fleets was even more exceptional. Those serving under Nelson all knew what to expect from a fleet action under his leadership. The bloody battles of the Nile and Copenhagen had cemented Nelson's reputation as an aggressive fighting commander, whose aim was to decisively defeat the enemy. Many were

[83] Gillespie to sister, 22 Jan. 1805, *Chambers's Journal*, 232.
[84] Royal College of Surgeons of England, Examination Book, 1800–1820, p. 72. Smith was unusual in taking the examination to become a member of the Royal College of Surgeons as well as the navy qualifying exam. Usually, naval surgeons did not obtain this certificate of distinction, if at all, until they were placed on half-pay.

familiar with his frequently declared determination to 'annihilate' the Combined Fleet, and of the tactics of close-range combat that he advocated to achieve it. Surgeon William Burnett of the *Defiance* had served at the battles of St Vincent and the Nile, and Forbes Chevers had fought at the Glorious First of June, but few other medical officers at Trafalgar had endured such an ordeal or knew precisely what to expect. On 21 October the 32-year-old Beatty faced the naval surgeon's rarest and most supreme test, the treatment of a heavy number of casualties in a full-scale, bitterly fought fleet action.

'VAULT OF MISERY'

When the *Victory*'s decks had been cleared for action, the sick berth was dismantled and all of its contents were removed below. Such was the state of the crew's health, that all ten seamen or marines on the sick list were convalescents, who Beatty reported were able to perform their duties during the battle. Beatty and his assistants prepared the cockpit of the orlop deck as an emergency surgery, which was below the waterline and considered safe from enemy gunfire. Those who visit the *Victory*'s cockpit today can see for themselves the conditions under which the surgeon worked (see Ill. 6). It was by no means an ideal place for conducting delicate operations and caring for the wounded. It was a very cramped space, dimly lit by lanterns or candles, poorly ventilated, and permeated by the damp, unwholesome smell of the hold, which was immediately below. The cockpit normally formed the living quarters of the midshipmen, master's mates, and assistant surgeons, and casualties were treated upon mess tables or makeshift platforms of chests lashed together. These were located near to the hatchway, down which the casualties were evacuated, and close to the dispensary and its medical supplies.

The set of surgical instruments that Beatty most likely used at Trafalgar has survived, contained in a portable wooden case which would have been placed upon one of the tables ready for use (see Ill. 7). The case was divided into two compartments, including long- and short-blade knives and a fine-toothed bow saw for amputation, a screw tourniquet, forceps, probes, trephines, and scissors. The inventory of Beatty's medical equipment recorded that fifteen tourniquets, splints of various lengths, 120 yards of linen, and 8 pounds of lint were available for the dressing of wounds and injuries. There were no anaesthetics in the modern sense: laudanum was all that could be offered to relieve pain. Olive or linseed oil and cold vinegar, often mixed with ceruse (which contained lead), were used to treat burns. Barrels and buckets of water for cleaning sponges, swabs, and instruments, vinegar for disinfection, and receptacles for blood and amputated limbs would also have been at hand. The cable tier, the area immediately forward, was prepared for the reception of the wounded, who were laid upon platforms or coils of rope covered with sailcloth, where they would await attention.

A contemporary textbook of naval surgery published by William Northcote in 1770 gives some insight into how Beatty may have prepared:

A surgeon of a man of war should have everything needful, in a sufficient quantity, always by him in readiness . . . His capital instruments should be constantly kept clean, bright, and in good order. His apparatus should consist of several tourniquets . . . crooked needles of all sizes threaded with proper flat ligatures . . . a large quantity of scraped (short) lint, some mixed with flour in a bowl; double- and simple-headed rollers (or bandages) of all breadths and lengths . . . for slight wounds those made of bunting will be sufficient; but for cases of more consequence, such as amputations, fractures, dislocations *etc.* the linen roller must be used. He ought to be furnished with common needles and thread, with pins in plenty . . . Splints of all sizes must also be at hand, and when used armed with tow or old linen cloth.[85]

Surgeon Edward Ives, who served in the Indian Ocean during the Seven Years War, went into battle armed with six amputating knives instead of the usual two or three, 'having learnt from experience, that the best of knives after an operation or two quite lose their keenness'. In the heat of battle there was simply insufficient time 'for properly restoring them to the hone'. The same advice applied to the number of saws, as the changing of blades 'is equally inconvenient in time of action'.[86] In obedience to a standing order that Nelson had first issued to his predecessor Magrath, Beatty probably had plenty of warm water ready in the event that the commander-in-chief had to endure another amputation:

Yet, of all the sufferings of the operation, and its subsequent facts, so strongly pressed upon his mind, he complained most of 'the coldness of the knife'. So painfully and deeply was the recollection engrafted on his feelings, that I had general instructions, in consequence, whenever there was a prospect of coming to action, to have a hanging stove kept in the galley, for the purpose of heating water, in which to immerse the knife, in the event of his being the subject of an operation, and on which he always calculated.[87]

---

[85] William Northcote, *The Marine Practice of Physic and Surgery*, 2 vols. (London, 1770), 445–6.
[86] Edward Ives, *A Voyage to India* (London, 1773), 453. [87] Nicolas, *Dispatches*, ii. 444.

The *Victory* had a limited medical staff in proportion to the approximately 820 members of her crew who sailed into battle, and even that was below strength. Beatty should have been able to rely upon the aid of a third assistant, according to regulations which assigned three assistants to three-deckers and two to two-deckers, but the Admiralty's failure to act swiftly enough to encourage recruitment of new medical officers before 1805 meant that many ships fought the battle with insufficient numbers. There were approximately seventy-one medical officers serving aboard the twenty-seven ships of the line at Trafalgar, one-fifth fewer than the total of eighty-eight that regulations demanded.[88] These surgeons were responsible for casualties suffered among crews whose total strength was approximately 20,000 men. None of Nelson's seven first- and second-rates had three assistants, and one of the most heavily engaged, the *Temeraire*, possessed only one. Eight of twenty third-rates lacked one of two assistants, including many which suffered the greatest losses such as the *Tonnant*, the *Belleisle*, and the *Bellerophon*. William Burnett had only one assistant on board the *Defiance*.

In addition to his assistants Smith and Westenburg, and the loblolly boys, there were a number of others present in the cockpit whom Beatty could turn to for some help. Richard Francis Roberts, an 18-year-old midshipman and Dorset neighbour of Hardy, was assigned to the orlop with a handful of men, probably to assist in the reception of casualties. Nelson's chaplain and personal secretary Alexander John Scott would provide comfort to the wounded and dying, and he was joined by Walter Burke the purser. It was not uncommon for the wives of warrant and petty officers, whom some captains allowed to accompany their husbands aboard ship, to serve as nurses during battle. Forbes Chevers of the *Tonnant*, who had only one assistant to help him treat seventy-six casualties, received much-needed aid from ... 'the Purser and a petty officer's wife, a very big woman, who, as fast as the unfortunate wounded were operated on, lifted them off the table bodily in her arms and bore them off as if they were children to their temporary berths out of the way elsewhere'.[89] Nelson had received a petition from a widow and mother of two, Christiaan White, who had acted as a nurse at the Battle of the Nile, where her husband was killed: 'I attended the Surgeon in Dressing the Wounded Men, and Like wise attend[ed] the Sick and Wound[ed] During the Passage to Gibraltar Witch was 11 Weeks on board his Majesty's Ship Majestic...'[90] Nelson did not like women aboard his ships, once famously

---

[88] McKenzie, *Trafalgar Roll*.
[89] Geoffrey Bennett, *The Battle of Trafalgar* (London, 1977), 181.   [90] WL, MSS 3677.

declaring: 'Every man became a bachelor after passing the Rock of Gibraltar.' But Hardy may have taken a more lenient view, for there appear to have been women with the *Victory* at Trafalgar, although they worked as powder monkeys, not as nurses. In 1843 a Mrs Sarah Pitt claimed to have been 'employed during the battle in carrying powder from the magazine, along with the other sailors' wives who were aboard'. She was probably married to the 18-year-old Bristol native George Pitt, who served as an ordinary seaman.[91]

William Beatty later wrote and published an extremely influential account of his experiences on 21 October, which has become one of the most widely cited sources in histories of the battle, the role played by the *Victory*, and the death of Nelson. In addition to his own recollections, the narrative incorporated the experiences of other members of the ship's company, including Hardy, Scott, and Burke. Beatty had been on the flagship's quarterdeck for most of the morning, marvelling at the impressive sight of the Combined Fleet. He was ordered to take up his station below by Nelson just before the enemy opened fire on the *Royal Sovereign* and the battle commenced. It is difficult to imagine Beatty's state of mind during the tense minutes of waiting, as the *Victory* slowly approached the enemy at a speed which never exceeded 3 knots, and he anticipated the impact of its shot, and the influx of casualties down the hatchway. Did his hand shake, and did he doubt his courage and ability to perform his very arduous duty?

Although Nelson's tactics were designed to focus overwhelming force upon sections of the Combined Fleet, initially it had the opposite effect, as it exposed the leading ships of his columns to the concentrated, undisturbed fire of a number of enemy ships before they would be able to penetrate the line and reply. Even when the *Victory* and the other leading ships had cut the enemy line, they risked defeat in detail, as they were confronted by a superior number of opponents until support arrived. The desperate struggle of Nelson and Collingwood's leading ships is reflected by the fact that they suffered the heaviest casualties and greatest physical damage. According to Beatty, the enemy began firing individual ranging shots a little before noon. Once they found the range, the *Victory* ran the gauntlet of the broadsides of the French and Spanish flagships the *Bucentaure* (80 guns) and the *Santissima Trinidad* (140), as well as the *Redoutable* (74) and several other ships. Marine lieutenant Lewis Rotely, who was stationed on the poop, wrote: 'Previous to breaking the enemy's line their fire was terrific . . . It was like a hailstorm of

[91] *Exeter Times*, 10 Oct. 1843.

bullets passing over our heads.'[92] It is surprising that neither Nelson nor Hardy instructed the *Victory*'s crew to lie down, to minimize casualties, given their otherwise exemplary concern for their men's safety, a precaution adopted by Collingwood and Captain William Hargood of the *Belleisle*. Rotely stated: 'no man went down until knocked down; had such orders been given many a life would have been spared.'[93] One of the early shots killed eight marines drawn up on the quarterdeck, and Nelson at least ordered the rest to be dispersed around the ship to make them less vulnerable. Beatty reported that the flagship suffered about twenty killed and thirty wounded, or roughly a third of her total casualties, during the approach, and it is difficult not to believe that some of these losses could have been avoided. Beatty's work had therefore begun well before the *Victory* severed the enemy line a little after noon, and fired raking broadsides into the *Bucentaure* and the *Redoutable*.

Unfortunately, Beatty's narrative does not precisely explain how he organized the cockpit as an operating theatre and his assistants for the treatment of casualties. It is sometimes claimed that casualties were attended by surgeons in the order in which they arrived, regardless of the severity of the wound, despite the dangerous consequences. The seaman William Robinson of the *Revenge* wrote: 'For the rule is, as order is requisite, that every person shall be dressed in rotation as they are brought down wounded, and in many instances some have bled to death.'[94] There may have been some sort of rough code of honour among seamen, as illustrated by an incident reported by Captain Henry Baynton of the *Leviathan*, when recommending his captain of the forecastle, Thomas Main, to the Patriotic Fund. Main's arm had been badly shattered, but he refused to allow William Shoveller to amputate it immediately: 'The Surgeon (who respected him) would willingly have attended him, in preference to others, whose wounds were less alarming; but Main would not admit of it, saying, *Avast, not until it comes to my turn, if you please.*'[95] Whatever seamen expected, Shoveller's behaviour suggests that naval surgeons did not follow such an arbitrary practice, but directed attention to where it was most urgently needed. The veteran surgeon John Atkins, who published a much-respected medical manual in 1734, advocated careful organization of the cockpit before battle, and the rapid, efficient division of casualties into three groups based upon immediate need, placing greatest emphasis upon staunching haemorrhage.[96] The most dangerous cases would

---

[92] 'Lewis Rotely', *Nelson Dispatch*, 6 (1999), 384.   [93] ibid. 384.
[94] Robinson published his naval memoirs under the pseudonym 'Jack Nastyface', *Nautical Economy* (London, 1836), 21–2.   [95] *NC* (1806), 16.
[96] John Atkins, *The Navy Surgeon* (London, 1742).

be dealt with by the surgeon, who assigned flesh wounds and minor injuries for dressing to his mates. Ives implemented a similar system, directing his mates to initially assess casualties, and only pass on those who 'were desperately hurt, and whose cares ... required an immediate operation'. Finally, William Northcote declared, 'if more than one wounded is brought down at a time, always first take care of him who is in most immediate danger, but otherwise dress them as they come, without distinction.[97]

Beatty's experience at Trafalgar must have been very similar to Robert Young's, surgeon of the *Ardent* at the Battle of Camperdown in 1797, who wrote an extremely rare personal account. Young's description of combat surgery emphasizes the extraordinary clear-headedness, self-control, and energy required to impose order upon the chaos of the cockpit during battle:

Melancholy cries for assistance were addressed to me from every side by wounded and dying, and piteous moans and bewailing from pain and despair. In the midst of these agonising scenes, I was able to preserve myself firm and collected, and embracing in my mind the whole of the situation, to direct my attention where the greatest and most essential services could be performed. Some with wounds, bad indeed and painful, but slight in comparison with the dreadful condition of others, were most vociferous for my assistance. These I was obliged to reprimand with severity, as their voices disturbed the last moments of the dying. I cheered and commended the patient fortitude of others, and sometimes extorted a smile of satisfaction from the mangled sufferers, and succeeded to throw momentary gleams of cheerfulness amidst so many horrors.[98]

The surgeon and his assistants at work were described by seaman Charles McPherson at the Battle of Navarino in 1827, who remarked upon 'their bare arms and faces smeared with blood'.[99]

As the preceding account demonstrates, Beatty required heroic self-possession, skill, and stamina to treat the approximately 100 officers and men wounded on the *Victory* during the battle (see Ill. 8). The circumstances in which he had to examine wounds, locate and remove wooden splinters and other foreign material, perform amputations, and tie arteries were appalling. The obscure, fitful light was an acute problem, so bad that Chevers carried out most of his operations with the aid of two candles held close upon either side of him by assistants. Only after the battle did he realize that they had singed all the hair from his eyebrows.[100] Lack of space to work was another severe

[97] Ives, *Voyage*, 453. Northcote, 449.
[98] TNA, ADM 101/85.
[99] Charles McPherson, *Life on Board a Man of War* (Glasgow, 1928), 158–9.
[100] F. M. Chevers, 'Memories of the Battle of Trafalgar', *Notes & Queries*, 6th ser. 4 (1881), 504.

constraint, as any visitor to the *Victory*'s confined cockpit will appreciate who tries to imagine the accommodation of approximately 100 wounded upon its deck. The normally close atmosphere of the cockpit would have been rendered even more stifling by the overcrowding, and the stench of the many partially naked casualties, sweating from pain and fear. Candles and lanterns consumed oxygen, and contributed to the excruciating heat. The ship's hull was shaken by the concussion of its gunnery, and the impact of enemy shot. The cockpit was located immediately below the lower gun deck, which mounted the 32-pound cannon, the heaviest guns aboard ship, each weighing several tons. The blast they produced was deafening, followed by the thunderous rumble of their recoil, reloading, and running out to fire again. Rotely, surrounded by fire from both broadsides of the middle deck, as well as from above and below, described it as 'louder than thunder'.[101] Well may the dying Nelson have purportedly cried out at the disorienting cacophony: 'Oh *Victory, Victory*, how you distract my poor brain.' Although gunners attempted to protect their ears by wrapping handkerchiefs or cloths around their heads, many suffered permanent damage to their hearing from the violent discharge of so many cannon in such a confined space.[102] The flagship's 22-year-old master's mate Henry Symons permanently lost the hearing in his left ear.

These were not the only disruptions with which surgeons had to cope. Despite being below the waterline, the cockpit was by no means safe from enemy gunfire, and the surgeon himself faced the constant risk of death or wounding. Beatty's colleague the army physician Sir James Fellowes, who distinguished himself in combating the yellow fever epidemic at Gibraltar during 1804–5, visited the *Victory* and several other ships when they arrived in port after the battle. Fellowes reported how hostile fire violently interrupted the work of two of the fleet's surgeons, who narrowly escaped injury themselves:

in the *Colossus* the Surgeon had just performed an operation, when a cannon shot passed thro the Cockpit, knocked down his Table, and wounded his assistant who was taking him some dressing. The unhappy brave fellows who were laying down on the deck after being amputated rolled over one another—on board the *Bellerophon* the same thing happened and the distress it occasioned cannot be conceived.[103]

[101] 'Rotely', 384.

[102] Lt.-General S. B. Ellis, who served as a marine lieutenant aboard the *Ajax*, *Notes & Queries*, 11 (1868), 357.

[103] NMM, MSS 73: James Fellowes to father, 5 Nov. 1805. To reduce these distractions and dangers, Ives advocated setting up the combat surgery in the hold, where the 'operator's mind as well as body ought to be as little agitated as possible': *Voyage*, 451.

Ten of the French fleet's eighty-eight surgeons, including two aboard the *Redoutable*, were killed during the battle, illustrating the destructive effect of British gunnery.[104]

Beatty's medical log includes a partial descriptive list of the wounds suffered by the *Victory*'s casualties (see Ill. 8). It gives an illuminating insight into the nature of the ship's struggle during the battle, and her surgeon's work. The majority of the *Victory*'s initial casualties, the fifty that Beatty reported before she broke the enemy line, would have been caused by cannon fire: either solid round shot, or bar or chain shot which were designed to inflict maximum damage upon masts and rigging. They either killed or maimed directly, as in the case of Nelson's secretary John Scott, who was cut in two early during the action, or by the lethal showers of wooden splinters scattered in all directions by their impact. Those on the upper decks were also injured by falling masts, yards, blocks, and other debris caused by enemy gunfire. Gunner William Rivers reported a marine who was impaled upon his own bayonet by the fall of the mizzen mast.[105] Midshipman Roberts, who did a detailed survey of the *Victory*'s battle damage, recorded that she was struck by at least 122 shot.[106] Flying splinters caused penetrations, contusions, lacerations, and fractured bones. Tiny fragments of wood were extremely difficult to remove from wounds, exposing their sufferers to infection with tetanus. Surgeons had long observed the relationship between the velocity of the ball and the severity of splinters it produced upon impact. Balls fired from a longer distance tended to punch great jagged holes in a ship's hull, scattering many large, deadly splinters in all directions, while balls fired from close range, travelling at higher speed, produced much narrower, cleaner apertures.[107] After breaking the enemy line, the *Victory* fell on board the *Redoutable*'s port side and the two ships became entangled together. The shocking casualties inflicted on the French ship may partly be explained by the fact that many of the *Victory*'s guns were double- or treble-shotted, and fired with reduced powder charges at a depressed angle to prevent them from passing completely through her opponent and injuring the *Temeraire* on her other side. Consequently, their penetration would have swept the *Redoutable*'s decks with a hail of splinters.[108]

[104] Jean Pierre Hamon, 'Les Chirurgiens Navigants Français de La Bataille de Trafalgar', thesis, University of Nantes (1982), 194, 197.

[105] NMP, MS 1998/41/1 William Rivers Gunnery Notebook.

[106] A. M. Broadley and R. G. Bartelot, *Nelson's Hardy: His Life, Letters and Friends* (London, 1909), p. 262.

[107] Gilbert Blane, *Observations on the Diseases Incident to Seamen* (1799), p. 79.

[108] Beatty, *Authentic Narrative*, 31.

One of the most poignant episodes in the battle, for Beatty, was the agonizing death of his close friend Lieutenant William Andrew Ram, which illustrated the horrific wounds inflicted by splinters. Ram, midshipman Robert Smith, and several seamen and marines had been on the gangway when a round shot fired from a gun on the *Redoutable*'s main deck, pointing upwards, penetrated obliquely through the quarterdeck, scattering a lethal shower of splinters. Smith was killed and Ram was cruelly wounded. The lieutenant was carried below, and Beatty applied ligatures in an attempt to staunch the severe haemorrhage from several wounds. Ram, however, who must have been driven mad with torment, tore them out, either in a defiant attempt to return to duty or when he realized he had no hope of living, and bled to death.[109] The 21-year-old Ram was a fellow Irishman, the second son of Abel Ram of Clonattin, who was MP for Wexford and colonel of its militia. Beatty and Ram had met while serving aboard the *Spencer*, which was not present at Trafalgar. Ram had been promoted acting lieutenant and transferred to the flagship in April 1805 as part of a series of moves to replace a lieutenant who had absconded from the *Hydra* at Malta, 'from an unfortunate desire to travel, and perhaps an imprudent attachment to an Italian female', according to Nelson.[110] The two friends could not have anticipated the consequences of their reunion. After burial at sea, Ram's body was washed ashore near Cadiz and identified by the name woven into his shirt. He was given a proper burial thanks to the generosity of the city's governor.[111]

It was not uncommon for combatants to be killed by the immense pressure exerted upon their internal organs by the close passage of cannon balls at great velocity, which was called 'wind of ball' by contemporaries. Hardy's clerk Thomas Whipple was killed by the near miss of a round shot that left no mark on his body, while speaking to midshipman George Westphal. In addition to being struck in the leg with a splinter, Collingwood was badly bruised in the back, 'which I think was caused by the wind of a great shot, for I never saw anything that did it'.[112]

---

[109] M. and A. Gatty, *Recollections of the Life of the Rev. A. J. Scot, D.D., Lord Nelson's Chaplain* (London, 1842), 185; 'Letters of Lieutenant William Andrew Ram Killed at Trafalgar', *Nelson Dispatch*, 6 (1998), 184–7; C.P. Addis, *The Men who Fought with Nelson in HMS Victory at Trafalgar* (London, 1988), pp. 102–3.

[110] Nelson to Marsden, 11 Apr. 1805, Nicolas, *Dispatches*, vi. 403.

[111] NMP, MS 1998/41/1: William Rivers Gunnery Notebook.

[112] Admiral Collingwood to Sarah Collingwood, 28 Mar. 1806, *Life and Letters of Vice-Admiral Lord Collingwood*, ed. O. Warner (London, 1968), 154.

The majority of the *Victory*'s casualties were suffered among those officers, seamen, and marines whose action stations were upon the upper decks. This was largely due to the gunnery tactics of the Combined Fleet, which fired high to halt Nelson's attack by damaging British masts, yards, and rigging. In addition, the captain of the flagship's principal opponent, Jean Lucas of the *Redoutable*, had concentrated his training upon boarding and the use of small arms. Soon after the *Victory* had run aboard the Frenchman's port side, Lucas ordered her lower gun ports on that side to be closed and her batteries abandoned, so that his men could be mustered for boarding. Large numbers 'climbed halfway up the shroud to open a musketry fire'.[113] Lucas's tactics help to explain Beatty's report that the only two men wounded on the lower deck were hit by musket balls.

If the *Redoutable* made limited use of her great guns, her small-arms fire and the 200 grenades that Lucas claimed were hurled aboard took a heavy toll upon those on the *Victory*'s forecastle, quarterdeck, and poop. Soon after the two ships became locked together, Beatty wrote: 'The *Redoutable* commenced a heavy fire of musketry from the tops, which continued for a considerable time with destructive effect to the Victory's crew.'[114] At approximately 1.15 p.m. Nelson was wounded by a musket ball, probably fired from the mizzen-top, which 'struck the epaulette on his left shoulder, and penetrated his chest'. In the next quarter-of-an-hour nineteen were killed, including Captain William Adair of the marines, and twenty-two more were wounded, most from the *Redoutable*'s musket fire.[115] *The Victory*'s crew repulsed a boarding attempt by Lucas's men, and then the French boarding parties were decimated by the broadsides of the *Temeraire*, which had run aboard the *Redoutable* on the other side. By about 2.20 p.m. the 522 casualties and intense damage inflicted by the two British ships' gunnery compelled Lucas to surrender.[116]

Nelson was carried below to the cockpit. He was undressed, laid upon a bed supported by Scott and Burke, and covered with a sheet. He was then examined by Beatty, who gently probed the wound with his right forefinger, and asked the admiral to describe his sensations. According to the surgeon, Nelson replied that: ' "he felt a gush of blood every minute within his breast: that he had no feeling in the lower part of his body: and that his breathing was difficult, and attended with very severe pain about that part of the spine

[113] Jean Lucas, 'Report', in E. Desbrière, *The Naval Campaign of 1805: Trafalgar*, trans. C. Eastwick (Oxford, 1933), ii. 215. [114] Beatty, *Authentic Narrative*, 31. [115] Ibid. 54. [116] Desbrière, *Campaign*, ii. 200–2.

where he was confident that the ball struck; for" said he, "I felt it break my back".'[117] Beatty's assessment of the musket ball's damage to Nelson's heart, lungs, and spine, and particularly of the internal bleeding, convinced him that the wound was fatal. Nelson lingered on in great pain, before dying at approximately 4.30 p.m. from 'a wound of the left pulmonary artery, which poured out its blood into the cavity of the chest'.[118]

Beatty could do nothing to save Nelson, and throughout the battle he was constantly drawn away from the mortally wounded admiral to treat other gravely injured men demanding his attention. He was called upon to perform of the amputation of nine legs and two arms during the battle or its aftermath, their timing reflecting most contemporary surgeons' opinion that these operations should be carried out immediately, before loss of blood, shock, and the effects of fear reduced the patient's chances of survival. Seventeen-year-old midshipman William Rivers, son and namesake of the *Victory's* gunner, had his left leg amputated below the knee. His father recorded an account of his behaviour as reported by his mate Thomas Bailey, who carried William below:

The foot hung by a Piece of Skin abought 4 Inch above the ankle. When in the Cockpitt call for Putty Nose, (Nick Name for Purser Steward), for a Knife to Cutt the foot off. Mr Beaty the Surgeon stop it. Say what are going to do with a Knife? Cut my foot off, it is no use. I say Docter—when will you take me [in] hand. Anser very Shortly. Abought An Houre after, when the Docter took him in hand, told him to Lay Down on the Table. His Answer was, I will sett on the Table, you may Cut where you Please. During his Amputation, say to the Ships Company that was wound'd, my Men, it is nothing to have a Limb off. You will find Pleasure, when you come here Men, to get Rid of your Shatter'd Limb. The Men among one an other [ask], Who was that was Taulking. They told it was Mr R. The Cock pitt was Quite Silent Afterward. When the Docter had saw'd the Bone off 4 Inch below the Nea, he put his Finger up, and said, Docter you have left me some Marrow. When taking up the Arters say, Docter, awast their belay. After being Dressed and the Action over, the Father went into the Cockpitt, Inquired after his Son. He call out on the Other side of Cockpitt, here I am Father, nothing is the Matter with me; only lost my leg, and that in a Good Cause.[119]

Later young Rivers interrupted the men, who had cleared the cockpit of dead bodies and amputated limbs, while they were throwing them overboard.

---

[117] Beatty, *Authentic Narrative*, 39.   [118] Ibid. 84: see Ill. 9.
[119] NMP, MS 1998/41/1 William Rivers Gunnery Notebook. (As in some other quotations from contemporary sources, punctuation has occasionally been modified for clarity.)

When he enquired after his own leg, one replied: 'I understand Old Putty Nose, was to have them, for Fresh Meat for the Sick.'

Rivers's fortunate escape was celebrated in a poem, written by a Miss Vigo, and transcribed into his father's journal:

> Dear Youth by all so tenderly Beloved,
> We morn you[r] loss which you so lately proved.
> Nought could avert the Direful Ball,
> That took thy Limb and has made Hundr'ds fall.
> But tho' thy Loss is Great, how Great thy Fame;
> Thy Matchless Valour will Each Tongue Proclaim.
> With manly Fortitude you View the Scar,
> And Dauntless [say] it is the Fate of War.

Perhaps Miss Vigo was a sweetheart, for the poem concludes with a hopeful vision of peace and marriage:

> May Every Comfort Bless thy futur life,
> And Sooth thy Cares with a fond & Tender wife.
> Heaven's choice Blessing Each Brave Tar attend,
> What does so nobley England Laws Defend.[120]

Rivers was promoted to lieutenant in 1806, but never rose beyond that rank. He was awarded a Greenwich Hospital pension in 1826, perhaps through the good graces of his former shipmate Beatty, who was now its physician. Rivers sat for an early photograph in 1844, and died in 1856, aged 78. There were other examples of extraordinary courage during amputation or excruciating operations. Baynton, the captain of the *Leviathan*, reported that Thomas Main, 'with great composure, smiling, and with a steady clear voice . . . sang the whole of *"Rule Britannia"*' while his arm was being amputated at the shoulder.[121]

As a source, Beatty's carefully constructed third-person narrative of his experience at Trafalgar is as fascinating for what it conceals as for what it reveals. A work intended to commemorate the heroism and self-sacrifice of Nelson and other veterans of the battle was hardly likely to describe behaviour in which the wounded failed to exemplify these ideals. It is hard to accept, however, that all of the casualties endured the pain of wounds and fear of death so stoically. Edward Ives recorded how he was constantly besieged by

---

[120] Ibid. If Miss Vigo did have designs upon Rivers she was disappointed, for he married a Miss Grace Gibson in 1809.   [121] *NC* (1806), 15–16.

suffering, apprehensive men desperate for assistance, and the same pleas must have been addressed to Beatty:

At the very instant when I was amputating the limb of one of our wounded seamen, I met with an almost continual interruption from the rest of his companions, who were in the like distressed circumstances; some pouring forth the most piercing cries to be taken care of, while others seized my arm in their earnestness of being relieved, even at a time when I was passing the needle for securing the divided blood vessels by a ligature.[122]

Following Ram's cruel death, Scott's nerve temporarily gave way, and unable to cope any longer with the appalling misery surrounding him, he rushed upon deck to escape. Scott had only managed to catch his breath when Nelson fell wounded, and he followed the commander-in-chief below. The chaplain was deeply traumatized by the sights and sounds of the cockpit, and the only recorded instance in which he ever spoke of his experience was to tell a friend 'that it resembled a butcher's shambles'.[123] Midshipman Richard Roberts was also shocked by the combat surgery, and he avoided any detailed account of his assignment to Beatty beyond the telling statement 'that I will not if possible be quartered there again'.[124] Roberts left the navy immediately after Trafalgar, perhaps to avoid sharing the fate of the many wounded and dying men he had helped to tend.

Although Beatty, Scott, Roberts, and Burke forbear from detailed accounts of the *Victory's* cockpit during the battle, 17-year-old Lieutenant Paul Nicholas of the *Belleisle* has left a graphic description of the transformation of his ship's midshipmen's berth, normally the site of cheerful conviviality, into a 'vault of misery':

...our cock-pit exhibited a scene of suffering and carnage which rarely occurs. I visited this abode of suffering with the natural impulse which led many others thither—namely, to ascertain the fate of a friend or companion. So many bodies in such a confined place and under such distressing circumstances would affect the most obdurate heart. My nerves were but little accustomed to such trials but even the dangers of battle did not seem more terrific than the spectacle before me.

On a long table lay several anxiously looking for their turn to receive the surgeon's care, yet dreading the fate which he might pronounce. One subject was undergoing amputation, and every part was heaped with sufferers: their piercing shrieks and expiring groans were echoed through this vault of misery; and even at

---

[122] Ives, *Voyage*, 451.   [123] Gatty, *Recollections*, 185.
[124] Quoted in Broadley and Bartelot, *Nelson's Hardy*, p. 242.

this distant period the heart-sickening picture is alive in my memory. What a contrast to the hilarity and enthusiastic mirth which reigned in this spot the preceding evening.[125]

Although the Battle of Trafalgar concluded at approximately 4.30 p.m. there was no rest for Beatty, Smith, and Westenburg, who struggled over the ensuing hours and days to save the lives of the *Victory*'s dangerously wounded. Beatty must have been exhausted by the intense physical and mental pressures of battle, aggravated by the death of Ram and other close personal friends, and of Nelson, his revered commander-in-chief, whom he was powerless to save. Beatty's ordeal again probably very closely mirrored Robert Young's after Camperdown: 'I was employed operating and dressing till near 4.0 in the morning, the action beginning about 1.0 in the afternoon. So great was my fatigue that I began several amputations under a dread of sinking before I should have secured the blood vessels.'[126] Such was the strain of coping with the *Victory*'s many casualties that the schooner *Pickle*'s surgeon, Simon Gage Britton, came aboard on the evening of the battle to assist Beatty in treating the rows of shattered men who covered the orlop deck. He remained until 24 October.[127] Once all the wounded were out of immediate danger, Beatty set about preserving Nelson's corpse for the inevitable public funeral. It was placed in a cask of brandy, and stored upon the middle gun deck.

When the battle finished the breeze was still westerly and very light, but a great swell was running. By next morning the wind was rising, and by noon the fleet was buffeted by powerful gales and heavy rain. The winds increased to hurricane force, and blew for seven days onto the hostile shore. On 24 October the *Victory* was in such distress that she was taken in tow by the *Polyphemus*, but the lines had to be cut because of the heavy seas. The storm finally began to abate on 27 October, when the *Neptune* took the ship in tow and carried her into Gibraltar on 28 October.[128] The storm caused great agony for the wounded in the British fleet, especially for those unlucky enough to be in completely dismasted ships, whose motion was even more violent. Many lying upon the deck were rolled along it, and those in

---

[125] [Lt. Paul Nicholas], 'An Account of the Battle of Trafalgar', *The Bijou* (London, 1829), 75–6.

[126] TNA, ADM 101/85.

[127] TNA, ADM 101/72. Britton is representative of the many highly qualified, gifted medical men who entered the navy during the later years of the French wars and retired to successful civilian careers. After going on half-pay in 1814 he earned a medical degree, and practised for many years in Newport, Devon, serving between 1848 and 1856 as physician of the North Devon Infirmary.

[128] ADM 51/1454.

hammocks were pitched against each other and the bulwarks, and some were thrown down. Wounds were reopened and several casualties bled to death. The storm made the surgeons' struggle to save the wounded even more difficult.

The high survival rate of the *Victory*'s casualties indicates the quality of care they received at the hands of Beatty and his assistants. When the ship was decommissioned in early January 1806, Beatty reported that only six of the 102 convalescents had died, five on board and one at Gibraltar Hospital. All of the rest recovered from their wounds while under his charge, except for five of the worst cases, who were left at Gibraltar, and five who were transferred to the *Sussex* hospital ship off the Nore. The fact that eight of the eleven amputees survived reflects very highly upon Beatty's judgement and skill as a surgeon, given the extremely adverse circumstances of the operations. Statistics collected after the Battle of Algiers in 1816 reported mortality rates of 46 per cent among patients whose amputations were delayed, and 33 per cent among those whose operations were immediate.[129] The 24-year-old ordinary seaman Richard Jewell died on 22 October, the day after the removal of one of his thighs. Beatty attributed his decease to the great shock of the operation, and the fact that 'he had lost a great deal of blood before he was brought to the cockpit'. Loss of blood was always a great danger to the wounded, especially those furthest from the orlop. Bearing casualties below was laborious and slow, and often inflicted further trauma, especially if the companion ladders had been destroyed by enemy fire. Blane and Turnbull advocated training a number of officers and men in the use of tourniquets, who could provide immediate first aid to the wounded before their evacuation to the cockpit, but it appears that this excellent advice was not widely practised.[130] The 22-year-old ordinary seaman William Smith, who also had a leg taken off at the thigh, died of an infection. Beatty must also have maintained the highest standards of hygiene during the treatment and dressing of wounds, for only two others—not amputees—for few were apparently lost to post-operative infection. The 21-year-old midshipman Alexander Palmer, who had been struck in the thigh by a musket ball, succumbed to tetanus, and the 22-year-old landsman Henry Cramwell died of gangrene after suffering several severe contusions, probably from splinters.[131]

---

[129] A. C. Hutchinson, *Some Further Observations on the Subject of the Proper Period for Amputating in Gun-Shot Wounds* (London, 1817), 1–64.
[130] Blane, *Select Dissertations*, 77; Turnbull, *Naval Surgeon*, 249–50.
[131] TNA, ADM 101/125/1.

CONCLUSION

Nelson achieved a resounding victory at Trafalgar, which confirmed British naval superiority over the French and Spanish. Superior British gunnery, seamanship, self-confidence, and high morale encouraged by Nelson's inspiring leadership had triumphed over a demoralized and divided foe. Above all, the battle was decided by the rapid close-range broadsides of the British gunners, whose rate of fire was two to three times faster than their opponent's. Lieutenant Humphrey Senhouse of the *Conqueror* wrote that his ship fired upon the *Bucentaure* at so 'short a distance, that every shot flew winged with death and destruction'.[132] The discipline exercised by most British ships in holding their fire until they reached point-blank range was extremely important, ensuring that their gunners were fresh and able to fire to the maximum effect, in contrast to their enemies, who had forfeited the advantage by opening fire at the maximum range. The safe, efficient teamwork of the *Victory*'s gun crews is emphasized by Beatty's report 'that not one casualty from accident occurred on board during the engagement'.[133]

Gilbert Blane studied how the difference in British and French gunnery tactics and proficiency influenced the casualty patterns inflicted in battle. Because the British usually preferred close-range combat, with a rapid rate of fire aimed at the enemy's hull to compel a quick surrender by causing heavy casualties and silencing guns, the ratio of killed to wounded suffered aboard French ships was very high, often reaching or exceeding 1 : 1. In contrast, because the French often fired high to immobilize their opponents, and were slower, less destructive gunners during point-blank encounters, they inflicted proportionately fewer fatal casualties. Therefore, the ratio of killed to wounded aboard British ships was much lower, roughly 1 : 3. Blane's observations are supported by an analysis of Trafalgar, where the British suffered approximately 449 killed and 1,242 wounded and their opponents roughly 4,530 killed and 3,573 wounded, as well as the other major battles of the French wars.[134]

---

[132] Humphrey Senhouse, 'The Battle of Trafalgar', *Macmillan's Magazine*, 81 (1900), 419.

[133] Beatty, *Authentic Narrative*, 61.

[134] Gilbert Blane, *A Brief Statement of the Progressive Improvement of the Health of the Royal Navy* (London, 1830), 40; James Watt, 'The Injuries of Four Centuries of Naval Warfare', *Annals of the Royal College of Surgeons of England*, 57 (1975), 3–24, and 'The Surgery of Sea Warfare from the Galley to the Nuclear Age', *Transactions of the Medical Society of London*, 97 (1980–1), 1–15.

Serving guns which weighed several tons demanded a high degree of physical strength and stamina. It was so exhausting that a high rate of accurate fire could not be maintained for very long. Some idea of the intensity of fire achieved by the *Victory* is suggested by the gunner Rivers's report that approximately 4,100 round shot and 338 rounds of grape shot were expended, propelled by 150 barrels of gunpowder, weighing over 6 tons.[135] The British fleet at Trafalgar, exemplified by the *Victory*, was manned by crews sustained by what Dr Snipe described as 'that Muscular Vigour, [and] spirit of courage and adventure so necessary on the day of Battle'.[136] The British fleet's great physical and mental fitness reflected its excellent health, a factor which was fundamental to its success. This was achieved by the close co-operation of the Royal Navy's executive and medical officers in attaining high standards of nutrition, hygiene, clothing, and morale, and in implementing effective measures for the prevention and control of disease. The considerable improvement in the health of the fleet which had been achieved since the beginning of the French wars was emphasized by Blane's calculation that the ratio of seamen and marines voted for service by parliament to those sent sick to hospital, had declined from 1 in 4 in 1794 to 1 in 8.33 in 1804.[137]

The impact of health upon the Trafalgar campaign is emphasized by a comparison with the Combined Fleet, which had been seriously weakened by disease during its voyage to the West Indies. At this time, neither the Spanish nor the French navies had adopted reliable measures for combating scurvy.[138] This is a surprising omission in the case of the Spanish, since Vice-Admiral Gravina himself had been advised of the efficacy of lemon juice during a visit to Portsmouth in 1793.[139] Consequently, the fleet suffered considerably from the disease. Dysentery and typhus were also present aboard the crowded ships, which carried approximately 3,000 troops for offensive operations against the British colonies. Once in the West Indies, the fleet became vulnerable to yellow fever and malaria during the approximately four weeks that it waited for Ganteaume. An increasingly serious shortage of provisions also undermined its health. Gravina cut his crew's rations by one-quarter.

---

[135] NMP, MS 1998/41/1: William Rivers Gunnery Notebook.

[136] WL, MSS 3680: Snipe to Nelson, 19 Sept. 1803.

[137] Blane, *Select Dissertations*, in Lloyd, 198–9.

[138] Julian de Zulueta, 'Health in the Spanish Navy During the Age of Nelson', *Journal of the Royal Naval Medical Service*, 86 (2000), 89–92, and 'Trafalgar: The Spanish View', *Mariner's Mirror*, 66 (1980), 293–319; Hamon, 'Les Chirurgiens', 198–9; Kenneth Carpenter, *The History of Scurvy and Vitamin C* (Cambridge, 1986), 96; Martine Acerra, 'Le Scorbut', *L'Histoire*, 36 (1981), 74–5.   [139] John Harbour, *Trafalgar and the Spanish Navy* (London, 1988), 21, 82.

The Spanish admiral evacuated 691 men to hospital at Martinique, and he warned the French minister of marine, Denis Decrès, of the rapid spread of disease: 'had we remained there a month longer, I believe that we should have lost half our crews and it might have made it impossible for us to return to Europe.'[140] The Spanish were compelled to leave a frigate at Martinique when its crew were reduced to a number too small to man it.

Scurvy and other diseases plagued the Combined Fleet during the return voyage to Europe, and after its battle with Calder. At Vigo, on 28 July, Villeneuve reported that there were 200 sick on board the *Achille*, 150 each on board the *Indomptable*, *Intrépid*, and the *Aigle*, and between 120 and sixty sick on all the other ships, making a total of approximately 1,200 or 10 per cent of their total complement.[141] When Villeneuve sailed from the port, 800 sick were crowded into the 74-gun *Atlas*, which had been badly damaged during the action of the 22nd, and left behind. These included eighty disembarked from the *Berwick*, according to her Captain Jean Filhol-Camas, 'presque tous scorbutiques'.[142] General Jacques Lauriston, the commander of the military forces on board the Combined Fleet, informed Napoleon that 470 ill soldiers of the 16th and 67th Infantry Regiments were evacuated in Vigo.[143] The French also suffered from a lack of food, which impinged upon the fleet's health. Villeneuve was forced to reduce the rations of his ships' companies from early August, and the acute French provisioning crisis was not resolved until early October, when sufficient funds were organized to pay Spanish contractors.[144] Almost paradoxically, because of Nelson and Collingwood's logistical ability and the perilous state of French finances, the blockading fleet was well victualled while the fleet in port was poorly supplied. An inadequate diet probably helps to explain why numbers on Villeneuve's sick list did not significantly decline after the fleet's return to Spain. In Corunna on 10 August he reported that the *Algésiras* had 114 sick and the *Achille* seventy-five. The crew of the frigate *Sirene* was broken up to reinforce the two sickly ships of the line, and it was left in the port to land the ill.[145] These ships probably suffered from a serious epidemic, because both were scoured and disinfected with lime-wash on 2 September. On 16 September, in addition to those mentioned above, Villeneuve identified the *Mont Blanc* as another ship whose

---

[140] Gravina to Decrès, 16 Sept. 1805, Desbrière, *Campaign*, ii. 94.
[141] Villeneuve to Decrès, 28 July 1805, ibid. i. 113; Hamon, 'Les Chirurgiens', p. 198.
[142] Filhol-Camas to Decrès, 4 Aug. 1805, quoted in Hamon, 'Les Chirurgiens', p. 198.
[143] Lauriston to Napoleon 28 Sept. 1805, Desbrière, *Campaign*, i. 169.
[144] Ibid. i. 168–72.   [145] Villeneuve to Decrès, 10 Aug. 1805, ibid. 128.

'crew is weak, having lost many through sickness'.[146] When the Combined Fleet reached Cadiz Lauriston landed more diseased soldiers, 'not in a state to support any fatigue, all having symptoms of scurvy'.[147] Cadiz's hospitals were so overstretched that the army patients had to be accommodated in two field hospitals. Nearly a month later, on 16 September, Lauriston reported that their recovery did not advance 'as rapidly as I had hoped', and conditions aboard the fleet were probably similar.[148]

On 28 September, as he prepared to confront Nelson, Villeneuve reported that there were 1,731 sick in the Combined Fleet, 649 of whom had been hospitalized.[149] In addition to this drain upon manpower, 311 ratings had deserted since the fleet had first sailed from Toulon. The French admiral resorted to soldiers to make up his total deficiency of 2,027 men, but confessed: 'they cannot supplement the small number of seamen left to us.' The Spanish ships particularly suffered from a dearth of skilled seamen. The yellow fever epidemic of 1804–5 had devastated the seafaring population of southern Spain, which made it extremely difficult for Gravina to muster experienced crews, and to replace losses from disease and desertion. Some sense of its ferocity can be gained from a report from Malaga in February 1805, which recorded the death of 9,326 of its 36,530 citizens.[150] This highlights the wisdom of Nelson's strict quarantine to prevent yellow fever from spreading to his ships. Similar safeguards to avoid infection must have been rigidly enforced by Nelson and the experienced Gillespie during the British fleet's briefer spell in the West Indies, to shield it from infection. Gravina was compelled to press many of Cadiz's poorest inhabitants and draft soldiers to man as many Spanish warships as possible. Prisoners from Cadiz's gaols were also conscripted, introducing typhus and other infectious diseases into the fleet.

A comparison of the sick lists of the Combined Fleet with those documenting the low incidence of illness aboard Nelson's ships reveals a sharp contrast in the relative health of the two combatants on 21 October. In addition to inferior gunnery and seamanship, the poor performance of the French and Spanish seamen must also be assigned to a want of Snipe's 'Muscular Vigour', or deep reserves of physical and mental energy, the results of a poor diet and debilitated health, which also weakened their morale.

[146] Villeneuve to Decrès, 16 Sept. 1805, ibid. ii. 94.
[147] Lauriston to Napoleon, 22 Aug. 1805, ibid. 118.
[148] Lauriston to Napoleon, 16 Sept. 1805, ibid. 123.
[149] Villeneuve to Decrès, 28 Sept. 1805, ibid. 100.   [150] Zuleuta, 'Trafalgar', 305.

4

Beatty and Nelson's Apotheosis

THE FUNERAL

The news that reached London in the first days of November 1805 was grim. Napoleon had confirmed his recently self-appointed title as emperor of France by inflicting a stunning reverse on Britain's ally Austria at Ulm, far away on the banks of the Danube. On the very day of Trafalgar the Austrian commander, General Mack, had been forced to capitulate and the French had captured 60,000 prisoners, along with much of the artillery and the vast baggage train of the Austrian army. Although the allies were massing an army of some 400,000 troops to move against the Grand Armée, there was now no guarantee of success. In celebrating their victory, the French poured scorn on the British, whom they accused of plotting and financing the Austrian attack. The implication was that when the enemy in the east was crushed, the emperor would resume his assault on Britain. William Pitt, the prime minister, and his government badly needed news of a victory at sea to restore public confidence in their conduct of the war and in the House of Hanover. Just after midnight on the morning of 6 November an exhausted Lieutenant John Lapenotiere, commander of the schooner *Pickle*, banged on the doors of the Admiralty in Whitehall demanding urgently to see William Marsden, the secretary. Marsden had just completed answering the evening mail and was leaving the boardroom for his private apartments, when Lapenotiere was ushered in and cried out: 'We have gained a great victory, but we have lost Lord Nelson.' He handed over Collingwood's dispatches containing the exciting news of the annihilation of the combined French and Spanish fleets off Cape Trafalgar a fortnight earlier, and noting that the body of the fallen hero, preserved by William Beatty, was being brought home by the *Victory* for burial.

From this moment on, Nelson's body ceased to be an object of devotion to the friends who loved him, and was transformed into a trophy for a national celebration and day of mourning. With Collingwood's well-chosen use of 'the Immortal Nelson', coined after the Battle of the Nile, ringing in his ears, Marsden hurried off, candle in hand, to rouse the first lord of the Admiralty, the 79-year-old Lord Barham, unsure where he had chosen to lay his head. Shaken from his slumber, 'the old Peer calmly asked: "What news? Mr. M." '[1] Well aware that this was the news that the people hankered for after the long, frightening months when invasion was hourly expected, Barham immediately sent word to Pitt in Downing Street. Pitt later told Lord Fitzharris 'that he had been called up at various hours in his eventful life by the arrival of news; but whether good or bad, he could always lay his head on his pillow and sink into sound sleep again. On this occasion, however, the great event announced brought with it so much to weep over as well as to rejoice at, that he could not calm his thoughts; but at length got up, though it was three in the morning.'[2]

Given the government's need for a morale-raising victory, it was inevitable that Nelson would be treated as the saviour of the nation and his body given a state funeral, even if the king only gave his consent grudgingly.[3] A national day of thanksgiving was declared for 5 December, which was to be a truly ecumenical occasion with services in churches and chapels of every domination throughout the new United Kingdom of Britain and Ireland. At the same time, it was decided that Nelson should be interred in St Paul's Cathedral rather than Westminster Abbey. Christopher Wren's masterpiece was ideally suited to a great national spectacle, with its wide-open vista to the high altar, uninterrupted by a medieval choir screen as at Westminster Abbey, and it had already been used successfully to host the thanksgiving service for the king's recovery from illness on St George's Day 1789. As the 1789 service had shown, it could seat thousands if temporary galleries were erected down the length of the nave and around the transepts. Moreover, the choice of St Paul's, in the heart of the City of London, was richly symbolic, linking Nelson's victory and death firmly with Britain's commercial prosperity, and with every section of society from the great merchant princes to the crowd itself. The funeral was to be an affirmation of Britishness in the country's only modern cathedral, and not an antique affair in St Peter's Abbey in Westminster, the centre of the English monarchy and government for a thousand years. When the news reached London in mid-December of Napoleon's

---

[1] Elizabeth Marsden (ed.), *Brief Memoir of . . . William Marsden*, (London, 1838), 116.
[2] Quoted in Philip Henry Stanhope, *Life of Pitt* (London, 1861), 343.
[3] A. Aspinall, *The Later Correspondence of George III*, vol. 4 (Cambridge, 1968), 365, n. 1.

crushing defeat of the emperor of Austria and tsar of Russia at Austerlitz on the second day of the month, the need to pull out all the stops in a great celebration of national unity became even greater.[4]

By a happy coincidence Nelson's body arrived on the *Victory* at Spithead on 5 December, the day of national thanksgiving. There the ship anchored for six days until Hardy received instructions that she should be sailed to the Nore. Since contrary winds prevented the *Victory* from rounding the South Foreland for a week, it was 23 December before the admiral's remains could be transferred to an Admiralty yacht and taken to lie in state in Greenwich Hospital, as had been arranged. The coffin was on public view in the Painted Hall from 3 to 7 January, then taken the following day by water up the Thames in a grand procession to the Admiralty, where it was rested, surrounded by candles overnight. The funeral took place on 9 January. A little before six o'clock the city resounded with the beating to arms of the several regiments of London and Westminster volunteers which were to line the route all the way from the Admiralty to St Paul's. By nine the whole route was guarded with detachments of mounted volunteer cavalry, on duty at every crossing in case of disturbances. Altogether some 20,000 volunteers were reckoned to be on parade, an impressive turn out of regiments which had only been recently raised to meet the invasion threat. In addition, every police constable in London and Westminster was on duty. While the volunteers were taking up their stations, swinging into Horse Guards' Parade came 8,000 regular soldiers with standards and ensigns with crêpe streamers flying, and bands playing 'Rule Britannia' with their drums muffled. Dressed in their kilts, the Highland soldiers of the 75th and 92nd Regiments created the greatest stir. The kilt had been proscribed from 1746 to 1783 as part of the government's efforts to rid the highlands of Scotland of Jacobitism, and were an unusual sight on the streets of London. By nine the regulars stood in line of battle, ready to move away at the head of the funeral cortege, which finally departed about 11.30 a.m. Altogether it took some three-and-a-half

---

[4] Apart from royal funerals, there had only been three state funerals since the restoration of the monarchy: in 1670 of the duke of Albermarle, who as General Monck had been largely responsible for negotiating the return of Charles II; in 1722 of the duke of Marlborough, the great military commander in Flanders; and in 1772 of the earl of Chatham, the prime minister's father, whose government had defeated the French in the Seven Years War. None of these had been in St Paul's Cathedral. For the development of St Paul's as the nation's church, see Holger Hoock, 'The British Military Pantheon in St Paul's Cathedral: The State, Cultural Patriotism and the Politics of National Monuments, *c.* 1795–1820', in Matthew Craske and Richard Wrigley (eds.), *Pantheons: Transformations of a Monumental Idea* (Aldershot, 2004).

hours for the procession to pass through the sorrowing crowds. The bier did not draw up before the mass bands at the top of Ludgate Hill until about a quarter-to-three. The funeral service, performed in the cathedral before a congregation of some 7,000 men, took the form of evensong, the *Magnificat* sung to a setting by the organist, Dr Thomas Attwood. The catafalque bearing the coffin was lowered into the crypt by machinery and the service was over by six o'clock. St Paul's was not finally cleared for another three hours.[5]

William Beatty's role in Nelson's funeral was minimal. He was only an attendant lord. It is significant, though, that he was actually present, and even given some prominence. When Nelson's body was taken up the Thames on 8 January, the surgeon was in the first barge which carried the admiral's standard and guidon. He sat in the cabin with two pursuivants-in-arms from the College of Heralds, other naval officers, Nelson's servants in mourning dress, and his chaplain, the Revd Alexander Scott. On the following day he took part in the funeral procession itself, riding alone in a mourning coach.[6] He was thus part of a very select band of royalty, aristocrats, churchmen, naval officers, members of Nelson's family, and the admiral's intimates on the *Victory* who accompanied the hero to his resting place. Given Beatty's relatively lowly status in the *Victory's* pecking order, presumably Hardy had been responsible for his presence. However, if his was just another face in the cortege for the crowd to gawp at, he must have taken a quiet satisfaction in the fact that the state funeral had really only been made possible through his care over the preceding months in preserving the admiral's body.

Victory took five weeks to make her way back from Gibraltar to Portsmouth, slowly sailing home under jury rig, with Nelson's pennant flying halfway up the mainmast. While the admiral's remains were the especial concern of his chaplain and close friend Scott, who kept vigil by the barrel on the middle deck in the company of a marine guard throughout

---

[5] Contemporary newspaper accounts of the funeral are given in Nicolas, *Dispatches*, vii. 399–418. *Bell's Weekly Messenger* printed a lavish popular account of the funeral in January, as did the monthly *Gentleman's Magazine*. A funeral programme appeared in the *London Gazette*, no. 15,881. For a full account of the event and its significance in the creation of Britishness, see Michael Moss, 'The Grand National Obsequies', unpublished paper. See also, Timothy Jenks, 'Contesting the Hero: The Funeral of Admiral Lord Nelson', *Journal of British History*, 39 (2000), 422–53; Gillian Russell, *The Theatres of War: Performance, Politics and Society 1793–1815* (Oxford, 1995).

[6] These details are taken from the British Library collections of cards, cuttings from newspapers, etc. at C.55.k.7.(2.), and at 10815.dd.1, and Archibald Duncan, 'A correct narrative of the funeral of Horatio Lord Viscount Nelson', in *The Life of Lord Horatio Nelson* (London, 1806). See also, *A Correct Account of the Funeral Procession of Lord Nelson etc.* (London, 1806). Francis William Blagdon, *Edward Orme's Graphic History of the Life, Exploits, and Death of Horatio Nelson, etc.* (London, 1806), contains an illustration of the procession with the individual participants.

the voyage, the preservation of the body was the surgeon's responsibility. Twice more on the way home William Beatty had to refresh the spirits in the cask. Legend suggests that he may have been helped by Mary Buick (or Buek), the wife of William Watson, a seaman in the *Victory*, and Mary Sperring.[7] More importantly, having arrived at Spithead he had to prepare the corpse for the lying-in-state at Greenwich, once he had learnt of the government's plans from a letter written to the Revd Scott by Nelson's clerical brother, Earl William, on 6 December.[8] As a result, Beatty sent ashore for cotton and linen wrappings to prepare the body. Lead was also carried on board to make a casket, which had to be large enough to encase Nelson's own wooden coffin, which was stored with the London undertaker, Mr Peddison, of Brewer Street.[9] Peddison no doubt sent the dimensions down with one of the many visitors who came on board during the week the *Victory* lay at Spithead to see the spot where the 'Immortal Nelson' fell. Then, on 11 December, the day the *Victory* sailed for the Nore, the body was taken from the barrel, presumably with the help of Smith and Westenburg, Beatty's assistant surgeons.

On inspecting the corpse, Beatty decided that if it were to be exposed to public view then the contents of the chest and abdomen would have to be removed to prevent further decomposition. While this was being done, curiosity got the better of him and he excised the musket ball, along with a piece of Nelson's coat and a gold epaulette. Probably as he worked, Beatty dictated an account of his findings, which he wrote up four days later under the title, 'a concise history of the wound', for Scott to send to the earl (see Ill. 9) This confirmed the devastating extent of Nelson's injuries:

The ball struck the forepart of His Lordship's epaulette; and entered his left shoulder immediately before the processus acromium scapulus, which it slightly fractured. It descended obliquely into the thorax, fracturing the second and third ribs: and after penetrating the left lobe of the lungs, and dividing in its passage a large branch of the pulmonary artery, it entered the left side of the spine between the sixth and seventh dorsal vertebrae, fractured the left transverse process of the sixth dorsal vertebrae, wounded the medula spiralis and fractured the right transverse of the seventh vertebrae, made its way from the right side of the spine,

[7] Roy Adkins, *Trafalgar: The Biography of a Battle* (London, 2004), 227–8.

[8] BL Add MSS 34992, Earl Nelson to Scott, 6 Dec. 1805. William had been made an earl by a grateful monarch.

[9] The coffin was a gift from Nelson's friend Captain Benjamin Hallowell, and was fashioned from a large piece of the mainmast and spar of the French flagship *L'Orient*, which had blown up at the Battle of the Nile.

directing its course through the muscles of the back; and lodged therein, about two inches below the inferior angle of the right scapula.[10]

The ball was given to Hardy, who immediately had it set in a crystal case then presented it to Beatty as a memento. (see Ill. 10)[11] This was to prove a piece of good fortune. Beatty must have very quickly come to appreciate the significance of the artefact, which he thereafter did nothing to keep hidden. Just like Nelson's sword given to him by his uncle Captain William Suckling, the ball became Beatty's lucky talisman. Elegantly mounted in a fob on a watch-chain, it allowed him to bask forever in Nelson's reflected glory. Every time that Beatty consulted his watch in future years, those around him were reminded that this was the man who looked after the hero of the age in his agony. Not surprisingly, on one occasion he was offered 1,000 guineas for the ball.[12]

When the autopsy was completed and the soft tissue removed from the cadaver, the body was surrounded with cotton and linen wrappers and rolled 'throughout with bandages of the same after the antient mode of embalming'.[13] It was next placed in the lead coffin, along with the bowels and other soft tissue wrapped in bandages, and the coffin filled with strong spirits and a solution of camphor and myrrh. In describing these events and the autopsy, for Scott to forward to the earl, Beatty commented that Nelson had: 'retained his wonted energy of mind and the exercise of his faculties until the latest moment of his existence and when victory as signal and decisive was announced to him, he expressed his pious acknowledgement thereof and heartfelt satisfaction at this Glorious event in the most emphatic language, he then delivered his last orders with his usual precision, and in a few minutes afterwards expired without a struggle.'[14] In his covering letter, Scott added that he did not consider it appropriate to expose Nelson's features during the lying-in-state, because they were beginning to decompose, reiterating a view that Beatty himself expressed in a letter to the Admiralty of the same day.[15]

The corpse remained in the lead coffin until 23 December, when the Admiralty's representative and Nelson's friend, John Tyson, chief clerk of

[10] BL Add MSS 34992, fo. 48. Beatty's memorandum, 15 December 1805. It was later reprinted in his *Authentic Narrative*, 68–71. For an uncritical medical review of Nelson's wounds see Harold Ellis, 'Famous Trauma Victims: Nelson', *Trauma*, 3:2 (2001) 127–31.

[11] Beatty, *Authentic Normative*, 71, n. 9.

[12] *The Times*, 9 Dec. 1806, p. 2, col. C: description of watch and chain.

[13] BL Add MSS 34992, fo. 49: Beatty to Scott, 15 Dec. 1805.

[14] Ibid., memorandum by Beatty, 'a concise history of the wound'.

[15] Ibid., fo. 47: Scott to Earl Nelson, 15 Dec. 1805; NMM MS 51/040/2: Beatty to the Admiralty, 15 Dec. 1805.

survey at Woolwich Dockyard, encountered the *Victory* at anchor in Nob Channel. The initial intention had been that the body was to be brought ashore in the lead coffin, then transferred to Nelson's own wooden one under the superintendence of Dr Moseley, the physician to the Royal Hospital at Chelsea, who had served with Nelson in Nicaragua. This, though, the *Victory*'s officers, with Tyson's support, seem to have considered inappropriate, and it was eventually agreed that the undertaker, Peddison, would effect the transfer on Nelson's flagship. On the very day that Tyson left Sheerness on board the Admiralty's yacht *Chatham* to look for the *Victory*, the chaplain Scott sent a further letter to Earl Nelson in which he offered Beatty's services in helping to remove the linen wrappers, as there was a danger of the 'skin coming away from the body'.[16] Beatty, therefore, had one final service to perform. Once Tyson was on board, he carefully removed the embalmed body from the lead casket and dressed it in a pair of silk stockings, uniform breeches, and a shirt. A white cambric handkerchief was bound round its neck and another round the forehead. The face was gently rubbed with handkerchiefs in a final effort to restore the features, just in case it was to be exposed to public view.[17] With his comrades in arms looking on for the last time, Nelson's body was then placed in his own coffin, which was sealed in the lead one. Tyson, Captain John Whitby (who had broken the news of Nelson's death to Lady Hamilton), and Nelson's servants went with the coffin while Beatty remained on board to attend to his duties.[18]

In the weeks before the funeral, moreover, Beatty had also played a part in ensuring that the body of the hero would survive forever as a visual icon. Amongst the visitors to the *Victory* at Spithead was a young artist, Arthur William Devis, who approached Lieutenant Edward Williams with a request to be allowed to stay on board for the passage round to the Nore so he could make sketches for a painting of the battle. According to an account given by Williams much later to Joseph Allen, who was writing a biography of Nelson, he was much too busy overseeing the repairs to reply, but sent Devis below to the wardroom. Once there, he 'ingratiated himself with the officers' and was allowed to remain on board.[19] This seems implausible, particularly as in the

[16] BL Add. MSS 34992, fo. 59: memo from Scott, 20 Dec. 1805.

[17] Nicolas, *Dispatches* vii. 259.

[18] Tim Clayton and Phil Craig, *Trafalgar: The Men, the Battle, the Storm* (London, 2004), 361. Nelson's retinue were Henry Lewis Chevalier, Thomas Dear, Robert Drummond, and Getano Spedillo, his Italian valet.

[19] Joseph Allen, *Life of Lord Nelson* (London, 1852), 229, fn. This is omitted in subsequent editions.

coming weeks Captain Hardy was a stickler for allowing no one on board to whom he had not specifically given permission. The most likely explanation is that Devis was sent on his errand by Nelson's friend and prize agent Alexander Davison, who probably wanted a pictorial record of the great victory.[20] Whoever it was who commissioned Devis, it had to be someone whom Hardy knew well. Moreover, he had to have the influence to arrange with the King's Bench for Devis's release from prison, where he had been incarcerated after the bankruptcy of his sister's dressmaking business two years before. Presumably, too, he had to provide him with funds to buy the materials he needed.[21]

Once on board, Devis decided not to paint a triumphant victory scene but to show the agony of the hero in the depths of his flagship, doubtless sensing that this was the grander subject, and remembering the young Benjamin West's triumph with the *Death of Wolfe*, exhibited in 1771.[22] Devis was probably present at Nelson's autopsy, but there is no evidence that he took a death mask when the body was removed from the barrel. Rather, he concentrated his artistic energies on recapturing Nelson's last moments on canvas. With Hardy's permission, he began to make sketches for the central image of his painting of the scene of death in the cockpit. The meticulous detail of the picture suggests that all the officers, from Hardy downwards, were only too willing to descend to the dimly lit cockpit during the voyage to be sketched in the positions they might have occupied when Nelson breathed his last. So concerned was Devis to leave an accurate record for future generations that he busied himself making a model of the cockpit to which he could refer in his studio. His primary informant must have been Beatty. The senior-ranking officer who had been present below decks in the cockpit throughout the battle, he was the artist's obvious guide in reconstructing the scene and positioning the players. Devis stayed on the *Victory* until shortly before the funeral. In the following weeks he and Beatty seem to have become close friends. Immediately or a few days after the autopsy, Devis provided the surgeon with a sketch of the bullet with the piece of uniform attached that he

[20] Charles Mitchell, 'Benjamin West's *Death of Nelson*', in Douglas Fraser (ed.), *Essays in the History of Art Presented to Rudolf Wittkower* (London, 1967), ii. 269. Devis was later to paint Davison's portrait as a colonel in the Volunteer Regiment.

[21] *Arthur William Devis*, exhibition catalogue, Hariss Museum & Art Gallery (Manchester, 2000), biographical introduction.

[22] C. Mitchell, 'Benjamin West's "Death of General Wolfe" and the Popular History Piece', *Journal of the Warburg and Courtauld Institute*, 7 (1944), 20 ff.; H. von Erffa, *The Paintings of Benjamin West* (New Haven, Conn., 1986), 55–60 and 211–16. The engraving was done in 1776, by Woollett.

had extracted from Nelson's body. More importantly, as the *Victory* sailed round to the Nore he agreed to paint Beatty a likeness of the dead hero in return for access to the corpse. A year later, towards the end of 1806, he would paint Beatty's own portrait (see Ill. 2).[23]

In giving his professional advice, Beatty must have been well aware that he was doing more than helping in Nelson's apotheosis. By placing the hero's agony correctly but unromantically in the cockpit, Devis ensured that the surgeon could claim a prominent place in the visual narrative. And Beatty capitalized on the possibility. In the eventual painting, completed in the summer of 1807 and exhibited at the British Institution in 1809, the dying Nelson is at the centre of the composition, lit by the light of an overhead lantern (see the Frontispiece). Immediately surrounding him is a tableau of five figures, all but one gazing towards the hero: Hardy standing over his friend, a little way back; Scott massaging Nelson's chest; Burke the purser supporting the dying hero with a pillow; the admiral's steward, Henry Lewis Chevalier; and Beatty, taking his pulse. Three of the five—Hardy, Scott, and Beatty—through their positioning, dress, and colouring are clearly dominant: they are the figures who actually frame the expiring hero. But it is Beatty alone whose action places the painting in time: he is either pronouncing the hero dead or signifying that the end is near. Significantly, Chevalier crouches beside him, looking not at Nelson but at Beatty, for confirmation. In what was a detailed but clearly posed representation of Nelson's death—no one of Hardy's size could have stood upright in the cockpit—Beatty had secured a defining position in the iconic moment. Moreover, unlike Scott, who knelt on the other side of the admiral, it was obvious who Beatty was: he was the *Victory*'s surgeon.[24]

NARRATING THE DEATH OF NELSON

The funeral over, Beatty did not return immediately to the *Victory* to resume his duties. He remained in London for some days, long enough at least to

---

[23] Beatty, *Authentic Narrative*, 71, n. 9. See below, p. 148, and Ch. 5, p. 161.

[24] Sydney H. Pavière, *The Devis Family of Painters* (Leigh-on-Sea, 1950), 132–3; Algernon Graves, *The British Institution 1806–67: A Complete Dictionary of Contributions* (London, 1908), 156. There are three copies extant of the Devis painting: one owned by the Crown, one at Greenwich Hospital, and one in private hands. An engraving by William Bromley appeared in 1812 with the telling caption: 'Mr Devis has adopted the plan of making TRUTH alone the object of his delineation, and has consequently depicted this awful scene exactly as it occurred.' See James

visit his friend the Revd John Evans, a Baptist minister in Islington, to show him the bullet. After he had gone, Evans penned a letter of appalling senti-mentality, which he sent to the *European Magazine and Literary Review*.[25] Once back on board, Beatty can have spent only a few days among old friends discussing the momentous events of the previous days, because the *Victory* was decommissioned at Chatham at the end of January and the crew and officers paid off. He himself tells us that he was immediately posted to the *Sussex*, the hospital ship lying off Sheerness, where he seems to have served as the surgeon in charge until the following September. It is possible, though, that he spent most of this time on leave, since he disappears from the navy's records for the next six months.[26] Wherever he was, he was not idle, for it was during these months that he made a much more personal contribution to the apotheosis of the admiral Nelson by penning the *Authentic Narrative of the Death of Lord Nelson*, which eventually appeared in early 1807.[27]

From the moment that the news of Nelson's death reached England the press and public were eager for information about his final hours, and various versions were flying around. The first published account of Nelson's dying words were reported in the *Gibraltar Gazette* of 24 October in both English and French: 'Thank God I have outlived this day, and now I die content.'[28] These, though, were not the last words first relayed to the British public through the leading Whig newspaper, the *Morning Chronicle*, on 9 December, which carried a description 'from an officer who was with him', and claimed, inaccurately, that Beatty had extracted the bullet rather than simply probed the wound. The account ended with news of the victory being conveyed to the dying hero. Nelson reportedly replied: 'Victory! But upon attempting to repeat it, he convulsed, grasped the hand of one of his friends near him, and the blood rushed from the lungs into the throat, and he expired calmly and without a groan.'[29] This account accords with that in Chaplain Scott's letter to his uncle, Rear-Admiral Scott, written on 27 October, six days after the battle: 'I knew not until his loss, how much I loved him! He died as the battle

Greig (ed.), *The Farington Diary* (London, 1922–8), iv. 151. For the NMM copy, see http://www.nmm.ac.uk/mag/pages/mnuExplore/PaintingDetails.cfm?letter = d&ID = BHC2894.

[25] *European Magazine and London Review*, 14 Jan. 1806, p. 24. Evans was a Fellow of the Society of Antiquaries: see *DNB*, *sub nom*. We do not know how the two were acquainted.

[26] Beatty, in the *Authentic Narrative*, reveals that he was transferred to the *Sussex*, but there is no reference to this in his service record: p. 65.

[27] It was published in January 1807: see below, p. 146.

[28] Oliver Warner, *A Portrait of Lord Nelson* (London, 1958), p. xx.

[29] *Morning Chronicle*, 9 Dec., 1805.

finished, and his last effort to speak, was made at the moment of joy for victory.'[30] The only addition was a preamble in which the *Victory*'s officers tried in vain to persuade Nelson not to wear his dress jacket with the woven insignia of his four orders of knighthood. Nelson is reported by the anonymous officer to have responded:

No whatever may be the consequences, the insignia of the honours, I now wear, I gained by the exertions of British seamen under my command in various parts of the world; and in the hour of danger I am proud to shew them to the enemy of Old England, I will never part from them, if it please God I am to fall, I will expire with these trophies entwined around my heart.

Although the officer was not named, when his account was republished in 1806 he was identified as Nelson's signal officer, whom the admiral had intended to promote for his meritorious conduct. The author was probably, therefore, Lieutenant John Pasco, who had composed the famous 'England expects' signal and who, severely wounded with grape shot, had lain near the dying Nelson in the orlop.[31]

This version of events was followed in the *Morning Chronicle* the next day by a completely different and fuller narrative from Walter Burke, the purser, who claimed for himself the leading part in the drama. In his version it was he who carried the dying Nelson to a midshipman's berth in the 'wings' of the cockpit and was by his side throughout his final agony. The surgeon, who is not named, is only referred to once and Scott's presence is not mentioned at all. Hardy, it is revealed, briefly attended the admiral's bedside and was commanded to bring the fleet to anchor. When he said he would come back, Nelson replied, 'I will be dead before you return'. According to Burke, Nelson died in his arms with the final exclamation: 'I have done my duty, I praise God for it.'[32]

Further information leaked out privately through letters home from sailors and officers in the battle. According to Lieutenant Humphrey Senhouse of the *Conqueror*, who wrote home on 27 October, Nelson's last words were: 'I see the day will be a glorious one; my ship is much disabled and may be more so, but never strike my flag. Let her go down. Anchor, Hardy, anchor.'[33] Midshipman Norwich Duff, in contrast, whose father, the captain of the *Mars*, had been killed, told his mother from on board the *Euryalus* that he

---

[30] M. and A. Gatty, *Recollection of the Life of the Rev. A. J. Scott, D. D., Lord Nelson's Chaplain* (London, 1842), 195.   [31] Blagdon, *Graphic History*, p. 37.
[32] *Morning Chronicle*, 10 Dec. 1805. The account originally appeared in a Portsmouth newspaper.
[33] Humphrey Senhouse, 'The Battle of Trafalgar', *Macmillan's Magazine*, 81 (1900), p. 419.

had heard Nelson's final words were: 'I die happy since I die victorious.'[34] Just before Christmas, too, Chaplain Scott revealed fuller details of the hero's dying moments himself in a long epistle to Nelson's friend, the MP George Rose. The latter had been visited by Hardy at Cucknells, his home in the New Forest, a few days after the *Victory* anchored off Spithead, where he had been given an account of Nelson's last moments and told of the hero's particular wish that the MP should promote Lady Hamilton and their daughter Horatia's case with a grateful nation.[35] On 10 December Rose wrote to Scott on the *Victory*, presumably seeking confirmation, and the chaplain duly replied on the 22nd.

The letter begins by saying that Nelson 'was compelled to speak in broken sentences which pain and suffering prevented him from always connecting', but then goes on to record some remarkably lucid moments. He recalled the dying Nelson's first command to him was: 'Remember me to Lady Hamilton!—remember me to Horatia!—remember me to all my friends. Doctor, remember me to Mr. Rose; tell him I have made a will, and left Lady Hamilton and Horatia to my country.' He then recounted Nelson's agitation at Hardy's failure to come to him, and for the first time in any written reminiscence of the hero's last hours mentioned Hardy kneeling to kiss him. The chaplain made no mention of Nelson learning of the victory, but recorded his command to bring the fleet to anchor. After Hardy left, Scott claimed that Nelson had confessed: 'I have not been a great sinner, Doctor'; then added: 'Doctor I was right,—I told you so—George Rose has not got my letter—tell him.'[36] Given Scott's state of mind during the action—it will be recalled he had had to rush on deck after Lieutenant Ram's death—there must be some doubt as to the veracity of his account. Probably the conversation about writing to Rose took place before Scott went to his action station in the cockpit.

Scott's letter was significant not only in introducing Nelson's mistress into the narrative but also in recording his partial confession. It was almost certainly intended to help Rose and Nelson's other close friends deal with the adverse publicity which would inevitably result from the publication of the hero's will and his bizarre request relating to Emma and their illegitimate

---

[34] Quoted in Adkins, *Trafalgar*, 293.

[35] Thomas J. Pettigrew, *Memoirs of the Life of Vice-Admiral Lord Viscount Nelson, KB*, 2 vols. (London, 1849), ii. 625: Rose to Emma Hamilton, 9 Dec. 1805. By then Emma had already been given an account of her lover's death. Nelson's steward Chevalier left for Merton immediately the *Victory* arrived at Portsmouth: ibid. 549–50: Hardy to Emma, 8 Dec. Nelson never acknowledged Horatia as his daughter: publicly, she was Emma's ward.   [36] Gatty, *Recollections* 189–90.

daughter. His infamous bequest of Emma to the nation had been penned by Nelson in his log on the morning of the battle, and witnessed by Hardy and Captain Henry Blackwood of the frigate *Euryalus*. It would seem that Hardy had the original copy, which was eventually given to Earl Nelson, but rumours were circulating about its existence virtually from the moment the *Pickle* arrived back in England.[37] Initially they had been stifled. The Whig *Morning Chronicle* tried to divert public attention from them on 19 November with the chilling news that Nelson had had intimations of mortality on the eve of the battle. First reports revealed that Nelson had told his surgeon, William Beatty, before the action that 'he felt the symptoms which he had been informed by him in a previous conversation presaged death'.[38] Three days later, the newspaper moved to silence criticism entirely: 'We mentioned some particulars of the Noble Lord's will, and several paragraphs have appeared in different Papers which tend to mislead the Public. The Lord Nelson's obligation to Sir William and Lady Hamilton were of a nature that drew from him at all times the most lively acknowledgement—They made an indelible impression on his heart.'[39] The first steps to prove the will, with its various codicils, however, were taken on the very day Rose had written to Scott, and it was inevitable that the terms would soon become public.[40] Arguably, by demonstrating Nelson's love of his mistress but emphasizing his contrition, however limited, Scott hoped to salvage the hero's reputation, especially among Dissenters and Evangelicals.

Nelson's will, and the extraordinary bequest regarding Emma, appeared in the press on 23 December. Not only did he leave his mistress to the country, he made generous provision for her while leaving Fanny, his estranged wife, just £1,000 a year to live on. Many of his naval colleagues were horrified by his behaviour. Earl St Vincent, his patron and supporter, wrote to his sister: 'The Will of Lord Nelson has thrown a Shade upon the lustre of his service; that infernal Bitch Lady Hamilton would have made him poison his Wife and stab me, his best friend.'[41] We can guess that Hardy quickly orchestrated a response by getting Beatty and Walter Burke, the purser, to agree yet

---

[37] Pettigrew, *Memoirs* ii. 624–5, says the codicil was given to the earl by Blackwood. However, a letter from Lady Blackwood to Emma dated Portsmouth, 6 December, the day after *Victory* docked, reveals that Hardy had the 'papers of the last will of this ever to be regretted commander': ibid. 548–9. Also, BL Add MSS 34992, fo. 39: Scott to Earl Nelson, 5 Dec. 1805, says all Nelson's papers had been sealed up by Hardy in Scott's presence and were still on board.

[38] *Morning Chronicle*, 19 Nov. 1805.   [39] Ibid., 22 Nov. 1805.

[40] Probate was given on 21 December: TNA, Prob 1/22, 21 Dec. 1805.

[41] BL Add MSS 29915, St Vincent to his sister, 3 Jan. 1806.

another account of Nelson's final hours for release to the *Morning Chronicle*, which had defended Nelson's reputation when rumours about the contents of the will were circulating in November and had printed Burke's original version.[42] Since Scott had already left the *Victory*, he was not able to contribute his recollections. The account appeared after Christmas, and this time Beatty claimed the spotlight with his introductory note that 'the following is the substance of the conversation which really took place in the cockpit, between his Lordship, Captain Hardy, Mr. Bourke, and Mr. Beatty'. This account bore some resemblance to Scott's, but none to Burke's or that of 'the officer who was with him', and considerably embroidered the version Beatty had given to Scott. This time Hardy came to the cockpit twice, and for the first time the words 'Kiss me Hardy' were included, and the following exchange:

'I hope your Lordship will still live to enjoy your triumph.'

'Never, Hardy! I am dying—I am dead all over—Beatty will tell you so—bring the fleet to an anchor—you will have done your duty—God bless you!'

Captain Hardy now said, 'I suppose Collingwood, my dear Lord, is to command the fleet?'

'Never' exclaimed he, 'whilst I live;'—meaning doubtless, that so long as his gallant spirit survived, he would never desert his duty.

This part of the narrative can only have come from Hardy, as Beatty was later to admit that the noise of the gunfire and the shrieks of the wounded were so great it was impossible to hear very much.[43] This account ended with a moving description of Nelson's dying moments: 'What passed after this was merely casual: his Lordship's last words were to Mr. Beatty, whilst he was expiring in his arms, "I could have wished to have lived to enjoy this; but God's will be done!" "My Lord", exclaimed Hardy, "you die in the midst of triumph!" "Do I Hardy?"—He smiled faintly— "God be praised!" These were his last words before he expired.'[44]

This is a very different account from that which Beatty had given to Scott or that Scott had himself given to Rose. Presumably it served its purpose. It was just what the newspaper-reading public wanted to hear, although perhaps these accounts were beginning to record a 'descent from the cross' and not the Wolfe-like apotheosis Nelson had hankered after. West had painted Wolfe

---

[42] *Morning Chronicle*, as cited in nn. 32, 38 and 39 above.

[43] Beatty *Authentic Narrative*, 51, n. 8. According to the *Authentic Narrative*, Scott and Burke were present during this exchange but can hardly have heard much of it.

[44] *Morning Chronicle*, 28 Dec. 1805.

dying on the Heights of Abraham surrounded by his men, a soldier running towards him from the left carrying a captured French standard and bearing news of victory. It was an image Nelson cherished. Reputedly he had met West at a big dinner shortly before Trafalgar and confessed his admiration for the painting: 'There is one picture whose power, I do feel. I never pass a print-shop with your "Death of Wolfe" in the window without being stopped by it.' The ageing West, now the country's most famous historical artist, had promised to paint a similar scene for Nelson if he died in action.[45]

Finally, at the beginning of the new year, Beatty's own medical account of Nelson's death and of the autopsy appeared in the newspapers. Under pressure from the press for more details of the circumstances of Nelson's death, Beatty, when he arrived at Greenwich, seems to have released an account of the admiral's condition from the time he was carried into the cockpit, possibly through Devis. The surgeon stated that Nelson's respiration was short, his pulse weak, and that 'he felt every instant a surge of blood within his breast'. After an hour his pulse became 'indistinct and was gradually lost', and he became extremely cold. No reference was made to the excruciating pain Nelson must have been suffering, given the extent of his internal injuries. Beatty gave no indication of when the admiral died, but repeated his assertion in his memorandum to Earl Nelson that 'he retained his wonted energy of mind until the last'. This statement began to appear in the press, conflated with the others, from 3 January. Readers were warned not be put off by the reminiscences of a medical man: 'The description of the surgeon . . . is so accurate and scientific that, by his permission we thankfully give it.'[46]

Clearly, then, by the time the people's hero was lowered into the crypt of St Paul's there were a variety of disjointed and contradictory stories about his death in circulation. There was an evident need to clear up the confusion and provide Nelson's adoring public with a stable and permanent narrative, and Beatty, the captain of the cockpit, was the obvious man to do it. Whether the Ulsterman would have ever put pen to paper without prompting will never be known, but his hand was forced by James Stanier Clarke. Clarke, a former naval padre and co-editor of the six-monthly *Navy Chronicle* (the periodical which charted the navy's activities during the French wars), was the librarian

---

[45] Mitchell, 'West's *Death of Nelson*', 265. If this conversation occurred then it possibly dated from 1800: see Erffa, *Paintings*, 222.

[46] See e.g. *Glasgow Herald*, 6 Jan. 1806. Presumably the statement was released with the earl's permission or even released by the earl himself.

and chaplain of the prince of Wales, who had been commissioned, along with his fellow editor John McArthur, former secretary to Lord Hood, to produce a sumptuous official biography of Nelson. Earl Nelson had been anxious that an authentic and grandiose life of his brother should appear as soon as possible, and satisfactory terms were agreed with the distinguished London printers, Thomas Cadell and William Davies, who were also the publishers of Thomas Trotter, the naval physician, and William Wilberforce, the leading Evangelical.[47] The biography was announced and the first subscriptions were paid on 16 January 1806.[48] In March the biography received the blessing of the prince of Wales, and McArthur and Clarke got down to seeking out assistance to fill the gaps in their own knowledge and ordering the engravings.[49] Probably almost immediately, Beatty was approached to write up Nelson's dying moments. The two authors would have had to move fast. There were other, more commercially minded competitors ready to rush a biography of the hero into print to capitalize on the public interest. They would have needed to engage Beatty before one of their rivals obtained his services.

Beatty must have spent the next few months composing his account, for it was ready by the summer of 1806. At this juncture, however, he decided that he wanted to publish the narrative as soon as possible. Its publication, Beatty declared in the first of a number of surviving letters he wrote to Emma Hamilton in the years after Nelson's death, was a national duty: 'I'm strongly recommended by several eminent characters to have it Published immediately in my name, as they say it will be read all over the world before Mr Clark[e]'s life of our lamented lord possibly makes its appearance, [which] when it does, must from the price of the work, be confined to but a small part of the community.'[50] Almost certainly, this was disingenuous, even though the subscription work was definitely expensive and Clarke and McArthur's life would obviously not be published for some time.[51] It is much more likely that Beatty had consulted with Hardy and Scott in writing the

---

[47] The *Navy Chronicle* had already published a long biography of Nelson which stopped with the Battle of the Nile. Nelson seems to have commissioned McArthur to write his biography before he died: see McArthur to Earl Nelson, 10 Feb. 1806, BL Add. MSS 34992, fo. 95.

[48] J. S. Clarke and J. McArthur, *Life of Lord Nelson*, 2 vols. (London, 1809), vol. I, subscription list.

[49] BL Add MSS 34992, fo. 120: McArthur to Earl Nelson, 21 Mar. 1806. The earl insisted that Clarke's name appear first.

[50] WL, MS 6242: Beatty to Emma, undated, but definitely pre-September 1806. Beatty's correspondence with Emma Hamilton is discussed below, Ch. 5, pp. 160, 167–9.

[51] See n. 48 above.

account, and was then pressurized by them and other of Nelson's friends to put an end to the rumours floating around about the hero's last moments by getting the narrative into print as soon as possible. Moreover, it is not difficult to see why Beatty would be easily persuaded.

In the first place, the surgeon must have quickly realized that going it alone offered him an unparalleled opportunity to place his name firmly in the public mind. The Irishman's own experience of Nelson's obsequies would have impressed upon him—if he had not properly realized it already—the incredible national significance which would thereafter be attached to the Battle of Trafalgar and Nelson's death in the hour of victory. For the son of an exciseman from a small town in Ulster, who had spent most of the last twelve years as part of a cramped society afloat, the sheer size and grandeur of the funeral must have been overwhelming. Sitting in solitary splendour in his carriage, a participant in a piece of theatre played out before hundreds of thousands of ordinary people, a self-confident, ambitious man in the prime of life cannot but have felt a heightened sense of pride and importance. And having experienced, however fleetingly and vicariously, the sweet taste of popular adulation, it is hard to imagine that Beatty would have been content to slip away into obscurity. The publication of his account of Nelson's death under his own name was his chance to link that name with the public hero's indelibly. Devis's painting of the scene in the cockpit, when it was eventually exhibited at the British Institution in 1809, would guarantee that his likeness would not just be glimpsed by the crowd and forgotten.[52] But in the painting he would just be one among many faces surrounding the dying admiral.

In addition, Beatty would have been galvanized into action by the appearance of a clutch of unofficial biographies of the hero, most of which claimed authenticity but contrived to include conflicting accounts of Nelson's death. *The Authentic History of the Gallant Life, Heroic Actions and Sea Fights of the Right Honourable Horatio Lord Viscount Nelson, K.B.*, published as early as December 1805 for Anne Leomine White, reported that he lived for about an hour after being wounded, and at the end exclaimed: 'But the will of God be done. He laid his head upon the shoulder of Captain Hardy, who remained with him to the last.'[53] Edward Orme's magnificently illustrated *Graphic History*, which appeared on 1 June 1806, with a text by Francis Blagdon, who had been imprisoned during 1805 for slandering St Vincent,

---

[52] Mitchell, 'West's *Death of Nelson*', 269.
[53] *The authentic history of the gallant life, heroic actions, and sea fights, of . . . Horatio, Lord Viscount Nelson . . . chiefly compiled from his own letters and official papers* (London, 1805), 36.

included without comment the account of the signal officer and the Beatty–
Burke narrative. However, by placing the signal officer's version first, he gave
a strong hint as to which he felt deserved the more credence. Adam
Collingwood, on the other hand (not to be confused with the admiral), who
published another 'authentic' account in 1806, conflated the Burke and
Beatty–Burke narratives, and cited Burke's 'final words' in reported speech:
'[Nelson] thanked God that he had outlived the action, and had been enabled
to do his duty to his country.'[54] In contrast, James Harrison, whose two-
volume *Life of Nelson* also appeared in the course of the year, must have relied
almost entirely on Scott, for his description of Nelson's death follows closely
the account given by the chaplain to Rose in the letter of 22 December 1805.

This was the only authorized biography to appear in 1806. Commissioned
by Emma Hamilton, it was reputedly partly written at her dictation.[55]
Although her object was to vindicate the reputations of her lover and herself
before the publication of Clarke and McArthur's book, Harrison con-
scientiously interviewed some of those who had known and worked with
Nelson.[56] In Harrison's account of the hero's agony and death, Beatty made
only one appearance at the outset to pronounce the wound fatal. Thereafter
Scott remained beside the dying Nelson, who spoke 'in low broken tones and
unconnected speech'. Apparently, Nelson had revived when he heard the
cheering presaging victory, but had been disappointed on Hardy's arrival at
4.30 p.m. to learn that there were only twelve prizes. In the subsequent *tête-à-
tête*, both Hardy and Scott were admonished to remember Nelson to
Lady Hamilton and Horatia and to inform them that he had 'left them
a legacy to my country'. Next, Harrison revealed, Nelson, on the point of
death, made his confession to his chaplain: 'Dr. I've not been a great sinner.'
Then, shortly before dying, he uttered his last words, which were taken again
from Burke, but were now transformed into the heartfelt exclamation that
every reader will know: 'A paroxysm of pain now suddenly seizing him, he
exclaimed, in a loud and most solemnly impressive tone "Thank God, I have
done my duty".'[57]

[54] Blagdon, *Graphic History*, 7; Adam Collingwood, *Anecdotes of the late Lord Viscount Nelson;
including copious accounts of the three great victories obtained . . . off the Nile, Copenhagen & Trafalgar,
also, of the various engagements and expeditions wherein his Lordship signalized his courage. An
authentic account of his death . . . To which is added, the ceremonial of his funeral . . . Also, select poetry,
etc.* (London, 1806), 68.
   [55] James Harrison, *The Life of . . . Horatio Lord Viscount Nelson* (2 vols.; London, 1806); Coleman, *Nelson*, 408–9.
   [56] See e.g. NAS, GD51/9/3/10, Letter from James Harrison, Richmond, to Lord Melville, 17
June 1809.   [57] Harrison, *Life*, ii. 501–4.

In such circumstances Beatty would have felt a compelling need to place his own story in the public domain as soon as possible, all the more so in that the waters were being muddied further by visual misrepresentations of Nelson's death. The London engraver and entrepreneur Josiah Boydell, as early as 22 November 1805, had advertised a competition for the best painting of the hero's dying moments.[58] According to the contemporary art critic Joseph Farington, the patron-engraver James Heath immediately sought out Benjamin West and urged him to take up the challenge. West took the commission seriously and apparently assembled and studied all the authentic records and reports of the battle and Nelson's death. He even invited many of the *Victory*'s crew to his house to tell their tale and have their portraits taken. The painting was finished on 11 May and then exhibited in West's home for ten days. (see Ill. 11). Hardy, Beatty, Scott, and the assistant surgeon Smith must have sat for him, as they occupy centre-stage, cradling the dying hero. So too must have assistant surgeon Westenburg, who stands just to the left of the group. Hardy kneels at Nelson's side, reading a message with the number of enemy ships that have struck. The painting was an instant success, and 30,000 people saw it in a month.[59] The *Morning Chronicle*, reviewing the painting on 12 May, declared: 'It is a wonderful work and will raise the fame of the master to a very high point . . . Upon no former occasion has he had so good a subject, and upon no former occasion has he so highly distinguished himself.'[60]

The painting was, however, a fake, for West had deliberately decided to show Nelson dying on deck. His study also differed from Devis's as-yet unfinished narrative of the scene, in that neither Purser Burke nor Nelson's steward, Chevalier, were depicted. The change of location was partly to allow as many people as possible to be depicted, including others amongst the fallen—Nelson's secretary John Scott, Captain Adair of the Royal Marines, and Beatty's friend, Lieutenant Ram—whose likenesses he presumably had to invent. But the fraud was also perpetrated for aesthetic reasons, as West explained to Farington:

[T]here was no other way of representing the death of a Hero but by an Epic representation of it. It must exhibit the event in a way to excite awe & veneration & that which may be required to give superior interest to the representation must be

[58] Boydell's uncle had made a fortune out of Woollett's engraving of the *Death of Wolfe*.
[59] Erffa, *Paintings*, 220–2. West's painting was engraved in 1811 and provided with a key identifying all the figures. It is now in the Walker Art Gallery, Liverpool.
[60] *Morning Chronicle*, 12 May 1806.

introduced, all that can shew the importance of the Hero. Wolfe must not die like a common soldier under a bush; neither should Nelson be represented dying in the gloomy hold of a Ship, like a sick man in a Prison Hole. To move the mind there should be a spectacle presented to raise & warm the mind, & all shd. be proportioned to the highest idea conceived of the Hero. Nobody, sd. West, wd. be animated by a representation of Nelson dying like an ordinary man. His feelings must be roused & his mind inflamed by a scene great & extraordinary. A mere matter of fact will never produce this effect.[61]

William Craig, the hack illustrator used by Orme, took the same line. Beatty's Ulster Protestant conscience cannot but have been mortally offended. A man whose understanding of art would almost certainly have been gained from looking at illustrations in the family Bible, he would have expected a historical painting to be locationally accurate. Biblical illustrations were visual presentations of a moment in the text, not imaginative reconstructions.[62] Indeed, West's paintings were later to be condemned on just such grounds.[63]

Not surprisingly, Clarke and McArthur were annoyed at being pre-empted, but they could do nothing to stop the separate publication of Beatty's narrative. What must have been most galling was that their publisher, Thomas Cadell, agreed to take it on at his own risk without a subscription. Beatty had had the good sense to let the prince of Wales have a sight of his manuscript, and Prinny raised no objections to its going straight into print. As a result the *Authentic Narrative* was published by Cadell on 15 January 1807, the bookseller presumably sensing that the short work— about 100 pages—would have an entirely different market from the richly illustrated and highly priced two-volume *Life*. It was priced at 7*s*. in boards or 10*s*. 6*d*. on royal paper, and advertised in the *Morning Chronicle*.[64] By then, too, Cadell was marketing an author with a higher public profile, since Beatty's role in the death scene had also been flagged in the periodical press. In March 1806 the *Gentleman's Magazine* republished Beatty and Burke's account of the death of Nelson, which had originally appeared in the London *Morning Chronicle*, along with the autopsy report that the surgeon had sent

[61] Greig, *Farington Diary*, iv. 155.

[62] Henry Howard, 'The English Illustrated Bible in the Eighteenth Century', D.Phil. thesis, University of Oxford (2005).

[63] S. Uwins, *A Memoir of Thomas Uwins RA* (London, 1858), ii. 202.

[64] *Morning Chronicle*, 15 Jan. 1807. The publication was no doubted timed to coincide with the resumption of the London season on the postponed birthday celebrations for the queen on 18 January. A notice also appeared in the *Edinburgh Review* (Oct. 1806–Jan. 1807), 494.

Nelson's brother. As the *Gentleman's Magazine* was the favourite monthly of the gentry and aspiring middle classes, Beatty's name would thereafter have had a resonance far beyond the capital and his native Ulster. Then, in the summer of 1806, the *Navy Chronicle* also carried these accounts, which were accompanied for the first time by Devis's engraving of the bullet with its tear jerking piece of gold epaulette attached. This was important. Hitherto, Beatty's centrality had not been endorsed by his own service's journal. The second 1805 issue of the *Navy Chronicle*, which probably appeared just before the funeral, had given a short account of Nelson's death but made no mention of Beatty personally. Moreover, it built the death scene entirely around Hardy, although there was no mention of the kiss. 'He [Nelson] desired his blessings to be conveyed to all who were nearest to his heart, and whom he could have wished to embrace—"but the will of God be done". He had his head upon the shoulder of Captain Hardy, who remained with him to the last, and in a few minutes his gallant soul escaped for ever.'[65] The summer issue of the periodical, therefore, placed Beatty's name squarely before the navy and the Admiralty, and irrevocably located the scene in the cockpit. In September, furthermore, Beatty gained promotion to physician of the fleet. Cadell was no longer publishing the testimonial of a humble surgeon but one of the leading figures in the naval medical service.[66]

THE AUTHENTIC NARRATIVE

As a book intended to lay to rest any debate among the public about the events surrounding Nelson's death, Beatty's *Narrative* was careful to make the reader in the new British state created by the Act of Union of Britain and Ireland of 1801 understand from the beginning that only the surgeon could tell the world the true story of 21 October. In his preface 'To the Public', Beatty presented himself implicitly as a modern professional man, unwilling to be placed in the limelight, but one who had no choice but to go into print.

The Surgeon of the late illustrious Lord Nelson feels himself called upon, from the responsible situation which he held on the eventful day of the 21st of October 1805, to lay before the British Nation the following Narrative. It contains an account of

---

[65] *NC*, xiv (1805), 414; *Gentleman's Magazine* (Mar. 1806), 278–9: the periodical also published extracts from Nelson's will and the codicil of 6 Sept. 1803 which left money to Lady Hamilton to bring up Horatia.   [66] For Beatty's promotion, see below, Ch. 5, pp. 159–61.

the most interesting incidents which occurred on board the *Victory* (Lord NELSON's Flagship) from the time of her sailing from England in the month of September, till the day of Battle inclusively; with a detail of the particulars of his Lordship's death, the mode adopted for preserving his revered remains during the subsequent long passage of the *Victory* to England, and the condition of the body when it was deposited in Greenwich hospital.

This short statement of Facts is deemed a small but necessary tribute of respect to the memory of the departed Hero, as well as a professional document which the Public had a right to expect from the man who had the melancholy honour of being his principal Medical Attendant on that occasion....

It was originally intended that the Narrative should be published in the *Life of Lord Nelson* undertaken by the Rev. J. S. CLARKE and J. McARTHUR...; but from the length of time which must necessarily elapse before so extensive and magnificent a Publication can be completed, the Author has been induced to print it in a separate form.[67]

To heighten interest, the small volume included an engraving of a portrait of Lord Nelson as its frontispiece, 'in the dress he wore, when he received his fatal wound' (see Ill. 12). This in fact was not a life portrait at all but an engraving of the painting done for Beatty by Devis, referred to earlier in the chapter, which had been worked up from sketches of the corpse and information supplied by the surgeon. The artist must have finished it in the summer of 1806, since the engraving by Scriven was published by Cadell and Davis on 17 November, a month or so before Beatty's text appeared. Besides being the last of the many portraits of the hero, it was also the only one to depict Nelson sporting his green eyeshade. According to Nelson's nephew, the third earl, who apparently received an annual visit from Beatty for the rest of the surgeon's life, the portrait had a chequered history:

The likeness, Sir Wm told me was the only true one he ever saw, and Lady Hamilton was so pleased with it that, though Sir Wm refused to give, he was as yet induced to lend it to her.... On her passage from England to France [when she fled her creditors in 1814] the box containing it and many other relics fell overboard. Fortunately the artist broke his promise to Sir Wm and painted a second picture (at the same time as he was at the first) for Admiral Page.[68]

[67] Beatty, *Authentic Narrative*, preface.

[68] R. Walker, *The Nelson Portraits* (London, 1998), 160–6, 264. According to Walker, Devis made a number of copies of the original. He also distrusts the earl's memory and suggests that Beatty might only have lent Lady Hamilton a copy. A version was displayed at the Royal Academy exhibition in 1807: Algernon Graves, *The Royal Academy Exhibitions*, 8 vols. (London, 1906), ii. 316. Pettigrew, *Memoirs*, i. p. xiv, gives a different history of the portrait, which does not involve

The first third of the narrative covers the days before the battle and the early stages of the engagement; the second takes the reader from the moment Nelson is felled on the deck by the bullet until he dies in the cockpit; while the third provides an account of the *Victory*'s casualty list, the return to Portsmouth, and the autopsy, and concludes with a description of Nelson's physical habits and state of health. The portrait painted by the text is of a Nelson who was every inch a hero. Perspicacious, prophetic—'The 21ˢᵗ of October will be our day'[69]—humane, loyal, stoical, and God fearing, Beatty's Nelson was exactly the admiral the public already believed it knew and loved. Their hero was even robust, for Beatty used his account of the autopsy for the first time to declare that Nelson's viscera were all in good order and that he had had the 'body of a youth',[70] who would have lived to a ripe old age, thereby quelling rumours that he had been failing in health. In an important respect, therefore, the text reinforced an image which had already begun to be developed long before Trafalgar. The originality of the text, however, and its historical status as a canonical document lay in the careful, clear, and apparently authoritative way in which Beatty narrated the drama of Nelson's death. Whereas earlier reports had been content to offer general remarks about the admiral's state of his mind as he lay dying, or recorded at best snatches of his conversation, Beatty provided the reader with neatly turned dialogues in which Nelson is always lucid, and continues to portray his heroic virtues until the last. Moreover, by deliberately writing in the third person, Beatty gave his narrative a compelling but spurious objectivity. Beatty the author cunningly separated himself from Beatty the actor. Beatty the surgeon is just one of the players who appears in the drama, albeit one with a particularly 'juicy' part. Beatty the author, on the other hand, hovers objectively above the scene and knows to perfection the lines of the dying Nelson and all his attendants. He is the all-seeing, all-knowing outsider with a perpetual eye on the clock. All the action in the cockpit occurs in distinctive segments of time, and the account is closed, not with Nelson's death itself, but with the cold statement of fact that from the time he was wounded until the time he died two hours forty-five minutes had passed. At the same time the reader is never allowed to forget that the two Beattys are one and the same. The point is even

---

Beatty. Rather, the biographer claims the portrait had been begun by Devis while Nelson was in England before Trafalgar, but had not been finished before the admiral's departure. One copy was owned by Sir Thomas Bladen Capel, commander-in-chief at Portsmouth, which Pettigrew used as an illustration in his own text. The Maritime Museum owns a copy of a copy by an amateur artist.

[69] *Beatty Authentic Narrative*, 13.   [70] Ibid. 83.

hammered home graphically in the form of two illustrations of the bullet which killed Nelson, which first appeared in the *Naval Chronicle*. The first, a note reveals, 'represents the ball in the exact state in which it was extracted'. The second 'shows the ball in its present state; as set in crystal by Mr YONGE, and presented to the writer of this Narrative by Sir THOMAS HARDY'.[71]

In other words, the *Authentic Narrative, pace* its title, is a piece of creative writing. No one who had spent all or most of the afternoon of 21 October 1805 in the horror of the *Victory's* cockpit, amid the stupendous noise of the guns, the heat, and the cries of men in their agony, could have had such a perfect recall. Even if Beatty had pooled together the recollections of all the many individuals present at the scene and not just relied on his own, he could never have been given more than a brief, skeletal framework on which to hang his series of poignant tableaux—the narrative, as it were, for Devis's still unseen 'Adoration'. Nelson was dying. It is possible, in that the bullet had pierced a vein (the pulmonary artery), that he could have lived for several hours, but he was slowly bleeding to death in incredible pain, and his words, even in perfect conditions, would have been disjointed and difficult to hear. This is not to say that Beatty invented the *Authentic Narrative*. It is reasonable to assume that his story is largely chronologically accurate. What he did was to turn a series of sketches into a play. Doubtless well schooled in the histories of the classical world, and all too familiar with his Bible, he took the liberty of embellishing half-remembered snatches of dialogue so that the reader would be given an account of Nelson's death which would make sense of the conflicting reports and gell with the received image of the hero. It would also allow Beatty himself, with his austere, low-church upbringing, to come to terms with the ambiguities in a man he so much admired. Although he may well have met Emma Hamilton on Nelson's last visit to England, he had not been with the hero in the heady days in Sicily and would have found it hard to forgive his infidelity in the same way that his chaplain, Alexander Scott, most certainly did.[72]

Essentially, the account marries together Scott's letter to Rose and Beatty and Burke's original narrative. Since Scott, and later Harrison, had evidently made public Nelson's fixation with Emma in his dying moments, the fact could not be ignored, as it was in the *Morning Chronicle* article of 28 December 1805. Instead, it had to be used to bring out Nelson's humanity, frailty, and godliness, as no doubt Scott and Hardy intended.

---

[71] *Beatty Authentic Narrative*, 62.
[72] It is possible that Beatty only met Emma after Trafalgar: see below, Ch. 5, p. 160.

Early in the text, therefore, as Nelson prepares for battle, he orders various fixtures in his cabin to be taken down, including specifically Emma's portrait: 'Take care of my Guardian Angel.'[73] He then writes a prayer in which he commits himself to his Maker, 'a devout and fervent ejaculation, which must be considerably admired as truly characteristic of the Christian hero',[74] before penning the unfortunate codicil to his will in which he leaves his mistress and their child to the nation. There is a ring of truth in this. From his childhood Nelson was undoubtedly God-fearing, in a very English sort of way that borders on the secular but brings great emotional comfort at times of crisis. As his friends knew only too well, he had indeed fallen genuinely in love with Emma. The reader is thus well prepared for the admiral's constant concern for her well-being as he lies dying, as first Scott, the chaplain, then Hardy, then Scott again are exhorted to look after his mistress and their illegitimate infant daughter, Horatia. This is the vulnerable familiar Nelson, seeking protection from his closest friends who are his to command, with whom all ordinary Britons can identify, irrespective of the fact that his inamorata is not his wife. His final plea in his personal crucifixion is for the welfare of Emma and her young daughter, which is combined with the confession to his chaplain: 'I have not been a great sinner.' And all but the most flinty Evangelical heart has been primed by then to cry: 'No! No!'

At the same time, the Ulsterman confirms the earlier Beatty–Burke narrative in keeping Hardy centre-stage. In the *Authentic Narrative* Scott is given an important role in the drama, whereas in the *Morning Chronicle* account his presence had been completely ignored. But this does not mean that Hardy's lines are cut. The loser is Burke, the purser, who is in the wings but no longer a leading participant. Hardy in fact is Horatio to Nelson's Hamlet. Having been beside the hero at his station, pacing the quarterdeck with him when he falls, he is the one member of the cast who is absent at the beginning of the final act and whom Nelson is desperate to see. On numerous occasions messages are sent to the captain begging him to come below, but always he is too busy fighting the battle. At one stage he even sends Midshipman Bulkely in his place, which gives the dying Nelson the opportunity to show his most human side by asking the young man to remember him to his father. Then, after one hour and ten minutes, Hardy makes his first entrance, by which time Nelson is visibly failing. Their meeting is professional and unsentimental, even if the subject of Emma intrudes: 'Pray let my dear Lady

---

[73] *Authentic Narrative*, 14.   [74] Ibid.

Hamilton have my hair, and all other things belonging to me.'[75] Captain and commander talk together about the state of the engagement, they shake hands and Hardy leaves—an all too British gesture. But this is not the farewell. Whereas in the Beatty–Burke account and later descriptions Hardy and Nelson only meet once before the hero dies, in the *Authentic Narrative* the captain returns for a second visit fifty minutes later. And this time the tone of the meeting shifts, as the two professional officers are transformed into everyman at the bedside of his dying friend, and the scene becomes mawkish. Nelson refuses to relinquish command to Cuthbert Collingwood, one of his closest colleagues, and orders Hardy to anchor the fleet. He next, rather dramatically, begs his friend not to have his body thrown overboard— as if he would. Finally he asks Hardy 'to take care of poor Lady Hamilton', then requests that he kiss him.[76] This done, the hero is satisfied and Hardy leaves to carry out Nelson's dying orders. In the Beatty–Burke account Hardy is present when Nelson dies. Now he is back on deck, winning the battle.

However, Beatty the narrator is not just shaping a story in which Scott and Hardy are given the leading parts. He is also weaving a narrative in which Beatty the surgeon is continually at the centre of the event, and whose pro- fessionalism, like Hardy's, must always trump his love for his commander. In the early part of the *Authentic Narrative*, Beatty recounts various conversations of a non-medical kind that he had had with Nelson in the days leading up to the battle, suggesting that he was a man in the admiral's confidence, not just a surgeon. He was a man, too, willing to brave the lion's wrath, as indeed he had done earlier in his career. As the British fleet steers towards the enemy, he alone has the nerve, we are told, to warn the commander of the dangers of wearing a coat displaying his decorations, but fails to find the opportunity when pre- senting the daily sick list. When Nelson is brought down to the cockpit, a handkerchief covering his face, this missed opportunity is once more referred to, when Beatty the narrator has Scott, on seeing the wounded admiral, exclaim to Beatty the surgeon: 'Oh, Mr Beatty, how prophetic you were!'

In the cockpit, however, Beatty the surgeon no longer has time for such useless thoughts: he becomes the cool, competent professional, on hand and always right, even though it is his friend who is dying. Listening to Nelson explain his symptoms, he knows immediately that the wound is mortal. 'These symptoms [no feeling in the lower part of the body, severe pain in the spine, and difficulty in breathing], but more particularly the gush of blood

[75] *Authentic Narrative*, 42. In fact, all Nelson's papers were snaffled by the earl.
[76] Ibid. 48–9.

which his Lordship complained of, together with the state of his pulse, indicated to the surgeon the hopeless state of the case.'[77] Initially, Beatty does not want to alarm his patient unduly: he says nothing and leaves to inspect the other wounded, while Nelson is cared for by Burke and Scott. When he returns, Nelson begs him to go once more and attend to other cases. The hero knows that he is dying and wants the surgeon to confirm the prognosis and no longer pull the wool over his eyes. This Beatty does, but then the man temporarily betrays the professional. '[H]aving made this declaration he was so much affected, that he turned round and withdrew a few steps to conceal his emotion.'[78] But he is soon back under control. Thereafter he is the competent surgeon who moves in and out of the scene around the dying admiral, finally pronouncing him dead at 4.30 p.m. Necessarily, in this account, Beatty cannot hold the dying Nelson in his arms. This is left to the non-medical men in the cockpit—Scott, Burke, and Nelson's steward, Chevalier. Instead, he returns from time to time, checking progress, too conscious (the text seems to say) of the needs of the living—let the dead bury the dead. Indeed, throughout the *Authentic Narrative* the emphasis is on Beatty's abilities as a doctor. At the beginning we are informed of how healthy the *Victory*'s crew have been under his care, the narrator in a footnote citing Hardy as witness. 'The *Victory*'s casualties from 29 December 1804 to 20 October following, were only five fatal cases (one of them by accidental injury) and two patients sent to a naval hospital.'[79] Similarly, the narrator informs us towards the end of Beatty's success in quickly restoring to health all but a handful of the 102 sailors, marines, and officers wounded in the action.

In the *Authentic Narrative*, then, Beatty is one of a trio of characters who assist Nelson in his passage to the next world: precisely the three who are the dominant figures of the five surrounding the dying hero in Devis's painting. This is the story of the admiral, his captain, chaplain, and surgeon, the faithful few at the foot of the true cross, not a romanticized panorama. No one else has a proper part in the play. But Beatty, as narrator as well as actor, does more than simply present the 'gospel' reader with a compelling account of their respective roles. He not only conflates and embellishes two existing narratives, one peddled by Scott, the other by Beatty–Burke. He also adds his weight to Harrison's version of the 'dying words'. In the course of 1806 there were evidently several versions of Nelson's final words going the rounds: Lieutenant Pasco's 'Victory!'; Duff's 'I die happy since I die victorious'; Senhouse's

---

[77] Ibid. 38.   [78] Ibid. 44–5.   [79] Ibid. 21

'Anchor, Hardy, anchor!'; White's 'the will of God be done'; Beatty–Burke's 'God be praised!'; Burke's 'I have done my duty, I praise God for it'; and Harrison's alternative rendering: 'Thank God, I have done my duty!'[80] It was the last which Beatty opted for in the *Authentic Narrative*, and which historians, on his authority, have accepted ever since.[81] Beatty has Nelson exclaiming these words for the first time after Hardy has kissed him, although he apparently expressed Burke's earlier variant immediately after the surgeon confirmed his dismal prognosis. Once Hardy has gone, the words become a constant refrain, and are the mantra which Nelson utters as he dies and his voice gives way:'[H]e every now and then, with evident increase of pain, made a greater effort with his vocal powers, and pronounced distinctly these last words: "Thank God, I have done my duty;" and this great sentiment he continued to repeat as long as he was able to give it utterance.'[82] It is not difficult to see why Beatty settled on these particular last words. For an author who had framed his narrative around the eternal conflict of love and duty, the only choice lay between Burke and Harrison. In some form or other, they were exactly the dying words Nelson ought to have said. The battle had begun with the famous signal: 'England expects that every man will do his duty.' It was fitting and perfect that the hero should die in the arms of his chaplain thanking his Maker that he had obeyed unto death his own exhortation. And of the two variants, Harrison's was the more sonorous and memorable. Whether Beatty actually believed that he had heard these words himself, or been assured by Scott that they were authentic, is irrelevant. This was the perfect line on which to bring down the curtain on the life of a God-fearing hero.

Not surprisingly, Beatty's reconstructed account quickly won public approval and his version of the last words became standard. Almost immediately the *Authentic Narrative* was reviewed enthusiastically in the *European Magazine and London Review*, where it was hailed in the February issue as 'one of the most perennial monuments that can be attributed to excite the glow of exaltation, or stimulate the sighs of sensibility in the millions, who will perhaps, exist in centuries so remote from the present scene, that they can

---

[80] The gunner William Rivers, in his MS notebook containing reminiscences of the battle, records Nelson's last words as: 'I have done my Duty I praise God for itt', and states that they were said to Hardy. There is no way of knowing Rivers's source for this, or when the words were written down: see NMP MSS 1998/41/1. His son the midshipman, in his own 'Notes on Trafalgar', some of which were derived from his father, recorded Nelson's dying words on two occasions. In the second, they are given as: 'Hardy, The Lord be Praised I have done my Duty': NMM Wel/30.

[81] e.g. R. Southey, *The Life of Nelson* (London, 1813), 370–7; Captain A. T. McMahon, *The Life of Nelson* (London, 1899), 735–41; and Andrew Lambert, *Nelson: Britannia's God of War* (London, 2004), 306.   [82] Beatty, *Authentic Narative*, 50.

scarcely, by any mental effort, be dragged within the grasp of contemplation'.[83] We do not know how many copies Cadell published of the *Authentic Narrative*, but a second edition appeared in 1808 and a third, by another publisher, in 1825, so it must have sold reasonably well. As it was, the actual sales did not matter, for in April 1807 a long extract was published under Beatty's name in the *Gentleman's Magazine*, which contained all the set-piece dialogue and the last words. Thereafter Beatty's account was the property of the well-to-do in the United Kingdom and nothing could shake its influence.[84]

When Clarke and McArthur's *Life of Nelson* appeared in 1809, it leaned heavily on Beatty's narrative, but tried to rework it by dropping Nelson's effusions about Emma, giving Burke back his more positive role, and restoring the purser's version of Nelson's dying words. '[T]hese last words were distinctly heard, I have done my duty, I praise God for it. Having said this, he turned his face towards Mr Burke, on whose arm he had been supported and expired without a groan.'[85] The two authors also eschewed Devis's portrayal of the death scene, and published an engraving of Nelson's last moments in the cockpit from a specially commissioned imitation by West, which was exhibited to coincide with the biography's launch (see Ill. 13.).[86] In this new painting the composition was significantly changed. A gang of five now forms a human halo around the expiring Nelson, and it is Hardy, not Beatty, whose physical contact with the hero the painting freezes in time.

The wounded admiral is represented laid on a pallet, on the larboard side of the cockpit, with pious resignation in his dying moments, his hand in Captain Hardy's. Mr Burke, the purser in a reclining position in front, is supporting him with pillows. The Rev. Dr. Scott, the chaplain, is behind supporting his head. Mr Beatty, the surgeon, having a right hand with a handkerchief placed on the wound, expresses in his countenance that the vital spark is almost extinguished. Next to him stands Mr Smith, the assistant surgeon, apparently listening to the last words articulated by the dying Hero...'[87]

---

[83] *European Magazine and London Review* (1807), 131.

[84] *Gentleman's Magazine* (Apr. 1807), 335–8.

[85] Clarke and McArthur, *Life* ii. 453. Both Pasco and Scott had claimed that Nelson expired without a groan; so too did Rivers, father and son: see above, n. 80.

[86] Theodore Besterman (ed.), *The Publishing Firm of Cadell and Davies: Select Correspondence and Accounts, 1793–1836* (London, 1938), 176.

[87] Erffa, *paintings* 222–3. This paintings was presented to the Maritime Museum in 1849. See http://www.nmm.ac.uk/mag/pages/mnuExplore/PaintingDetails.cfm?letter = d&ID = BHC0566: the website makes much of the *pietà* theme. Reference to the exhibition accompanying the launch of the biography is given in a letter from McArthur to Davies in June 1807: see Besterman, *Cadell and*

But the official account of Nelson's death never replaced the 'authentic narrative', just as West's subsequent pastiche did not succeed in undermining the Devis original.[88] A few carping voices greeted Beatty's account. The Evangelical *Monthly Review*, which carried an account of Beatty's work in the course of 1808, was clearly disappointed not to have discovered fuller evidence of the dying hero's contrition in the text, sniffily commenting on Nelson's confession to Scott: 'No further reference to his situation, in a moral point of view, appears to have been testified to him.' In a similar vein, the *Gentleman's Magazine* in January 1809 carried a letter from one AH of Leicestershire, who complained about the inclusion of Nelson's dying words concerning Emma and her daughter: 'The book would have sold without it'.[89] This, though, was not the normal verdict. A few years after Beatty's death in 1842, his account even became canonical, when it was reprinted virtually word for word by Nicolas in the final volume of his *Letters and Dispatches of Lord Nelson*, and its accuracy applauded.[90] A couple of years later, too, Thomas Pettigrew, the first biographer to use Nelson's private correspondence extensively, again relied on Beatty exclusively in describing Nelson's last hours. 'Sir William Beatty, the surgeon, to whose care he was now entrusted, has furnished us with every particular in relation to his condition, and this cannot be stated better than in his own words.'[91]

Beatty, who would publish nothing else in his life, had fashioned a minor literary masterpiece. The British public had taken his account to their hearts and refused to let go. The man who had looked after the body of the dying Nelson, cared for his corpse, and been part of his funeral cortege had found public fame and recognition, not as a surgeon but as an author. Beatty and the death of Nelson had become inseparable. Even if, in the early twenty-first century, we have forgotten his name, Beatty's narrative is well remembered, particularly by the generation who were brought up in the shadow of the Second World War.

Davis, 176. The information on the figures in the painting is given in Clarke and McArthur, *Life*, i. pp. xliv–xiv: Beatty *et al.* were painted from life. The engraving of the painting in the biography carries the alternative last words as the caption.

[88] There was clearly a fear that the Clarke and McArthur version would become the authoritative account of Nelson's life and death *tout court*. Lady Hamilton had planned to undermine its publication by immediately issuing a second, illustrated edition of Harrison's biography, but this never materialized: see Harrison to Dundas, 1809: NAS GD51/9/310.

[89] *Monthly Review*, NS 56 (1808), 306; *Gentleman's Magazine*, 79: 1 (1809), 404–5.

[90] Nicolas, *Dispatches* vii. 244–52.

[91] Pettigrew, *Memoirs*, ii. 530–7. Pettigrew knew Beatty: see below, Ch. 5, p. 180.

5

Later Career

PHYSICIAN OF THE FLEET

Nelson's funeral was the culmination of Pitt the Younger's efforts to forge a new British state which could withstand the threat from post-revolutionary France. It was a manufactured, but nonetheless powerful, display of national harmony, where the monarchy, the political nation, the armed forces, and the London crowd came together to celebrate Britishness and its adamantine protector, the wooden walls of the Royal Navy. It was not—whatever some participants might have thought—a celebration of victory, but merely a great national gasp of relief that invasion had become henceforth unlikely. In fact, in the course of 1806–7 Napoleon's position in Europe would go from strength to strength. Having destroyed Britain's Austrian and Russian allies even before Nelson's obsequies were complete, he proceeded to annihilate the Prussians at Jena at the end of 1806, then humiliate the Russians once more at Friedland the following year. Thereafter, he had the power to hit his British enemy where it hurt by attempting to close the continent to her goods, meeting a naval by a commercial blockade. It would take another ten long years of war and an unprecedented British commitment to a land war in Portugal and Spain before Bonaparte would be forced to quit the European stage for good. And the new United Kingdom had to face its imperial rival without Pitt at the helm, for the country's longest-serving prime minister died on 23 January 1806, only two weeks after Nelson's funeral. The upshot was that for the next six years the war was prosecuted by a series of short-lived and divided ministries, as first the ex-Pittite Lord Grenville took office at the head of the Whig-dominated 'Ministry of All the Talents' (February 1806–March 1807), followed by the Tory Lord Portland (March 1807–September 1809) and finally the Tory Spencer Perceval (October 1809–May 1812), who had to weather the permanent emergence of the Prince Regent onto the political scene after George III went mad for a second time. It was only when the Tory Lord Liverpool became prime minister in 1812—a position he would occupy for fifteen years—that the governmental stability of the 1790s was restored.

The political tergiversations of the period could not but have an effect on individual naval careers. The state still wanted a large navy, but the odds were stacked against rapid promotion up the naval ladder. There were four different first lords of the Admiralty in the years 1806–12, the commander of the Channel Fleet was changed virtually every year, and there were far more post-captains than ships in service. The patronage game must have been much more difficult to pursue than normal. Although merit and length of service would always have played some part in progress in the service at all levels, rapid advancement must have been either the result of inordinate luck, consummate judgement in choosing the right commander to cultivate, or a good mix of political patrons. In consequence, when the *Victory* was paid off at the end of January 1806 its officers were not necessarily guaranteed a long and successful career in the navy, however much they might bask in Nelson's reflected glory.

Inevitably, then, the years that followed Trafalgar brought mixed fortunes to the small group of people who had gathered round the dying hero in the *Victory*'s cockpit. Purser Burke, purportedly a distant relative of the Whig politician Edmund, was 67 in 1805 and the oldest man aboard the flagship: after the battle he retired from the service and lived for a further ten years, dying near Rochester.[1] Captain Hardy received a baronetcy in February 1806 and married well, but only slowly climbed the promotional ladder under the constraints of the system of seniority: he was still a relatively junior captain in 1805. For his next post he was given command of the 74-gun *Triumph* and sent off to the North American station for three years. Thereafter he commanded a number of different ships of the line, but was only made commodore in 1819 and rear-admiral in 1825. The chaplain, Alexander Scott, who had been the admiral's secretary, interpreter, and intelligence-gatherer, fared considerably worse. According to his daughter, Nelson had intimated that Scott should inherit the canonry at Canterbury held by his clerical elder brother, on the assumption that the latter would be made dean by the king once victory had been gained at sea. But William Nelson refused to resign his

---

[1] He had two sons: Henry, a naval commander, and Walter, a naval lieutenant, who were both killed during the French wars. Addis, *The Men who Fought at Trafalgar*, 22.

position, even when elevated to the peerage by a grateful monarch , and the Crown, in whose gift the canonry was, made no effort to coerce him. As a result, Scott was left in the wilderness. Despite the best efforts of Nelson's friends and patrons, he never secured high ecclesiastical office and eventually had to settle for the comfortable Crown living of Catterick, Yorkshire, where he languished amid an ever-growing library. Although his daughter and biographer would have the world believe that he ended his days reconciled to his lot, it is difficult not to feel he died a bitter man.[2]

The careers of the assistant surgeons Smith and Westenburg were equally unspectacular, according to the naval service documents in the National Archives. Westenburg served as acting surgeon on the sloop *Atalante* for the two years 1808–10, then disappears from the records: presumably he eventually went back to Holland, which seems to have been his country of birth. Smith, on the other hand, was promoted to full surgeon after Trafalgar and posted to the Leeward Islands, where he was surgeon to the Martinique Hospital and served on the *Pegasus*. This was as high as he rose, however, and he gained little material reward from his seventeen years in the navy. When he died, a general practitioner at Forres on the Moray Firth, in 1819, four years after being placed on half-pay, his effects were insufficient to pay his debts. His wife Ann had nothing but his £40 pension on which to bring up their two daughters, until the Admiralty graciously increased the amount by £10 per annum on grounds of hardship.[3]

For William Beatty, in contrast, the battle was not the climax of his career but merely the end of the first act. After the *Victory* had been decommissioned at Chatham and the officers and crew paid off in January 1806, Beatty might have expected at the very least to have endured a short period of half-pay until he secured another surgeoncy. He might easily have had to contemplate becoming a civilian practitioner. In fact his luck held, and promotion rather than retirement beckoned. Instead of being released, he was transferred to the *Sussex*, a hospital ship lying off Sheerness. Then, in the following September, probably having spent much of the interim on leave, he was created physician of the Channel Fleet on 25 September.[4] Beatty served in this capacity until the end of the French wars, when he was initially discharged in October 1814, reappointed in May 1815, and eventually released the following August as part of the general reduction in naval personnel once the war against

[2] Gatty, *Recollections*, chs. ix–x, esp. p. 203.
[3] TNA, ADM 11/40, fo. 461; ADM6/326; ADM 104/30, fo. 411.
[4] TNA, ADM104/30, fo. 122.

France was finally over.[5] The new posting was a significant advance in the Ulsterman's status, now in his prime at the age of 33. Few naval surgeons could expect to rise to the rank of physician.

To become eligible for the promotion Beatty had to gain a medical doctorate. This he did on 28 February 1806, when he obtained a degree from the University of Aberdeen through the sponsorship of two London practitioners, James Laird and the mineralogist and FRS William Babington (1756–1833), an ex-naval surgeon and physician at Guy's Hospital, who himself hailed from Ulster and had been apprenticed in Londonderry. Since there is no evidence of his travelling north to obtain the diploma, it can be assumed that he took his doctorate by letter.[6] There can be no doubt, however, that Beatty owed the promotion itself to Nelson's friends, although who in particular lobbied on his behalf is impossible to say. It is evident that at some stage in his career—perhaps only in the summer of 1805, when the *Victory* was being refitted at Portsmouth—Beatty was introduced to Lady Hamilton. The impression left by the surviving correspondence between the two in the Wellcome Library is that this was a relationship which he assiduously cultivated after Trafalgar, and one that eventually became close.[7] Emma had little or no influence herself, but she was the conduit to Nelson's friends and associates who did. From the letters that cover the years 1806 to 1811, it would seem that Beatty was on good terms with a number of the admiral's circle: Dr Baird, inspector of navy hospitals and a confidant of St Vincent, Captain and Mrs Hardy, George Rose MP, vice-president of the Board of Trade and treasurer of the navy, and the northern Irishman Viscount Castlereagh, secretary of war, whom Nelson had visited in London before embarking on his last voyage.

This was a powerful bloc of allies, and one or all could have helped Beatty secure his promotion. Still, at the end of the day it would have been the backing of St Vincent, the grand old man of the navy and Nelson's patron, which guaranteed success. St Vincent had held no office during Pitt's second

---

[5] TNA, ADM104/30, fo. 122; ADM 97/88, Transport Board, unnumbered collection of letters: Beatty to Commissioners for Transport Service and Sick and Wounded Seamen, Plymouth Dock, 23 Oct. 1814, 1 May and 31 Aug. 1815.

[6] Peter John Anderson (ed.), *Officers and Graduates of University and King's College, Aberdeen, 1495–1860* (Aberdeen, 1893). Babington's sponsorship suggests that Beatty had trained at Guy's, either before joining the navy or, more likely, while on leave in 1802–3.

[7] WL, MS 6242. The correspondence is incomplete. Initially Beatty begins and ends his letters formally, but from the spring of 1808 he addresses Emma as 'My dear good lady' and signs off begging her to accept his 'inveterate love, affection and friendship'. It is clear from the content of the letters that he got to know Emma well and visited her whenever he could.

ministry (1804–6), but when the prime minister died in January he once more assumed control of the Channel Fleet, albeit only until March 1807. This was a tremendous stroke of good fortune. It is quite clear from Beatty's first surviving letter to Emma, which was written some time during the summer of 1806, that there was initially opposition in the Admiralty to his elevation. All the same, he was sanguine. In that he had secured St Vincent's approbation for his appointment as physician of the fleet, he was sure the hostility would eventually whither away.[8]

Once confirmed in his new post, Beatty almost immediately had his portrait painted, resplendent in new uniform, by Arthur William Devis (see Ill. 2). The man who stares out of the canvas is in the prime of life, handsome, alert, and charming. Unless the artist waived his fee or charged a nominal sum for acquaintance sake, this portrait must have represented serious expenditure for the new physician. Devis was a society painter, whatever the ups and downs in his career, and Beatty was not rich, for all the prize money he had garnered while serving on frigates. Presumably Beatty felt it was a necessary investment. The portrait was purely for his own pleasure; it was not a gift to a wife or parent. Thereafter, presumably hung in the physician's study or salon, it was a visible and permanent reminder to himself and visitors that he had arrived.[9]

As physician of the Channel Fleet, Beatty was based most of the time on shore at Plymouth, the fleet's home base. His official letter book for the first eighteen months of his tenure survives in the manuscript collection of the Royal Naval Museum at Portsmouth, and gives a good indication of the range of his duties. The ships of the fleet were primarily involved in blockading the ports of western France and northern Spain, and Beatty's principal task was to inspect the health of the crew when a vessel put in to Plymouth to refit and take on supplies. Each month in rotation a squadron of some ten ships would be sent back to base, often bringing with them the long-term sick of ships still on station. On their arrival in Causand Bay or Plymouth Sound, Beatty would go on board to inspect the sick and see which members on the list needed to be transferred to the hospital. Initially, his standing orders from St Vincent, his first commander, only permitted him to visit the sick, but on

[8] WL, MS 6242, no. 1: London (undated). This was the letter in which he announced that he was being urged to print the *Authentic Narrative* at once: see Ch. 4, p. 142.

[9] The portrait is considered to have been painted in 1806. There is no sign that Devis exhibited it at the Royal Academy. Sitters could often negotiate lower rates if they agreed to allow their portraits to appear in the Academy's annual exhibition.

his request they were soon extended to allow him to inspect the ship as a whole. Beatty was a disciple of Trotter: he believed that the best way to prevent disease was to keep a vessel well-ventilated, clean, and dry. His new standing orders left him free to roam around at will, checking that all parts of the ship, especially the orlop, wings, tiers, and storerooms, were properly looked after.[10]

When a squadron was forced to put into a neighbouring port or took shelter off Torbay, Beatty was expected to visit the ships where they had dropped anchor. One of his first tasks in late October 1806 was to travel by sea to Falmouth and await the arrival of four vessels, including the *Gibraltar*, which was supposed to have been struck by a scurvy epidemic.[11] Beatty was also required to keep a weather eye on the overall state of health of the Channel Fleet's crews, and every month he was sent a report by the surgeons of ships on station. From time to time, too, he was ordered to put to sea to inspect conditions on particular ships mounting the blockade, and for several weeks would live aboard the *St Josef*, the fleet's flagship. Furthermore, he could be asked to visit navy ships that put into Plymouth that were not part of the Channel Fleet. This, though, was not in his official remit, and when he suggested to the Admiralty on 27 July 1807 that his powers of inspection should be extended to include other vessels, he was sharply reminded that the Transport Board employed two roving inspectors to cover such eventualities.[12] Finally, he immediately gained the right to visit sailors from the Channel Fleet while they were in Plymouth Hospital, and to assist the medical officers of the hospital in deciding when patients could be invalided out.[13]

Essentially, Beatty's duties were administrative and advisory. Besides his work as an inspector, most of his time would have been spent in writing formal letters to the commander of the fleet (with a copy to the Transport Board), in which he would outline the state of the health of the crews and pick out surgeons for praise or blame. If he felt there were measures that could be taken to improve health on a particular ship, he would also write formally to the surgeon on board. Beatty must have found the posting a welcome change from the rigours of continual service at sea, especially as he now enjoyed a salary of £383 per annum, rising after three years to £520 and

[10] NMP, MS 418/88/2, pp. 1, 12–13: St Vincent's standing orders for the physician of the fleet, 22 Oct. and 24 Dec. 1806; Beatty to St Vincent, 16 Dec. 1806. The standing orders were maintained by later commanders of the Channel Fleet.
[11] Ibid. 4–5: St Vincent to Beatty, 29 Oct. 1806; Beatty to St Vincent, 9 Nov. 1806.
[12] Ibid. 34–5, 40: Beatty to Marsden, 27 July 1807; Transport Board to Beatty, 1 Aug. 1807.
[13] Ibid. 2: Beatty, letters to and from St Vincent 25, 26 Oct. 1806.

after ten to £766, plus a guinea a week lodgings allowance while on shore.[14] He was even able to take short periods of leave. On a number of occasions he travelled to London and stayed at an address in Surrey Street, off the eastern end of the Strand, from where he would network and see his friends.[15]

Beatty's position inevitably gave him the power to make or break careers. Although he appears to have been very solicitous for the welfare of surgeons who were injured or fell sick in the course of duty, he could be also officious and self-righteous with those whose care he found wanting, especially just after he had been appointed physician and was trying to impress. When the *Gibraltar* eventually docked in Falmouth, Beatty went on board and concluded that the crew had been struck down by an epidemic of malignant ulcers. In his opinion the surgeon, one Cunningham, had wrongly diagnosed scurvy and mistakenly tried to cure the outbreak with large doses of lemon juice. Cunningham was forced to admit his error, adopt a variety of more 'useful' therapies (which included placing his patients on a meagre diet, properly dressing their sores, and keeping their bodies and bedding clean), and write a grovelling letter to St Vincent begging forgiveness.[16] Back at sea, however, Cunningham recanted and maintained, from the progress of the invalids in his sick bay, that he had been right all along. In the letter he wrote to Beatty informing him of his change of heart, he claimed that he had accepted the physician's advice only under duress: 'In that opinion [that the disease was scurvy] I remained firm, until you told me I stood alone in an obstinate contention on a point of error, and threatened me with a court martial in case of persistence. For the sake of peace and to gain time for reflection, and more particularly to observe what advantage could be obtained from these refreshments [remedies], I gave in to your opinions.'[17] Beatty was incandescent, and replied with an excoriating letter in which he defended his own judgement and ridiculed Cunningham's. He also wrote to St Vincent, marking out Cunningham as a subversive, and loftily declaring that the surgeon's views 'convey a tendency not happy [*sic*] calculated to evince much zeal for the benefit of the service'.[18]

[14] Under the 1805 regulations: see Ch. 1, p. 16.
[15] For the first time in January 1808. NMP, MS 417/88/2, fo. 60: Beatty to Lord Gardner (St Vincent's successor as commander of the Channel Fleet), 8 Jan. 1808; Gardner to Beatty, 13 Jan. 1808. Another inhabitant of Surrey Street was the naval agent John Copland, who probably acted for Beatty.
[16] Ibid. 7–10: Beatty to St Vincent, 10 and 16 Nov. 1806; Cunningham to Beatty, 16 and 28 Nov. 1806; St Vincent to Beatty, 19 Nov.
[17] Ibid. 13–14: Cunningham to Beatty, 17 Dec. 1806.
[18] Ibid. 15–16, 19: Beatty to Cunningham, 28 Dec. 1806; Beatty to St Vincent, 27 Jan. 1807.

Some physicians of the fleet used their position to promote reform within the naval medical service or to gather information about the incidence and treatment of disease which might help to forward medical science generally. Beatty, however, does not seem to have been interested in making his mark in either respect. Tellingly, the surviving correspondence in the National Archive from physicians of the fleet to the Transport Board during this period contain surprisingly few unsolicited letters from the man in charge of the Channel station. This is not to say he was idle or inefficient. Clearly, as his official letter book reveals, he was careful and conscientious, meticulously carrying out whatever his commanding officer or the Board requested. But if he was Trotter's disciple, he was not Thomas Trotter, endlessly interfering in the work of his subordinates and firing off imaginative memos to his superiors. Nor was he a Burnett, his opposite number in the Mediterranean from 1810 to 1813, who used the experience to lay the foundations of his study of malaria. Beatty was simply a busy, good administrator and a bit of a martinet.

Beatty's correspondence with the Transport Board suggests that for most of the time the commissioners left him to get on with the job, and that communications were chiefly one way. Beatty, as he was expected to do, kept the commissioners informed about surgeons whom he had to certify unfit for service, potential candidates for promotion, and the various inspections that he undertook in accordance with the standing orders of his commanding officer. Except for routine enquiries and requests that he look into the sick list on a particular ship, the only known occasion he was approached by the Board for information about the general health of the fleet was in the summer of 1811, when he was asked to comment on the practice of vaccination in the navy. Apart from scurvy, smallpox was the one scourge of the eighteenth century which the armed forces managed to bring under control in the era of the French wars, thanks to Jenner's discovery of the prophylactic properties of cowpox in 1796. In 1811 the National Vaccine Establishment wanted to outline the success in eradicating the disease in the navy in its annual report to parliament, and the physicians were asked to forward their views. Beatty had been an enthusiastic supporter of vaccination for several years. In February 1807 he and a number of naval surgeons based at Plymouth had written to the Royal College of Physicians in London fulsomely endorsing the practice, although admitting limited experience with the technique.[19] Four years later

---

[19] NMP, MS 417/88/2, no pag. (end-page): letter 21 Feb. 1807.

the Ulsterman was clearly much better informed, and had obviously been promoting the innovation. On 27 July 1811 he reported back to the commissioners that 'the practice of Vaccination is very generally adopted on board His Majesty's ships composing the Channel Fleet', and that he was not acquainted with any instance of its failure. As a result, although cases of smallpox still occurred from time to time, 'the Disease is by no means so prevalent nor consequently so fatal'.[20] He also had a suggestion to improve matters further. Since he had often had great difficulty in procuring vaccine for the surgeons under his charge, he believed 'that it might promote and give facility to a more general practice if the Surgeons of His Majesty's ships be supplied with Vaccine Virus from the Royal Hospital [at Greenwich], as I have often found great difficulty in procuring it for them'.[21]

From Beatty's letter book, it would seem that the Channel Fleet in his first years at Plymouth was remarkably healthy. In December 1807 he reported with satisfaction that there were only sixty-seven sailors in the hospital.[22] Besides occasional signs of scurvy, which seemed to occur whenever a ship ran out of lemons, the main problem affecting the crews were malignant (that is, contagious) ulcers. The *Gibraltar* was only one of a number of ships whose men evinced signs of the complaint. According to Beatty, an explanation for the malady could be found in the men's over-rich diet. Malignant ulcers were an inflammatory disease: they were the inevitable result of young, plethoric sailors unused to living off animal fat being given large portions of fresh beef and strong liquor. The problem, as he outlined to St Vincent in January 1807, could be solved by a change of regime:

I beg leave to submit my opinion to your lordship that if fresh animal food was more sparingly supplied to our ships during the summer season (which proves more favourable to the generation of the ulcer) allowing at the same time a more frequent and liberal supply of fresh vegetables, and the issuing of beer as often as possible during the warm weather [rather than spirits] [, these] would prove measures highly instrumental in preventing the occurrence of a contagious ulcer which annually deprives the country of so many hundred valuable men.[23]

Since St Vincent agreed with Beatty's analysis, it is possible that the sailors' diet was duly changed.[24] Certainly, there are no reports of malignant ulcers in the physician's correspondence with the transport commissioners in the years

[20] TNA, ADM 97/88, unclassified.   [21] Ibid. Another letter the same day.
[22] NMP, MS 417/88/2, fos. 56–7: Beatty to Lord Gardner, 20 Dec. 1807.
[23] Ibid. 17–18. Beatty to St Vincent, 6 Jan. 1807.
[24] Ibid. 18: St Vincent to Beatty, 10 Jan. 1807.

after 1808, though admittedly the correspondence in the National Archive is far from complete. Rather, the principal epidemic disease affecting the Channel Fleet in later years was typhus (which Beatty often called typhoid), particularly prevalent in ships carrying troops and prisoners who brought the affliction on board with them. This was dealt with by 'purification': bedding and clothing had to be kept dry and clean, the air allowed to circulate freely, and the ship thoroughly lime-washed. But this was not always possible, given the state of many of the navy's ships, so that Beatty usually blamed the bad condition of many of the crews who docked in Plymouth on the low level of maintenance, as he explained in a report on the *Diadem* on 1 October 1812:

When Typhus fever is discovered on board of ships recently employed in conveying Troops, or Prisoners of War there is too much reason, in general, to ascribe its source to latent contagion; but in this instance, the damp state of the Diadem below, was sufficient, in my judgment, to produce Fever of an aggravated character, among her company. The ship had been leaky for some time past, requiring to be Pumped out twice a day, and in consequence of the defective state . . . of the Pumps, the water has escaped, on every occasion, in considerably [*sic*] quantity over the Deck, and the Bed fixtures had rendered it difficult if not impossible to thoroughly dry it afterwards.[25]

If the ship was watertight, then Beatty found other reasons to explain the failure to contain the disease. Required by his then commander, Sir Robert Calder, to inspect the *Romulus* in January 1811, and finding that her surgeon, one McFadden, had done all in his power to purify the vessel, he ended by attributing the virulence of the epidemic to the fatigue of the crew, inclement weather, and the lack of good bedding and change of clothes. No more than five of the crew had ever served on a ship of war before, and most of them could not afford to buy new clothes having had already spent more than their wages on their 'slops'.

Normally Beatty was content to inspect the ship and file his report. But as he grew more experienced, there are signs that he became more proactive. On 29 January 1814 he wrote a letter to Admiral Viscount Keith, his last commanding officer, suggesting ways in which troop ships (that is, the less seaworthy vessels used to transport the army overseas) might be kept free from disease. From his encounter with typhus on the *Diadem* and other ships, he was 'fully satisfied that their frequent unhealthiness is in a great

[25] TNA, ADM 97/88, unclassified.

degree attributable to the mode of fitting them with Cribs or Bed fixtures which renders it impossible to keep the Troop Decks clean, dry or in a proper state of Ventilation'. He therefore proposed that the troops should sleep in hammocks, like the crew. This would not only improve the soldiers' health but be a saving to the public purse. 'The loss and inconvenience incurred by the Troop Bedding on board these ships is likewise very considerable, as the Mattresses and Pillows soon become damp and dirty, furnishing a Nidus [nest] for contagion and filth, and in a short time are totally destroyed.' He further believed that once the troops or prisoners had left the ship, the troop decks should be thoroughly fumigated by lighting stoves, some of whose flues should extend through the decks to the open air.[26] Beatty had clearly developed a good political sense. In an age when measures which might reduce the expenditure on the army and navy were always guaranteed a fair wind, a suggestion which combined, in his own words, 'humanity' and 'economy' was likely to be particularly well received.

Beatty might have shown a greater commitment to reform in the first years of his office, had he not spent so much time networking with Lady Hamilton. Although their correspondence is too incomplete to grasp his intentions, it is clear that in January 1809, he was seeking a favour of some kind from the Admiralty, and that Rose provided him with letters to Lord Mulgrave, the first lord (1807–10), Sir Harry Neale, one of the junior lords, and Lord Gambier, a committed Evangelical and at that date in command of the Channel Fleet. He also secured an interview with Mulgrave on a day when the nobleman did not normally receive. Perhaps at this juncture Beatty wanted out.[27] He was certainly ambitious to become part of the court medical establishment, even if only in an honorific capacity. The year before, on one of his many trips to London, he had written to Emma just before he left to rejoin the fleet, asking her to lobby the Prince of Wales for a position.

Permit me to solicit your kind interference and good offices in my behalf, with His Royal Highness the Prince of Wales, to confer on me the distinguished honour of being appointed one of the Physicians extraordinary to the Prince, a mark of attention which would be highly gratifying to my feelings, and flattering to my reputation as the last and Professional friend of Nelson, whose memory His Royal Highness on all occasions honoured with respect: with such an advocate as your ladyship, I feel confident that my request cannot fail of being graciously received.[28]

---

[26] Ibid.   [27] WL, MS 6242, no. 5: Beatty to Lady Hamilton, 31 Jan. 1809.
[28] Ibid., no. 3: Beatty to Lady Hamilton, 2 Feb. 1808.

In this case, too, Beatty's lobbying seems to have been successful, for either then or later he gained the coveted position.[29] Presumably Beatty had counted on Prinny responding positively, given his courtesy in presenting the prince with the manuscript of the *Authentic Narrative* prior to its publication. He must also have known that the prince of Wales had a soft spot for Irish doctors: one of his Brighton set was the Edinburgh graduate Dr John Gibney, from County Meath.

To be fair, Beatty did not just use his acquaintance with Lady Hamilton in these years for his own advancement. He was also keen to forward the careers of his friends. In particular, he was anxious to help his fellow Ulsterman George Magrath, who had been his predecessor on the *Victory* and who had almost certainly played a role in his own elevation. By late 1806 Magrath's career had stalled. He was no longer surgeon at the navy hospital at Gibraltar but had been transferred to the Mill Prison Hospital outside Plymouth, where he presumably had renewed his acquaintance with Beatty. The physician of the Channel Fleet was anxious that one of Nelson's favourite medical men should not languish in obscurity, so he wrote to Emma asking that she press Magrath's case for promotion with the then first lord of the Admiralty, Thomas Grenville (served 1806–7, elder brother of the prime minister). Beatty himself had already sounded out the first lord through his wife and the Whig MP Samuel Whitbread, and all that was needed was Lady Hamilton's support:

Well knowing your Ladyship's excellence of heart I have taken the liberty of enclosing a letter from our dear Lord as well as Mr Grenville's letter, that your Ladyship may, from the latter see the nature of Mr Magrath's expectations, and noting that by the good offices of your Ladyship in transmitting the former to Mr Grenville with such comments as you deem proper, that Mr Magrath's preferment will be much promoted by it; my friend felt delicate in approaching your Ladyship on the subject but he has at my entreaty permitted me to make his communication to your Ladyship, who well knows the high opinion Lord Nelson entertained of his conduct and Professional acquirements, proof of which appear to be the only points on which Mr Grenville seems to look for further communication.[30]

---

[29] Beatty is described as physician extraordinary to the prince of Wales in the proposal he be elected an FRS: see below, n. 48. On the other hand, Beatty is never listed as one of the Prince Regent's physicians extraordinary in the annual *Royal Kalendar*, which gave details of his household. Perhaps he was only given an honorary title.

[30] WL, MS 6242, no. 2: Beatty to Emma, 15 Oct. 1806. Beatty had sent a signed copy of the *Authentic Narrative* to Grenville, now in the BL.

Moreover, Beatty's commitment to Magrath remained steadfast in the following years, long after Lady Hamilton's dubious charms had understandably failed to work their magic in a period when the lords of the Admiralty were continually changing. By the summer of 1811 he seems to have been determined to see what his own professional influence could do, and wrote to Emma requesting that she send him the letters from Nelson to Magrath that she possessed among her papers. Beatty did not forget friends to whom he was beholden.[31]

PRIVATE PRACTICE

Beatty was placed permanently on half-pay on 23 August 1815, on terms of 15s. per day.[32] At this juncture—now in his early forties—he could have gone back to County Londonderry and lived out of the rest of his life in his native town. It is easy to see, however, that a return to his homeland would have had little charm, for few immediate family members lived there any more. His uncle and putative master, the naval surgeon George Smyth, was still in the city and would only die in 1821, while his cousin Vincent, son of the exciseman Ross, was resident in a neighbouring county and briefly served as captain of militia in the 1st Provisional Battalion.[33] But Beatty's father and mother must have been dead, and of his three brothers only James, who had become a merchant, was still based in his home town, living in Bishop Street, and he too would die in 1818.[34] Brother George had moved away when he entered the marines in the 1790s, while Vincent had in turn joined the armed forces

---

[31] Ibid., no. 6: Beatty to Emma, 30 Aug. 1811.

[32] TNA, ADM 104/30, fo. 122: Beatty's career record.

[33] TNA, Prob 11/1644: will, proved 30 May 1821. IGI, under Vincent Beatty; http://homepages. rootsweb.com/~bp2000/summaries3.htm (lineage 180) (Jan. 2005). Cousin Vincent was born in County Monaghan in 1778 and attended Trinity College Dublin: presumably he lived from private means: G. D Burtchaell, *Alumni Dublinenses: A Register of the Students, Graduates, Professors and Provosts of Trinity College in the University of Dublin (1593–1860)* (Dublin, 1935), 53: his father was described as a gentleman; the *Army List* (1814–43), records his military career: commissioned 25 Dec. 1814, on half-pay the following year; death 1843. TNA, PMG 4/209: grant of administration to his sister, Margaret.

[34] Beatty Family at http://homepages.rootsweb.com/~bp2000/summaries3.htm (lineage 180) (Jan. 2005). A James Beatty, either William's father or brother, was listed as living in Glendermot, Waterside, among the 1796 Ulster flax-growers' index held in PRONI. There is an obituary for James in the *Londonderry Journal*, 1 Dec. 1818, where he is described as being of a 'mildness of disposition, sincerity of heart and rectitude of conduct'. Bishop Street is one of the four main streets of the walled city. His will was proved on 13 Jan. 1819 and he left everything to his sister, Anna Baker: Crossle, 'Beatty Genealogical Notes': NAI, vol. 2, fo. 4.

in 1800, when he became an adjutant in the Light Dragoons, making the rank of captain in 1807, probably with William's help.[35] Beatty's two sisters had also moved elsewhere. On 11 July 1805 Anna had married a naval lieutenant called John Popham Baker, whom she had presumably met when his ship, the *Venus*, was patrolling the Irish station, while on 1 October 1808 Eliza had married her distant cousin Robert Beatty, archdeacon of Ardagh since 1805 in succession to his father Robert.[36] Eliza went to live in her husband's rectory at Moydow, County Longford. Anna possibly initially stayed at home while her new husband returned to duty, but at some time before the end of the French war she went to live with her sister, since her son, Frederick Walter Baker, was christened in her brother-in-law's church on 15 January 1815.[37] She may even immediately have gone to England, for her husband came from a respectable Somerset family. Popham Baker was the second son of Aaron Abraham Baker, a DCL of Wadham and All Souls, who was rector of Burnet outside Bath and became a prebendary of Wells, a JP, and a deputy lieutenant of the county. His elder brother, Aaron Webb Baker, attended Corpus Christi, Oxford.[38]

In addition, surely well aware of the divisions within the Ulster Protestant community regarding the French Revolution and the recent Union with Britain, Beatty might have been reluctant, given his family's traditional commitment to the Hanoverian state, to show his face in a county where many Presbyterians had supported the United Irishmen. Moreover, had he gone home he would have had to go into semi-retirement, like so many naval surgeons on half-pay. As a physician of the fleet, it would have been beneath his dignity to set up in Londonderry as a surgeon as his uncle had done. But Londonderry was a small town. There would have been limited opportunities to practise physic alone. Understandably, therefore, Beatty decided to settle in England.

However, Beatty did not set up his plate immediately, but travelled north to Edinburgh, where he spent the academic years 1815–17 attending courses in the medical faculty.[39] This was a curious move. In the summer of 1814,

[35] *Army List* (1800–17). Vincent Beatty began in the 27th and moved to the 25th Light Dragoons in 1805 when he became a lieutenant. It is possible that William paid towards purchasing his various commissions. Curiously, no service register survives for Vincent.

[36] Beatty Family Website (n. 34 above); William Richard O'Byrne *A Naval Biographical Dictionary* (London, 1849), 39; Henry Cotton, *Fasti Ecclesiae Hibernicae: The Succession of the Members and Prelates of the Cathedral Bodies of Ireland*, 3 vols. (Dublin, 1845–78), iii. 193; Fig 1.1, above, p. 37.

[37] IGI, under Frederick Walter Baker. He was born on 16 April 1814 in Ireland.

[38] Joseph Foster, *Alumni Oxonienses, 1715–1886*, 4 vols. (Oxford, 1888), i. 49.

[39] Edinburgh University Library, Faculty of Medicine, Index of Matriculands.

doubtless thinking that the war was over with the first abdication of Napoleon in April, and that retirement consequently loomed, he had begun to take steps to secure his future in Civvy Street by becoming a fellow of the Royal College of Physicians of Edinburgh on the strength of his Aberdeen degree. He received his licence to practise on 2 August and was made a fellow on 1 November. Interestingly, his patron-become-client, George Magrath, who had been retired from his position at the Mill Prison on 24 June 1813, was received on the same day.[40] Presumably, Beatty had no intention of practising in the Scottish capital; he simply wanted to be able to write FRCPE after his name. Why, then, should he enrol in the Edinburgh faculty once placed on half-pay? Perhaps he genuinely wanted to mug up on the latest medical ideas after more than twenty years in the navy. More likely, he had already decided that if he wanted to build a solid clientele in England as a physician and not an apothecary-surgeon, he would have to become a licentiate of the prestigious Royal College of Physicians of London, not just an FRCPE. The college expected its licentiates to have studied at a respectable university. If Beatty was one of those entrants to the naval service who had not been to Edinburgh before they joined up, then his ambitions required that he regularize his position.

The Irishman became a licentiate of the London college on 22 December 1817.[41] In order to qualify, it seems that he had to take a second medical degree, for on 14 October 1817 he was awarded an MD *in absentia* by the senate of the University of St Andrews:

There was presented to the meeting a Letter from Dr Outram Physician in London, requesting the Degree of M.D. for Dr. William Beatty & stating that he has already a Diploma from the University of Aberdeen dated some years since, but that being about to become a Licentiate of the London College, he is required to have another dated subsequently to his residence at Edin[burgh] where he has studied proforma and obtained his certificates for the years 1815 and 1816. Dr Outram farther states that his Education, manners and character are in the highest degree respectable, & that he is fully convinced, no one is more worthy of a Diploma in Medicine. The University having taken these circumstances into consideration, resolved to grant the Degree; & being satisfied as to the plea of urgency stated in the Rectors Summons, they hereby confer it without farther delay.[42]

---

[40] *Historical Sketch and Laws of the Royal College of Physicians of Edinburgh from its Institution to 1925* (Edinburgh, 1925), 7, list of fellows. TNA, ADM 104/12: Magrath's service record.

[41] William Munk, *The Roll of the Royal College of Physicians*, 3 vols. (London, 1878), iii. 177.

[42] University Library, St Andrews, UY452/131-2: Senate minute-book, *sub dat.*

Beatty's sponsor, Outram, it will be remembered, was another naval surgeon, who had unusually decided to become a London physician and had been practising in the capital since 1809, when he had taken his MD in Edinburgh. Himself a licentiate of the London Royal College of Physicians from 1810, he resided in fashionable Hanover Square. Outram and Beatty were presumably close friends: they had been medical students together, either before 1791, when Beatty joined the service, or in 1802–3 when he was on half-pay, or perhaps in 1806, when the Irishman may or may not have had leave.[43] Outram's assistance, though, went no further than vouching for Beatty's abilities as a physician. Possibly Beatty dreamt of becoming a London practitioner in turn, but there is no evidence that he ever practised in the capital. Instead he returned to Plymouth Dock, where he could expect to find a ready clientele among ailing naval officers, serving and retired, and where his near neighbour in Plymouth town was his erstwhile colleague Magrath, who had similarly returned to his old haunts. Evidently ex-naval surgeons from Ulster, however distinguished their career, had little hope of setting themselves up in the metropolis.[44]

Beatty seems to have been in civilian practice in Plymouth for nearly five years. His friends included the local MP and naval officer Sir Thomas Byam Martin, but we know next to nothing about his clients.[45] Frustratingly, we only have one window onto his practice in these years, which comes from the notebooks of the Birmingham-born naval officer William Henry Dillon, later knighted and vice-admiral of the Red. In 1821, when Dillon was a captain on half-pay, he consulted Beatty over his violent headaches: 'He ... promised to cure me, and would not accept the usual fees. The Doctor evidently mistook my complaint. My having rather a sanguine complexion, and being, in body, of square frame, he thought that Plethora [over-rich and thick blood] was the cause of my suffering, and reduced me to the lowest degree of debility, but would not change his system.' For three months Dillon was placed on a strict diet, without much relief. In the end, when Beatty decided that his patient should be bled in the jugular vein and turned up with an apothecary with lancets and bandages, Dillon demurred and refused further treatment. 'I then showed him one of my legs, the calf of which had disappeared. "When I placed myself under your care", said I, "I had a good stout limb. It is now a

<hr>

[43] See Beatty's handwritten dedication to Outram's 1825 copy of the *Authentic Narrative* in the NMM.

[44] *Court Kalendar* (1819), 286; (1821), 286: list of members of the London Royal College of Physicians with their place of residence.

[45] Martin was MP for Plymouth, 1818–31: for his association with Beatty, see below, n. 61.

broomstick. Pray let me know what I am in your debt." . . . The Doctor in spite of all his professions, made me pay more than the usual fees'. Dillon then departed to the continent on the advice of a Dr Freeman, who prescribed a diametrically opposite regime of food, wine, and sea-bathing. When he came back to England in January 1822 he claimed to be completely cured, and on bumping into Beatty at a later date took the opportunity to upbraid his former physician for his inadequacy: ' "There," said I, pointing to a pint of Port Wine on my table. "Since I have renewed my former habits, I have recovered my health and strength." My medical friend retired in ill humour, and never forgave that observation of mine.'[46]

It is unfortunate that the one surviving account of Beatty as a civilian practitioner is such a negative one. However, patient dissatisfaction was an occupational hazard in an era when the sick were free to choose and drop their practitioners at will, and Dillon's testimony should not be taken as evidence that the physician of the fleet was incompetent, especially given the fact he was scornful of doctors. Rather, the narrative is of greater interest for what it reveals about Beatty's practice. The fact that he employed an apothecary to bleed a patient emphasizes that he took his dignity as a physician seriously. Phlebotomy was a commonplace remedy for most diseases in the early nineteenth century, and Beatty would have performed hundreds, if not thousands, of bleedings as a surgeon afloat. But in his new role as a civilian physician he examined and diagnosed; he was too grand to treat his patients himself.

We know nothing, too, about how Beatty reacted to the charged political atmosphere of the period. The post-war years were ones of economic depression and growing radicalism, as the Tory Liverpool government reduced expenditure by 50 per cent and refused to countenance any relief to Catholics or any reform of the traditional political system. London in particular was the home of a vibrant underground press, energized all the more by George IV's attempt, when he ascended the throne in 1820, to impeach his Whig-consorting wife for adultery. Beatty must have either applauded or been appalled by such events as the Peterloo Massacre at Manchester in 1819, but we have no idea where he stood, beyond a general association with the cause of improvement. This is evident from the fact that Beatty successfully negotiated his way into the capital's medical and scientific elite. Not content with being a licentiate of the Royal College, he also had himself elected a fellow of the Linnean Society of London on 7 April 1818, although there is

---

[46] William Henry Dillon, *A Narrative of My Professional Adventures 1790–1839*, ed. Michael A. Lewis, Navy Records Society, 2 vols. (London, 1953–6), ii. 478–9.

no evidence that he had a particular interest in natural history. Beatty may have picked up some acquaintance with the subject through his years afloat, but neither before nor after joining the society did he provide any sign of his commitment in print. His sponsors were the society's long-standing secretary, the entomologist Alexander McLeay, who was also secretary of the Transport Board, and two unremarkable members, G. Milne and G. Roddam.[47] A few weeks later he landed an even bigger honour, when he was accepted as a fellow of the Royal Society on 30 April.

In the early nineteenth century, entry to the Royal Society was relatively easy for those with an interest in science and the right social connections. Although the members included men of the eminence of Sir Humphry Davy, the majority were cultivated hangers-on, for whom being a fellow was a sign of their commitment to progress and modernity. All that an aspiring candidate required to be elected was the support of a handful of fellows who would be willing to put forward his name. The society's records reveal that Beatty, when first proposed in the preceding January, was able to assemble a powerful phalanx of well-wishers to promote his cause (see Ill. 14). Among the other fellows with naval connections, he was sponsored by William Babington, who had recommended him for his Aberdeen doctorate, John Barrow, second secretary of the Admiralty, Rear-Admiral Lord Amelius Beauclerk, and McLeay. In addition, Beatty was backed by the strongly Whig Henry Cline, surgeon at St Thomas's, John Rennie, the civil engineer who had just completed Waterloo Bridge, and the ornithologist John Latham. His ability to assemble such a heavyweight crew is testimony to his successful networking as physician of the fleet. Once again he presented himself as a naturalist, his sponsors claiming he was a 'Gentleman well acquainted with various branches of Natural History'. It is to be hoped his knowledge was never closely tested by the society's ageing president, Sir Joseph Banks.[48]

Obviously, living in Plymouth Beatty could play little part in either society's activities in the following years, but he was not totally comatose. In 1819 he was one of those who sponsored the election of his friend Magrath to the Royal Society, while two years later he joined many other fellows in contributing to the erection of a statue in the British Museum of its now defunct president, Banks.[49]

[47] Information supplied by Lynda Brooks, Deputy Librarian, Linnean Society of London: email to the authors, 26 Jan. 2005. The Linnean Society had been founded in the late eighteenth century, and contained many physicians.   [48] Royal Society Library, London, EC/1818/02.
[49] Ibid., EC/1819/09; *The Times*, 10 Sept. 1821, p. 2, col. A. Beatty gave 3 guineas. Most gave more: St Vincent offered £10.

PHYSICIAN AT GREENWICH

Beatty remained in private practice until September 1822, when he re-entered the service as physician to Greenwich Hospital in succession to Dr Robert Wright, who had only served two years in the post. Of all the postings a physician of the fleet could receive, this was the most prestigious, for Greenwich was the senior naval hospital, located close to London, and involved no seaborne duties. Why Beatty should have gained the position above others of his rank—at this juncture he was only the eighth in seniority—is unclear, but his elevation must be closely related to the appointment the year before of Sir Richard Goodwin Keats (1757–1834) as governor. Keats, captain of the *Superb*, was one of Nelson's favourite officers in the Mediterranean: 'I esteem his person alone as equal to one French 74, and the Superb and her captain equal to two 74-gun ships.'[50] And Keats returned the compliment. At the Battle of San Domingo, on 6 February 1806, as the *Superb* engaged with the enemy, he brought out a portrait of Nelson and had it hung from the mizzen stay, where it remained throughout the action. It is likely, too, that Keats knew Beatty fairly well, because the *Superb* had accompanied the *Victory* back to Portsmouth in August 1805 to refit. It was understandable, then, that the new governor would want the surgeon who had nursed the dying hero as his hospital physician. Keats, too, probably played a part in Beatty's elevation to the post of physician extraordinary to George IV in Scotland, and in 1827 or 1828 to the office of physician extraordinary to the duke of Clarence, soon to be William IV.[51] Sir Richard was a favourite of the duke, having been for some two years the lieutenant of his watch when Prince William Henry served as a midshipman on the *Prince George* in the American War of Independence. Presumably he played some part too in Beatty's eventual knighthood in 1831.

Beatty remained at Greenwich for seventeen years. This was his longest posting, a period which saw the last years of Liverpool's long Tory ministry,

---

[50] Nelson to Hugh Elliot, Britain's representative at the Neapolitan Court, 11 July 1803: Nicolas, *Dispatches*, v. 130.

[51] William Beatty, *Authentic Narrative of the Death of Lord* Nelson (London, 1825), title-page: we have been unable to discover when Beatty received the Scottish appointment. *Court Kalendar* (1828), 127; (1829), 127: household of the duke of Clarence. The post-holder is described as MD Will. Beattie, but there is no doubt that this is the Greenwich physician. Magrath held a similar position in 1829.

the swift dismantling of the confessional state, and the first bout of parliamentary reform in 1828–32, and a decade of almost unchecked Whig government under Grey and Melbourne dedicated to institutional modernization and secularization without further extending the franchise. Beatty's duties were essentially twofold. On the one hand he was responsible for checking the health of seamen who sought admission to the hospital, and of the boys and girls proposed for the two naval schools, from 1821 both located in the Queen's House. On the other, he was in charge of the infirmary, situated on the London side of the hospital, to which pensioners were transferred when sick, and the separate school sanatorium. In addition, he had to pay a monthly visit to the handful of inmates who had been certified lunatics and moved to the Bethlehem Asylum in Lambeth, which now shelters the Imperial War Museum. The position was far from being a sinecure. The foundation in Beatty's day contained some 2,700 veterans and 1,000 children (800 boys and 200 girls), and was staffed by several hundred administrators, clerks, medics, teachers, maintenance men, and female nurses (who were always wives of seamen). There was even an organist and two chaplains to maintain divine service, which the pensioners were expected to attend daily. Admittedly, the care of day-to-day admissions—there were at least 300 new pensioners a year—was presumably left to medical subordinates, but the physician was always more than a hospital manager. Besides the continual grind of form-filling and report-writing, he was directly responsible for the pensioners and schoolchildren suffering from physical ailments. Twice daily, when in residence, he had to do his rounds of the physical wing of the infirmary.

The infirmary had been built in 1763 to a design by the then hospital surveyor, James Stuart, a neoclassical architect, and completed under the direction of the clerk of works, Robinson (see Ill. 15).[52] It was originally a two-storey, quadrangular brick building with a double row of rooms on each level. Each room had a shuttered window and a fireplace with an aperture near the ceiling to allow extra ventilation, and could accommodate four patients in iron bedsteads. When full, the infirmary could house 256 pensioners. The sick were placed on the ground floor, convalescents on the first. The east wing of the building, nearest the hospital, was devoted to physical cases, the west to surgical ones, which, according to an 1819 report, were

---

[52] The most recent account is John Bold, *An Architectural History of the Royal Hospital for Seamen and the Queen's House* (London, 2000), 207–14.

usually double the number.[53] There was also a 'helpless' wing, only completed in 1808–10, which housed pensioners too weak to live in the main hospital. The physician's wing contained the infirmary hall, while the surgeon's wing, to emphasize the difference in status between the two branches of medicine, contained the kitchens. The rest of the building comprised the dispensary, the operating theatre, a good medical library, and the apartments of the medical staff, who received free accommodation. Besides the physician, the foundation in Beatty's day supported a deputy physician, a surgeon and two assistants, and an apothecary and assistant dispenser.[54] The physician's apartment was in the south end of the east wing and the surgeon's at the south end of the west.

Major modifications were made to the infirmary in 1811 after a disastrous fire, which led to the surgeon's wing being raised to three storeys. For the first part of Beatty's tenure there were no further changes of any significance, but in 1834–5 Joseph Kay, the hospital surveyor, put forward plans for large-scale reconstruction. Although these seem to have been initially opposed by the medical staff, who presumably objected to the upheaval it would cause, they were quickly given a green light. During Beatty's last years as physician the infirmary must have been a building site and the patients been continually moved around as construction progressed. By the end of 1836 his own wing had been given an additional storey, while work was well under way on converting the sanitation block in the middle of the courtyard. Beatty had retired by the time all the hospital's rooms were refurbished in 1840–4, leading to the permanent decampment of the physician to the south-west end of the building.

Next to nothing has survived about Beatty's hospital practice, just as we know virtually nothing about his civilian patients. In the early nineteenth century, when Robert Robertson (1742–1829) was the long-standing physician in charge, the infirmary had played a small part in the promotion of medical science. In 1807 Robertson himself contributed to understanding about the diseases of old age by publishing four volumes of medical observations based on the cases that he had treated there. These emphasized the high level of alcoholism among the pensioners and the consequent number of accidents, as well as the frequency of lethal pulmonary infections and influenza.[55] Four years later the directors tried to improve on the low rate of success

[53] TNA, ADM 105/24.

[54] *Navy List* (1823 and subsequent years), 126: list of personnel at Greenwich.

[55] *Observations on the Diseases Incident to Seamen, Retired from the Actual Service, by Reason of Accident, Infirmity or Old Age*, 4 vols. (London, 1807). Robertson was an FRS in 1804.

in cataract operations at the infirmary by engaging the much-vaunted Exeter ophthalmologist William Adams, later Sir William Rawson, to demonstrate his skill on twenty blind volunteers and teach the surgical staff his technique.[56] Neither Beatty nor his assistant physician, William Gladstone, however, seem to have been interested in revealing their activities to a wider public, suggesting again that Beatty was a conservative rather than innovative practitioner.

The surviving letters, now in the archives of the National Maritime Museum, which Beatty wrote to the governor of Greenwich during his stay show a competent and humane man, interested in the promotion of deserving staff and the well-being of his patients. Surprisingly, they also reveal that his patients were not always seamen and schoolchildren. Although officers who had not risen from the ranks could not be admitted to Greenwich Hospital, it would appear that they felt free to consult its medical establishment. One letter to the governor concerns Beatty's investigation into a complaint made by a rear-admiral about medicines that his nurse had received from the dispensary. According to Beatty the fault lay with the dispenser's assistant, who had failed to ensure that the measuring glass used in making up the prescription was properly cleaned. The mistake, the letter indicated, was par for the course: the assistant was disrespectful to superiors and absented himself without permission.[57]

Sadly, detailed information about only one of Beatty's infirmary patients has survived. This was James Ward, a 44-year-old single man of Croydon, who had entered Greenwich Hospital on 6 December 1832 after nearly thirteen years of service. His was a peculiar instance, in that his medical history was unveiled in the course of a coroner's inquest into the murder in January 1834 of another infirmary patient, John Bailey, a one-armed married man of 64 from America with a leg wound, who had been at Greenwich since 6 March 1824. Ward had been found with the knife that had killed his comrade, and admitted his guilt, so that the purpose of the inquest was to establish whether he was insane. In the course of the trial Beatty, Gladstone, two female nurses and the assistant surgeon, James Domville, all gave evidence on the state of Ward's mind and his previous ailments, and threw interesting light on the infirmary's day-to-day routine. According to Beatty, Ward had been 'a patient under my care in July and August last, during a spasmodic affection of the bowels, but he did not then labour under any complaint of the head'. He had then been

[56] *Official Papers Relating to Operations Performed by Order of the Directors of the Royal Hospital for Seamen at Greenwich on Several of the Pensioners Belonging Thereto* (London, 1814). The Greenwich surgeon at this date was one McLaughlin.   [57] NMM, KEA/18/1-4.

admitted for a second time on the morning of the murder (which took place in the late afternoon), and had been visited by the physician on his round: 'On that morning I visited Ward; he had then an ordinary febrile complaint from cold, exposure or drinking. He did not then labour under Insanity, or any other serious complaint. I was in the infirmary at half-past 4 in the afternoon, but as I did not observe that anything of consequence ailed Ward, I did not call upon him.' An earlier witness confirmed Beatty's account by swearing that Ward, on being admitted, had 'answered the usual questions as to his age, mess, country etc, with the greatest accuracy'. It was also revealed that if Ward had exhibited any symptoms of insanity, he would have been immediately removed on Beatty's standing order to the infirmary's strongroom to await examination by a doctor. A later witness, one of the nurses, similarly backed up the physician's evidence. 'In the course of the day leeches were applied to Ward's head for a slight fever, but he did not exhibit symptoms of delirium.' The second nurse, however, who had dealt with Ward's twelve leeches on several occasions in the late afternoon, bathing his head, thought his behaviour decidedly odd. Beatty concurred. He had interviewed Ward in the lunatic asylum to which he had been transferred, and concluded from his conversation that he was definitely mad and a totally unreliable witness to the event. In his evidence, true to the humanitarian instincts he had displayed at other moments of his career, he did his best to get his patient off a capital charge. 'I visited Ward, shortly after the murder, he was then evidently deranged, but whether it was a permanent or temporary fit of insanity, I am not prepared to say. I can only attribute his conduct to a sudden fit of delirium.' The jury did not agree. Ward had been brought back to the infirmary strongroom 'confined in a strait-waistcoat and strapped to down in bed', and was interrogated by the coroner in the presence of the jury. He explained that he had stabbed Bailey because he had been incensed by his fellow patient using the night-table close to his bed and demanding snuff, when 'he was better off than me'. Despite expressing sorrow and attributing his action to 'a severe injury which he received in his head by falling from his hammock in Chatham, when on board the *Atlas*', the jury found him guilty of 'Wilful Murder'. He was ordered to be conveyed to Maidstone Gaol to be tried at the assize, where he was condemned as a lunatic, confirming Beatty's opinion.[58]

[58] *The Times*, 29 Jan. 1834, p. 5, cols. E and F. Domville revealed that there was a bell placed at each patient's bed-head, and assistance could be obtained night and day in less than a second. Gladstone backed up Beatty's opinion that Ward was insane after the murder: http://www.murderresearch.com/index/uvw.htm (Feb. 2005).

On re-entering the service Beatty had to give up his civilian practice, since under the 1805 regulations hospital physicians were not allowed to have private patients. This did not mean, though, that he cut himself off from the outside world, for his move to the outskirts of London gave him the opportunity to mix permanently with the capital's scientific and medical establishment for the first time. Admittedly, he still played little active part in the intellectual activities of the Royal Society: he never presented a paper and was never chosen to be on the Society's governing council. But he did show concern for its good administration. On 23 November 1830 he wrote a letter from the United Services Club in Pall Mall to a fellow member of the Royal Society, the surgeon and antiquarian Thomas Pettigrew, in which he shared the latter's enthusiasm for the election of the duke of Sussex as the society's president.[59] He continued to take an interest, too, in the creation of new members: as late as 1838 he was one of those who sponsored the election of his friend Outram to the fellowship.[60]

Early on in his tenure at Greenwich, moreover, he endeavoured to place his name more broadly in the public domain by publishing a third edition of the *Authentic Narrative*, this time with the house of W. Mason off the Strand.[61] The publication is primarily of interest for the changes which were introduced. Although the text is largely word for word what had appeared in 1807 and 1808, except for a few added footnotes, significant lines had been excised. To all intents and purposes Lady Hamilton had been written out of the death of Nelson, and the narrative was no longer a story of love versus duty. To emphasize this the more, Beatty no longer included the final codicil to Nelson's will within the story. In the original edition the codicil, and an account of its composition, had been inserted in the text immediately after the Christian hero's prayer for victory. No reader could have doubted that Emma was deeply on Nelson's mind as he prepared for battle. In the 1825 edition Beatty merely writes that: 'This prayer and the codicil to his will were both written with HIS LORDSHIP's own hand, within three hours before the commencement of the engagement.' The codicil itself is now

---

[59] WL, MS 5371, fo. 20. We do not know when Beatty joined the club, which was founded in 1816 and open to medical officers of high rank. For its early history, see Maj.-General Sir Louis C. Jackson, *History of the United Service Club* (Aldershot, 1937), chs. 1–4.

[60] Royal Society, London, EC/1838/26.

[61] Beatty, *Authentic Narrative* (1825). The copy in the Brotherton Library, University of Leeds is a signed copy presented by the author to the Plymouth MP, Sir Thomas Byam Martin, with the ringing words: 'The glorious death of our glorious Nelson. His last day is an epitome of his whole life.'

buried at the end of the book. Even the footnote directing the reader forward gives the wrong page number.[62] Emma had died ignominiously in Calais in 1815, a bankrupt on the run. Evidently, with the Evangelicals ascendant in government, Beatty no longer deemed it appropriate to remind his readers of the hero's human frailty. Nor, presumably, did he want to embarrass Hardy in particular by telling the world that Nelson had entrusted his mistress to his care. The excisions were understandable, but they destroyed the drama.

This, though, was Beatty's only foray into print on his own account in his Greenwich years. If his name continued to come before the public in later years, it was not as an author but as public servant. Understandably, he was a physician whose medical views carried some weight. During the first cholera epidemic of 1831–2, his views on prophylaxis, which had been originally penned for the benefit of the governor of Greenwich Hospital, were published in the second number of the *Cholera Gazette*, an information sheet produced by the government's new Board of Health. Confronted by this new menace to the nation's health, moving towards London from the north, Beatty was confident that the peril could be kept at bay. In the past, he informed the reader, he had successfully used a mixture of Peruvian bark (which contained quinine) and capiscum (cayenne pepper) as a preservative against malaria, typhus, and something he dubbed remittent fever:

I am now impelled by these recollections, to express my opinion decidedly in favour of a like efficacy in this medicine, as preventative of Cholera, particularly with reference to the security of the attendants, nurses, as well as others having intercourse with the Cholera patients; and to be extended, likewise, to individuals generally, whose health may have been reduced below its usual standard, by previous indisposition, intemperance, or by other causes of debility.

Beatty remained as convinced as ever of the rectitude of his own judgement. He accepted that the medicine could not be used indiscriminately and should not be given to 'invalids with chronic affections of the lungs, other viscera, or organs'. Nonetheless, he was certain that its use would be positive.

Should occasion, therefore, present itself to this institution [Greenwich Hospital], for submitting this medicine to the test of exhibition against Cholera, I would deem myself warranted in recommending forthwith its adoption; and with so much

---

[62] Ibid. 15. The reference is to p. 99, while the codicil is printed on pp. 84–5. The copy in the Brotherton Library was given by Dr Philip Gosse, the widower of the authoress Anna Cooper Keown, who claimed to be a relative of Beatty.

confidence in its conservative influence, as to entertain but little doubt of its success in general, when duly administered.[63]

Moreover, throughout his tenure as Physician at Greenwich, Beatty was deeply engaged in the civic life of the national and local community as well. Only a few years after taking up his appointment he became one of the directors of the London-based Clerical, Medical and General Life Assurance Company. Beatty became involved with the company shortly after its foundation in 1824. The moving spirits behind its formation were Dr Joseph Pinckard and his brother, who became respectively the first chairman and treasurer. Pinckard had been a physician to the forces, accompanying Sir Ralph Abercromby on his expedition to the West Indies in 1795 and gaining promotion to deputy inspector of Hospitals. He left the service in 1799 and set up in practice in London. His objective in founding the Medical, Clerical and General Assurance Company, which soon changed its name to the familiar Clerical, Medical and General, was to provide life cover for members of the medical profession, who because of the nature of their calling had difficulty in getting the insurance they needed. The constitution stipulated that of the eighteen directors half had to be doctors.[64] Beatty, as a former physician to the fleet and now physician to Greenwich Hospital, with many contacts, would have been a natural recruit to the project. He was amongst the small band of proprietors (shareholders) who attended the first annual meeting in 1825.[65] Although the Clerical, Medical like other insurance companies of the period, had a distinguished president and vice-president, including Sir Astley Cooper, the work of running the company was in the hands of the board. In March 1828 George Vance of Saville Row, a former naval surgeon and erstwhile physician at Paignton Hospital, proposed Beatty for a seat on the board.[66] He was to serve the company until his death fourteen years later.

For Beatty to have been invited to join the board was a great honour, all the more so in that he was the only serving army and naval medical officer in

---

[63] *Cholera Gazette* (1832), 78–9 (all issues bound in one volume): letter dated 21 Jan. 1832. The information sheet only appeared for the first six months of 1832. The Central Board of Health was hastily created to organize the defence against cholera. The threat passed, it was dismantled. A permanent Board of Health was only created several years later.

[64] Arthur Digby Besant, *Our Centenary, Being the History of the First Hundred Years of Clerical, Medical and General Life Assurance Society* (London, 1924), 10, 79.

[65] CMG, general minute book 1, p. 34.

[66] Ibid. 90. George Vance is in the authors' prosopographical database: see Preface, n. 3, above. He was also probably of an Irish background.

the first half of the nineteenth century to be a director. It was testimony to the outside world's confidence in his administrative abilities and probity, and again emphasized that he moved in 'improving' circles. Among his fellow directors was the London physician George Birkbeck, who in the 1820s was one of the founders of the London Mechanics Institute (today Birkbeck College) and University College London.

Being a director of an insurance company was no sinecure. The Clerical, Medical board met weekly throughout the year to review applications for life cover. Applicants who had certain medical conditions or wished to insure their lives for large sums were required to attend in person, so that they could be examined by two of the medical directors and questioned as to their lifestyle and medical history by the whole board. In some instances two medical directors were instructed to attend on an applicant in their own homes at their convenience. Applicants paid the doctors directly for such examinations. Beatty took his new duties seriously. During his first year he scarcely missed a board meeting, and even when he was out of town he seems to have found time to prosecute the company's interest, particularly in recruiting local medical referees. He was able to use his position to reward his friends. During 1828 he arranged for his friend McGrath to acquire twenty shares.[67] On his recommendation McGrath was appointed medical referee in Devonport, Dr Lempriere (a former army surgeon) in the Isle of Wight, and a Dr McCabe in Hastings.[68] During 1829 and 1830 he recommended twenty-two of his friends for such appointments, mostly in the south-west of England and Wales.[69]

Board meetings were lengthy and often interrupted by the medical directors' examinations. Many of those who were asked to report to the board were members of the gentry or aristocracy, who, such as the Hon. Robert King, 'had lived freely'.[70] In November 1831 Beatty and his fellow director Dr Samuel Merriman, the distinguished physician and accoucheur, passed Lady Hales as fit, but she was dead by the summer.[71] He and George G. Babington, another medical director (and cousin of the historian Macaulay), were no more successful in approving the insurance of the life of Lord Glentworth, the eldest son of the earl of Limerick, in 1832 for £3,000. He was dead within two years.[72] These were exceptions, and in other cases,

---

[67] CMG minute book 3, p. 1212.   [68] Ibid. 1079 and 1106.
[69] CMG minute book B1, pp. 325, 374, and B2, pp. 11, 107, 114, 112, 133, and 199.
[70] CMG minute book 6, p. 328.
[71] CMG minute book 3, pp. 143 and 363. For Merrriman, see *DNB, sub nom.*
[72] CMG minute book B3, p. 373.

particularly where there was a doubtful medical history, Beatty was more successful, often recommending a higher premium rather than rejection. The board's ability to assess such risks was greatly helped by the presence of the physician Robert Bree, who suffered from asthma and devoted much of his career to its control.[73] Even after his retirement from Greenwich, Beatty remained an assiduous director, missing only fourteen meetings in the last year of his life. He attended his final board meeting on 16 March 1842, just a fortnight before his death. Being a director brought no great direct financial reward: there was an attendance allowance of some 5 shillings when Beatty first joined, which rose to over £1 by the time of his death.[74] However, indirectly he must have earned considerable fees. During his years on the board the assets of the society climbed from £28,632 to £477,160, at a time of virtually no inflation.[75]

A few years after joining the board of Clerical, Medical Beatty became the director of a second innovative company. The first railway to be built out from the capital was the London and Greenwich, which was given parliamentary approval in May 1833 and fully opened on Christmas Day 1838. It was only a 4-mile stretch of line, but a notable engineering achievement because for its whole length the railway ran on a viaduct. From the beginning Beatty was on the Directorial Board, along with two other naval representatives, Rear-Admiral William Hall Gage (1777–1864) and a Captain Cuthbert Featherstone Daly, who had been born about 1775 at Castle Daly, County Westmeath, and had commanded the sloop *Comet* in a notable small action in 1808. The navy's presence reflected the fact that Greenwich Hospital had a legitimate interest in the initiative, as did the army, as the intention was eventually to extend the line to Woolwich. But Beatty was no sleeping partner, simply there to make up numbers. Although he may have stood down from the board at the end of 1837, he had taken a leading role in its activities during the previous years. It was Beatty, along with two other directors, who organized the junket in December 1836 when the section of the railway from London Bridge to Deptford was opened by the lord mayor. In a secular ritual worthy of a man who had been a part of Nelson's funeral cortege, he helped to orchestrate an event where 1,500 of the great and good were herded into five trains for an inaugural journey down the line, then 400 conveyed back to Southwark for a grand banquet in

---

[73] For Bree, see *DNB, sub nom.*
[74] Besant, *Our Centenary*, p. 79; CMG general minute book 3, pp. 151–2: authors' calculations.
[75] CMG, general minute book. 1, p. 106, and 2, pp. 151–2.

the Great Room of the Bridge House Tavern. It was Beatty, too, who took the chair in July 1837 when a special general meeting of the shareholders was held to seek a futher £45,000 to complete the Greenwich extension.[76] The railway, futhermore, was not his only civic concern in these years. In 1834, according to an advertisement in the *Greenwich Gazette*, the Greenwich and Deptford Gas Company was formed. No trace of its activities has survived, but an undated prospectus in the British Library reveals that Beatty was the chairman of its board.[77] He was probably, too, on the directorial board of another gas company, formed the following year and discontinued in 1838, which planned to light the 4-mile viaduct of the Greenwich Railway.[78]

Beatty's involvement in such projects was important, for at the beginning of the 1830s Greenwich Hospital and the surrounding parish were at daggers drawn. Greenwich at this date was an expanding town, with a population of some 24,000. In the eyes of the good burghers of the community, the hospital was a drain on the parish's resources. It provided little financial benefit to the town, even if the pensioners spent their pocket-money there and the hospital employed local contractors and shopkeepers, because the inmates brought with them their dependants. If they were destitute, then under the terms of the Elizabethan Poor Law they could not be sent back to their original homes but had to be supported from the parish rates. In consequence, the pensioners and their families attracted the same kind of hostility as the modern asylum-seeker:

Many of the pensioners, on their admission, bring with them sick or aged wives, and burdensome families, which soon become chargeable. On the pensioner's death, it often happens that the clue to his place of settlement is lost, and it generally devolves upon Greenwich Parish to support his widow and children during the remainder of their lives; and a great proportion of those who quit the hospital for misconduct, or on account of insanity, are either Foreigners, or Men who cannot be removed because of their inability to depose to their real place of

---

[76] R. H. G. Thomas, *London's First Railway: The London and Greenwich* (London, 1972), 26, 57–61, 70. For Daly: IGI; William James, *The Naval History of Great Britain, from the Declaration of War By France in February 1793 to the Accession of George IV in January 1820*, 6 vols. (London, 1826), v. 77; www.cronab.demon.co.uk/INTRO.HTM: Maritime History, Naval Heritage Website: follow references to HMS *Comet*. Beatty and Daly were already acquainted: Beatty arranged for Daly to acquire 20 shares in Clerical and Medical in 1828: see CMG, minute book 3, p. 1079.

[77] Greater London Industrial Archaeology Society, *Notes and News* (June, 1996), no pagination (see www.glias.org/news/164news.htm).   [78] Thomas, *London's First Railway*, 72.

settlement, consequently they and their families become a fixed burden upon the Parish of Greenwich. In consideration of this part of the case, the character of the British Seamen, united to the weakness of human nature, must not be forgotten. A sailor is proverbially known to be prodigal and improvident; he cohabits indiscriminately with various women; one and perhaps more of whom, on his admission to Greenwich Hospital, follows him with her illegitimate offspring, and settles in the Parish; and some of the Pensioners, being young or middle-aged (admitted for some sufficient cause into the Hospital) form illicit connections afterwards, which entail upon the Parish a constant source of expense in the maintenance of an illegitimate progeny.[79]

To ensure that the community was not grossly out of pocket, the parish demanded that the hospital pay more than the legal rate. But in 1829 the governor, who argued that the complaint was greatly exaggerated, reneged on a deal brokered in 1807 and plunged relations between parish and hospital into chaos. The impasse seems to have lasted throughout the 1830s, for the hospital was still refusing to be surcharged to the tune of £2 per patient in 1838.[80] The fact that Beatty was closely involved with local citizens in schemes for improvement in this reforming decade suggests that he was good at building bridges and a recognized champion of civic progress.

The Beatty who spent the 1820s and 1830s at Greenwich was now in the autumn of his life, another reason, perhaps, why he seems to have shown little interest in medical innovation. Towards the end of the period he had his likeness painted again (see Ill. 16). This time he had himself presented as the elder medical statesman, seated before his desk, his identity clearly revealed through the iconic presence of the *Victory* seen through the window behind him. In these years the Greenwich physician must have been a man increasingly at ease with himself, doubtless content to enjoy the perquisites of his office: the free accommodation, the servants, and the large salary. As a man who had single-mindedly fashioned his public image as Nelson's surgeon, he must also have felt that he had come home. Greenwich Hospital was in the process of being developed into a monument to Nelson and Nelson's navy. In the King William Building, the Upper Hall had not yet acquired the coat and waistcoat that the hero had worn at the Nile and Trafalgar—these would be a later gift from Prince Albert in 1845. But the four corners of the Painted Hall were already adorned with the colossal statues of Nelson, Howe, St Vincent, and

---

[79] *Report of the Committee on the Subject of the Burden Sustained by the Parish of Greenwich in Relieving Poor Persons Connected with Greenwich Hospital* (Greenwich, 1831), 17–18.

[80] *Statement of the Case on the Part of the Commissioners of Greenwich Hospital in Regard to the Claims Made by the Parish of Greenwich Upon the Institution for Parochial Rates* (London, 1838).

Duncan, the victor of Camperdown.[81] The tympanum of the pediment above the entrance to the King William Building, moreover, had long been decorated with an emblematic representation of the death of Nelson, designed by Benjamin West in 1812 after his painting, and modelled under his direction:

In the centre is Britannia, seated on a rock washed by the Ocean, receiving from one of the attendant Tritons at the command of Neptune, the dead body of Nelson; Victory supports the body with one hand, while with the other she presents to Britannia the trident of the god, in token of the dominion of the seas: behind Neptune, who is seated in his shell, drawn by sea horses, is a British sailor, announcing 'Trafalgar' as the scene of the hero's death; to the left of Britannia is represented a naval genius recording the victories of the Nile and Copenhagen; before whom is a British lion, holding in his paws a tablet inscribed 'Nelson's CXXII Battle:' adjoining these are the sister kingdoms, England, Scotland and Ireland, with their emblems, the rose, thistle and shamrock; they are reclining affectionately on each other, and expressing their deeper sorrow. On the south side of the pediment are various naval implements of war, and on the north side is represented the destruction of the enemy's fleet at Trafalgar.[82]

Beatty would have seen the pediment every day he walked through the hospital. A glance up to the tympanum and a glance down at the bullet on his watch-chain would have forcefully reminded him of the part that he had personally played in settling the fate of the new British nation. Moreover, if he needed further reassurance, he had only to go and stand among the crowd in front of Devis's painting of the *Death of Nelson*, which the hospital had acquired in 1825 through the generosity of one of its directors, the former chancellor of the exchequer Nicholas Vansittart, Baron Bexley. In his final years, furthermore, he would have had the chance to share his reminiscences with an old friend. In 1834 Keats died. He was replaced by the *Victory*'s captain, now Admiral Sir Thomas Masterman Hardy, who would spend the last five years of his life as governor of Greenwich Hospital.

RETIREMENT AND DEATH

Hardy died on 20 September 1839 and was buried in the mausoleum in the hospital cemetery. Beatty, perhaps anticipating the imminent death of his

---

[81] *A Description of the Royal Hospital for Seamen, at Greenwich* (London, 1846), 14. The *Description*, originally published under the title *An Historical Account* by the chaplains of the hospital, John Maule and John Cooke, appeared for the first time in 1789 and was regularly reprinted in updated editions throughout the first half of the nineteenth century.   [82] Ibid. 9.

friend, had retired a few months earlier in July. Presumably, now aged 66, he had no desire to get used to the whims of a third governor, although he might have thought differently had he known that, after a brief interlude, the office would be given to his old captain on the *Spencer*, Sir Robert Stopford (governor 1841–7). In recognition of his forty-one years in the service Beatty was awarded a pension of £200 per annum from Greenwich in addition to his 21*s*. per day as physician of the fleet.[83] As soon as his retirement came through he departed to Germany for the sake of his own health, doubtless to take the waters at a fashionable spa. He was there on 16 October when *The Times* announced with sadness that he was dead, only to have to apologize to its readers two days later that it had made a mistake.[84] When Beatty finally returned to England is not known, but he was probably back early in the new year, and took a house in London's York Street, south of the Marylebone Road, off Baker Street. The 1841 census records him as living at No. 43, a male of independent means aged 60 (rather than 68). He had three live-in servants: Jane Jones (39), Ann Tew (25), and Caroline Hunt (20).[85]

This was a poignant time for a member of *Victory's* company to be residing in the capital, for Nelson's column was in the process of construction in Trafalgar Square. A monument to Nelson had been proposed as early as 1805, but it was only in 1838 that a subscription was raised with the duke of Wellington's support, Trafalgar Square chosen as the appropriate location, and architects invited to proffer designs in open competition. In the course of the following year, after numerous drawings and models had been scrutinized by the organizing committee, Railton's design was judged to be the best and work commenced. The Corinthian column and Nelson's statue, a staggering 173 feet high, took four years to erect, although the monument was not completely finished until 1852. It was also way over budget. £20,483. 11*s*. 2*d*. had been collected from the navy and well-wishers, including £500 from Tsar Nicholas I, but the monument cost an estimated £32,000. The rest was provided by the government, which took over the project in 1844.[86] Given that the tribute to Nelson was proposed and executed in the middle of the Chartist agitation for further parliamentary reform, it can be assumed that the monument was a deliberate sop to popular opinion in London. Parliament would not grant universal suffrage, but it was happy to honour the people's hero in the hope that this would draw the radicals' sting. It was also

[83] TNA, ADM 104/166, fo. 12.
[84] *The Times*, 16 Oct. 1839, p. 5, col. B; 18 Oct., p. 4, col. F.
[85] TNA, HO 107/680, fo. 17.   [86] http://www.victorianlondon.org/buildings/nelson.htm

an important visual buttress to the new reign. Victoria, the first queen since Anne, had ascended the throne in 1837, and her subjects needed to be reassured that she and her ministers would keep faith with the country's tradition of naval supremacy.

Beatty, in his last days at Greenwich, had played a significant part in the project's development. Although not one of the handful of grandees, led by Wellington, who initiated the movement to erect a monument to Nelson in the capital, he was among the host of naval worthies, including Hardy, who were invited to join the permanent organizing committee, which he did on 26 March 1838. It is possible that Hardy nominated him, or that he was judged a valuable addition, given his experience with Clerical, Medical and the London and Greenwich Railway. He proved to be an assiduous committee member, even if he was never placed on a subcommittee. Hardy dropped out after attending twice, but Beatty attended all the meetings up to and including the one held on 22 June 1839, when the monument's design was selected. Since the voting was secret there is no way of knowing whether Beatty approved the decision, but he had clearly played an important role in the preceding deliberations. Thereafter, his name ceases to appear in the minutes.[87]

Once back from abroad, we can assume that Beatty would have been a frequent visitor to Trafalgar Square to watch the column's slow erection. Sadly, however, the Ulsterman did not live to see the monument's completion or even the public exhibition of Bailey's 17-foot statue of Nelson before it was raised aloft. He died in York Street on 25 March 1842. Jane Jones, described as his housekeeper, was present at the agony and registered the death five days later. The cause of death on the certificate was acute bronchitis.[88] Presumably Beatty could have been buried in the Greenwich Hospital cemetery had he wished, but he was interred instead, doubtless on his own request, in Kensal Green, one of the new London burial sites some miles to the north-west of his house. Here he was laid to rest in an unmarked vault, presumably again on request. The present plaque identifying his grave was only placed next to the entrance of the vault at a much later date by the 1805 Club, a society devoted to maintaining the memory of the men of Trafalgar. The funeral was organized by his brother George, then a newly made colonel in the Royal Marines and based at Plymouth.[89] Who the other mourners were, besides the three

---

[87] TNA, Works 6/119: committee minute book.

[88] GRO [Marylebone District], 1842, fo. 464.

[89] TNA, ADM 196, *sub nom.* George's career had prospered during the latter years of the French war. He commanded the Royal Marines at the capture of Martinique in 1809. George was

servants, remains a mystery. Beatty's other brother, Vincent, on half-pay from 1818 to 1840, probably did not attend, for he was living in Tralee, County Kerry; while sister Eliza, who had married the archdeacon of Ardagh, was dead by 1820, and her husband, eventually an LL D, the following year.[90] Sister Anna, on the other hand, if she were still alive, and her husband John Popham Baker, who only died in 1859, could have travelled to London for the funeral, for at some time after 1815 they had set up house in Baker's home village of Burnett, Somerset. John Popham Baker was now a commander on half-pay, but he had only been promoted from lieutenant in 1821 when he had been superseded. He also, rather oddly, enjoyed an out-pension from Greenwich Hospital, which he had received in 1829, presumably through Beatty's patronage.[91] The Bakers' son, Frederick Walter, could also have accompanied his parents. After attending King's School Bath, he had gone up to Caius College, Cambridge, in 1832 before moving to Oxford and joining the Church in 1838, like his grandfather. At the time of Beatty's death he was curate of Bathwick, near Bath, a few miles from the family home.[92]

No will has been traced, but the death duty records in the National Archive reveal that Beatty's estate was valued at £3,000.[93] Although this was not a paltry amount, it was not a large sum for an unmarried man who had held one of the top posts in the navy medical corps. As there is no evidence that he drank to excess or gambled, it is likely that he spent most of his salary, especially in his later years, in building up a fine private library.[94] The three executors of his will were brothers George and Vincent and Captain Cuthbert Featherstone Daly, living at Hay's Place, Lisson Grove, west of Marylebone. As Daly, it will be recalled, was one of the navy representatives on the London and Greenwich Railway board, it must be assumed that he and Beatty were very close friends.[95]

mentioned in dispatches for his gallantry, and was presented with a £50 sword by the Patriotic Fund. In addition to fighting with Nelson, George later met Napoleon while serving aboard the ship which carried him to St Helena.

[90] *Army List* (1818–40). NMM, HSR/U/24: 'The administrative residuary account of the effects of the late Sir William Beatty, 1842', states Vincent's address. IGI, *sub* Eliza Beatty, b. about 1786, Londonderry. Cotton, *Fasti Ecclesiae Hibernicae*, iii. 193.

[91] O'Byrne, *Naval Biographical Dictionary*, 39. He had suffered a rupture in 1809, but as an officer it is difficult to see why he would qualify for an out-pension on top of his half-pay.

[92] J. A. Venn, *Alumni Cantabrigienses from 1752–1900*, 6 vols. (Cambridge, 1940–53), i. 126; Foster, *Alumni Oxonienses*, iii. 50. Venn gives his place of origin as Burnett.

[93] TNA, IR 26/255, fo. 123.   [94] For Beatty's library, see Afterword below.

[95] Daly died in 1851. He appears to have been living with his daughter, who was his sole legatee: see TNA, Prob 11/2143: will, proved 24 Dec. 1851.

When the assets of the estate had been liquidated, Vincent Beatty, who had travelled from Tralee to act as administrator, drew up an inventory documenting the transactions, dated 12 July 1842, the anniversary of the Battle of the Boyne.[96] William owned no real estate, for his house in York Street was rented from a Mr Rothe. The major part of his fortune, fittingly, consisted of 200 shares in the Greenwich Railway, which were sold for £1,445. In addition, he owned fifty Clerical, Medical shares worth £337 and had £80 in the Bank of England. Beatty's personal effects fetched £221. Brother George purchased three portraits (one, presumably, Devis's likeness) and Vincent an oil painting, while Beatty's nephew, the Revd Baker, bought the Clerical, Medical shares. Baker also temporarily took custody of the musket ball which killed Nelson and some articles of plate, which were returned to Vincent, then staying at 94 Sydney Place, Bath, on 10 July 1844. The funeral cost a modest £80, probate £90, and a sum of about £150 was set aside in trust to pay for the education of the daughter of William's housekeeper, Mrs Jones. When all outstanding debts and expenses were cleared—they amounted to £714—the residue of the estate was valued at £1,545, which was split four ways.[97] The beneficiaries are not recorded, but three must have been George, Vincent, and the Revd Baker. The fourth, from the provisions in brother Vincent's later will, may well have been Eliza Smyth Henderson, Beatty's niece and the daughter of sister Eliza. Eliza Smyth, who was born about 1810 and would only die in 1889, was the wife of the Dublin barrister William Carlisle Henderson, born in County Tyrone in 1801 and educated at Trinity College Dublin. They had married in 1835.[98]

Beatty's death went virtually unnoticed. The news quickly got back to Londonderry, for two short death notices appeared at the beginning of April in the city's press. Presumably they were placed there by the family for the benefit of local people who might still remember the gauger James Beatty and his sons.[99] On the other hand, the media does not seem to have been used to inform London society that he had died. *The Times*, which had already

[96] In fact not the literal anniversary: early in the eighteenth century Britain and Ireland had adopted the Gregorian calendar and the date had been advanced by ten days.

[97] NMM, HSR/U/24: perhaps one of the portraits was the 'lost' likeness of Nelson: see above, Ch. 4, p. 148, n. 68.

[98] IGI, under Eliza Beatty. Burtchaell, *Alumni Dublinenses*, 389: *sub* William Henderson, Irish Bar 1825; his father, another William, was described as a gentleman, 'generosus'. See the Beatty family tree, above, Ch. 2, p. 37.

[99] *Londonderry Sentinel*, 2 Apr. 1842; *Londonderry Journal*, 5 Apr. 1842. Neither mentioned that William was born in the town. The authors must have assumed that this was known. No obituary appeared in the *Londonderry Standard*.

pronounced the Irishman dead two years before, clearly feared to make the same mistake twice and left his passing unrecorded. So, surprisingly, did the *United Service Journal*, the organ of the army and navy, which might have been expected to mark his demise. At a meeting of the Royal Society on 30 November 1842 the secretary recorded his death on the list of fellows who had died in the previous year, but there was no encomium in the subsequent presidential address.[100] The Linnean Society equally made little of his passing, although the president on 24 May 1842 did at least remind the assembled company of his claim to fame when reading out a similar roll: 'Sir Wm. Beatty, Knt., M. D., F. R. S., well known as having been surgeon of the *Victory* at the memorable action off Cape Trafalgar, and as having in that capacity assisted at the last moments of Lord Nelson, of which he afterwards published an account.'[101] In fact, only two contemporary obituaries are known to have been published in the capital. The first appeared in the August 1842 edition of the *Gentleman's Magazine*, the other in the 1842 *Annual Register*, published the following year. Both, rather oddly, stated that Beatty had become physician at Greenwich in 1806, an error which has been repeated in all biographical entries ever since, including both the original and Oxford *DNB*.[102] Otherwise, the rest was silence. No pious descendant strove to keep alive Beatty's memory with a tale of his life and times in the senior service, and no biographer has taken up his cause before the twenty-first century. Nelson's surgeon quickly slipped into national oblivion, even if his narrative of the hero's death lived on.

This may partly have been Beatty's own design, as will be suggested below in the Afterword, but it was largely the result of biological accident. Unmarried himself, Beatty left no direct heirs to tell his story. Neither, too, did his brother James who had died in 1818, nor his two surviving brothers. Vincent had married a Frances Butler—whose family may have come from County Kerry—but there were no surviving children when he died on 21 August 1856 at Tenby in Pembrokeshire.[103] He made the most of being a captain in the dragoons and left a much larger fortune than his elder brother—at least £15,000, chiefly in Irish and English stock. He was also an

---

[100] *Proceedings of the Royal Society*, 4 (1843), 399.

[101] Source, as above, n. 47.

[102] *Gentleman's Magazine*, 18 (1842), 209; *Annual Register* (1842), pt. ii, p. 260.

[103] http://homepages.rootsweb.com~bp2000/summaries3.htm (lineage 180) (Jan. 2005). The Beatty website says he married a Belinda Butler, but his wife is called Frances in his will. He may have married twice. The IGI gives a Belinda Butler who marries a Valentine Beatty at St Anne's, Dublin, in 1812, who may be the Belinda Butler born at Rathkeale, County Limerick, in 1784.

orthodox Protestant, who remained true to the beliefs of his great-grandfather, William, hero of the siege of Londonderry. In his will, which he wrote himself at Bath in 1848, he displayed an exceptional religiosity, declaring in convoluted style: 'his firm and unalterable faith in Jesus Christ, the son of God and the Saviour of the believing world unto whom I commend my spirit [,] and to the Lord our God unto whom belong mercies and forgiveness although we have rebelled against him [,] and may he forgive us all our sins.' Under the terms of his will, he left legacies to a large number of Smyth cousins (relatives on his mother's side) and to two nephews and a niece through his wife. The bulk of his fortune, however, was eventually destined for the families of his only surviving blood kin. Eliza Smyth Henderson and her children ultimately received £6,000, including £2,500 for the children's education, while the Revd Frederick Walter Baker received £2,500, but only on the death of Vincent's wife.[104]

George Beatty, like William, never married. After a highly successful professional career, he retired from the marines in 1846 with the rank of colonel-commander and established himself in Bath. In the following years he was promoted, although on half-pay, and when he eventually died in Dublin, a year after Vincent, on 26 June 1857 he held the rank of general, obtained two years before.[105] He also left a huge fortune of £20,764, suggesting that he had been much more successful than William in using the navy as a launch-pad to riches. In that his niece, Eliza Smyth Henderson, was given the administration of the estate, she was presumably the chief beneficiary.[106]

It is interesting that the bulk of the brothers' fortunes does not seem to have passed to their nephew Frederick. As he was their nearest male relative, this seems odd. Perhaps they felt that Frederick was well enough provided for—certainly, when he died in Kent in 1878 his estate was initially valued at £25,000—or perhaps there had been a falling-out since William's death fourteen years before.[107] Either way, the omission may have played

[104] TNA, Prob 11/2337, fos. 91–3.

[105] TNA, ADM 195/58, fo. 6: George Beatty's Service Record. The marine's impressive career was recognized with a good service pension, which he received in Feb. 1857 (ibid., fol. 8). There is an obituary in the *Gentleman's Magazine* (Aug. 1857), 229, and in the *Annual Register* (1857), pt. ii, p. 316, which gives the date of his death as 26 July. Neither mentions that he died in Dublin.

[106] TNA, IR 26/285, fo. 335.

[107] First Avenue House, Administrations and Wills, 1878, *sub* Baker, Rev. Frederick Walter. Later resworn as under £14,000.

a significant role in ensuring that Beatty's story was never told. If his two surviving brothers, for whatever reason, did not rush into print, then the only other likely relative to keep his memory before the public was his nephew. If the Revd Frederick Walter felt that he had received insufficient material benefit from his Beatty uncles, he might have been understandably disinclined to immortalize the memory of Nelson's surgeon at Trafalgar.

Afterword

William Beatty was neither a pioneering surgeon nor an innovative physician. No novel surgical intervention has been associated with his name, just as there is no evidence that he developed any novel therapy, even though he was an ardent supporter of smallpox vaccination. Nor did he make any obvious contribution to the burgeoning medical science of pathological anatomy through the careful observation and later dissection of his many patients. In fact, except for his *Victory* surgeon's log and the letters he wrote as physician of the fleet (chiefly from Plymouth), he left no account of his activities as a medical practitioner whatsoever. True, within the limits of the knowledge of his age he seems to have been a considerate and competent doctor, *pace* the strictures of Sir William Henry Dillon. Above all, he had bottle. On the two occasions when he was definitely placed under considerable pressure—in the West Indies during the yellow fever epidemic and at the Battle of Trafalgar— he kept a cool head and dealt with the crisis as effectively as was humanly possible. Moreover, his sterling performance in the cockpit of the *Victory* immediately placed him among the elite of his profession. Since there were so few set-piece sea battles during the long French war, only a minority of naval surgeons ever had to deal with the horrific scenes he had manfully confronted on 21 October 1805. In other respects, however, Beatty was a typical surgeon in Nelson's navy, going about his job competently and leaving little trace of his activities. Even in his background he was unexceptional. An Ulsterman from the banks of the Foyle, he was just one of a large contingent of recruits to the service from small-town Ireland. Like most of his fellow medical officers, too, he came from the middling sort. There may have been few other sons of excisemen in the naval medical service, but the large majority hailed from families which were similarly modestly comfortable, loyal to the Crown, locally respected, and with access to networks of patronage.

Of course, Beatty's career was unusually successful. Very few of his peers rose to be physicians of the fleet, and even fewer became an FRS and a knight of the realm. But this was primarily the result of circumstance. The Irishman had the luck to be on board the *Victory* at Nelson's finest hour. By comforting the people's hero in his agony and being the guardian of his dying words, he had automatic entrée into Nelson's circle of admirers and friends back in England, particularly the king's sons. And he capitalized on his good fortune to the full, both in publishing his account of the events in the cockpit on the afternoon of 21October, and in using his contacts to pull strings with the Admiralty and royalty. This is not to say that Beatty's colleagues did not network just as energetically, as the machinations of Thomas Longmore illustrate only too well. Virtually every entrant to the service must have entertained hopes of rising to the top and knew that promotion depended on patronage. But in this competitive game Beatty, thanks to his association with Nelson, was in a particularly privileged position and able to leapfrog over rivals, such as his erstwhile patron-colleague Magrath. Indeed, Magrath must have thought himself singularly unfortunate. Had Nelson not moved him to Gibraltar at the beginning of 1805, he, not his fellow Ulsterman, would have scooped the professional jackpot. It is easy to imagine there were many naval surgeons who envied Beatty his success.

Yet if Beatty was a typical naval surgeon of his day, who knew, like many a fellow officer, how to make the most of a fortunate break, he was also, it goes without saying, an individual. Although this book is intended to be primarily a professional biography—an attempt to give the reader some idea of what it was like to be a medical officer in the Royal Navy at the turn of the nineteenth century—it behoves the authors in conclusion to write a few words about Beatty the man. This, though, is far from easy. While we know more about Beatty than about most naval surgeons of the period, we have relatively little information on him outside his professional activities. In many ways, the career is the man.

It is not hard to gauge Beatty's character. To begin with, he was tough. Although he was nearly constantly at sea for fourteen years, then spent several months a year afloat while physician of the Channel Fleet, there is no sign that he suffered any debilitating illnesses. And staying fit was essential if a surgeon wanted to make a successful career in the navy. Longmore was evidently weakened by his few years in the service, while the young Robert Young, who had performed wonders in the cockpit of the *Ardent* at Camperdown in 1797, was soon invalided out after contracting typhus and developing a hernia.[1] Beatty may have been in poor health during the last years of his life, but for most of his forty-one years in the navy he was fit and well. In addition—and the one follows on from the other—he was a man with energy. While afloat, his

[1] Lloyd and Coulter, *Medicine and the Navy*, iii. 60. Burnett thought that surgeons had the highest mortality in the navy.

professional duties may have been all-consuming, but on shore he had fingers in a number of pies. His role on the board of the London and Greenwich Railway demonstrates that even in his early sixties he could throw himself wholeheartedly into a new enterprise outside his professional sphere. Presumably, he had charm and chutzpah too. To gain the friendship of such a galaxy of medical, scientific, and political talents as he had evidently done by the late 1810s suggests he was prepossessing. Networking requires time and effort but is of limited effect without an attractive personality. The surviving portraits (see Ills. 2 and 16) support this conclusion. In his early thirties Beatty was a personable, fresh-faced, slightly built man with dark hair, who looked young for his age. In later life he had gone bald and put on a little weight, but still appears sprightly and approachable. There is no evidence, however, that he was unduly sycophantic. His clash with Captain Lord Fitzroy early on his career rather suggests he had a powerful sense of self-worth. The great-grandson of a defender of Derry was not going to kowtow before an English aristocrat.

We also have some idea of Beatty's general take on the world. In an age when the British political nation was becoming polarized into two camps—pro- and anti-reform, Whig and Tory—Beatty was on the side of change. His association with Nelson—always a suspect figure in the eyes of the Tory establishment—his Whig friends, and his enthusiasm for science and improvement mark him down as a progressive in many respects. Although he may have made little positive contribution himself to making Britain a better place—beyond serving on the board of London's first railway—he evidently believed wholeheartedly in the possibility of mankind taming and shaping its environment. At the same time, he was no radical. It can be assumed that he supported the First Reform Act in 1832. A real revolutionary, however, would have joined the ranks of London's simple general practitioners and become part of the circle of Thomas Wakley (1795–1862), whose journal the *Lancet*, founded in 1823, was the scourge of medical nepotism. He would not have hitched his wagon to the conservative London College of Physicians, whose corporate power and pretensions were the embodiment of William Cobbett's 'Old Corruption', an excrescence of privilege which no right-thinking person could support. Similarly, he seems to have been comfortable with the 1801 Act of Union. There is no sign that he resented the disappearance of the Irish parliament, even if he probably supported O'Connell's move for Catholic emancipation. Despite his ancestors' Presbyterianism, he showed no evidence of being an Irish patriot.

In fact, Beatty seems to have turned his back on Ireland altogether. It was not just that he decided to make a life in England and London after 1806—lots of Irishmen did the same in the early nineteenth century, Castlereagh and Wellington to name but two—but that he buried his Irishness. Not only did he probably never return to Ireland after 1794, but he clearly disguised his Derry origins once finally settled in the capital from 1822, even if he had relied on the assistance of at least one expatriate, William Babington, to advance his career after Trafalgar. He probably even lost his Ulster brogue. This can be the only explanation as to why his nationality has remained hidden until today. Whether he eventually saw himself as British or English is of little importance. Just like the two medical establishments of the armed forces, the regular officer corps of the army and navy were a mix of English, Scots, and Irish whose service together under the Hanoverian Crown must have helped to create a new supra-British identity. If and when the officers returned home on half-pay at the end of the French war, they would have played a pivotal role in forging a local allegiance to the new United Kingdom. Beatty, on the other hand, by establishing himself in England, can have done nothing to encourage Britishness. In this regard he was clearly different from his two brothers in the services, Vincent and George. Vincent, the army captain, lived in Ireland for a number of years, even if he spent time in Bath and died at Tenby in Pembrokeshire. George, too, eventually felt the lure of his home country, and retired to Dublin shortly before his death.

However, beyond the fact that Beatty was a healthy, energetic Unionist Whig with a taste for improvement, we know next to nothing about his private life. His religious faith, personal relationships, financial dealings, aesthetic taste—all the questions into which biographers customarily delve in pursuit of a rounded portrait of their subject—are beyond our ken.

The only thing that can be said for certain is that he had significant literary as well as scientific interests. His readiness to subscribe to Downey's volume of poetry in 1813 hints at a man with literary sensibilities.[2] So, too, does his friendship with the Burneys, a notable family of clergymen, antiquarians, and novelists in the early nineteenth century, whose relations with Beatty are revealed in a surviving letter in the Beinecke Library at Yale and an entry in Fanny Anne Burney's journal on 20 September 1831, recounting his presence at her father's dinner table with a number of literary lions.[3] More

---

[2] See above p. xx. Beatty was not the only naval surgeon to subscribe.
[3] Beinecke Library Yale University, New Haven, Conn., Burney Family Collection, Series 1, Box Folder 1/101: Beatty to Miss Burney, 16 Nov. 1832; Margaret S. Rolt (ed.), *A Great Niece's*

importantly, Beatty definitely had a fine collection of books, engravings, and manuscripts.

In 1828, at the same time as he became a director of Clerical, Medical, Beatty opened a current account with the Bank of England.[4] It is probable that he chose the Bank of England because he had lost money in the failure of one of the thirty-seven private banks that collapsed in 1826.[5] That he did not transfer any large sum into the account when he opened it supports this supposition. As a consequence of the financial crisis, the Bank of England was actively recruiting private customers.[6] Beatty remained on its books until his death in 1842. The internal evidence of his account suggests that this was his only bank account. The bulk of his income during these years was made up of his salary from Greenwich of some £600 a year and, after he retired, his pension, which was only a little less. He had other income from his railway investment and cash that presumably came from the work he did for Clerical, Medical. Altogether his payments into his account totalled £10,191, some £900 a year, given that there were few deposits in the first year. This was a handsome income for a single professional man. Remarkably, he spent almost all his income during these years, except for £70 collected by his brother after his death. Until he retired he would have had little need to spend money. He had a free house and could mess with his colleagues at the hospital. Moreover, he would not have needed to draw money from the bank, as he would seem to have received his expenses and fees for his work for Clerical, Medical in cash. Unfortunately, the ledger entries do not give the first names of those to whom he was making payments, but the surnames

---

Journals, Being Extracts from the Journals of Fanny Anne Burney (Mrs Wood) from 1832 to 1842 (London, 1826), 40–1. Fanny Anne (1812–60) was the great-niece of the famous novelist Frances Burney. Until her marriage in 1835 she lived at Greenwich, with her father, the Revd Charles Parr Burney, who kept a school, originally founded in the town in 1793 by her grandfather, the classicist and bibliophile Dr Charles Burney (d. 1817). The extract suggests that Beatty was a frequent visitor, in which case he would have been treated later in the year to an account of the Burneys' summer visit to the Lake District, where they stayed with Southey and met Wordsworth. The letter, presumably to Fanny Anne, discusses a position at the recently incorporated School for the Indigent Blind in St George's Fields Southwark—further indication of Beatty's interest in improvement. Beatty seems to be on the school's subscription list.

[4] Bank of England Archives, drawing office customer account ledgers, C98/3010, 1828–1829, 254, C98/3018, 1829–1829, 370, C98/3024, 1829–1830, 576, C98/3035, 1830–1831, 558, C98/3044, 1831–1832, 529, C98/3091, 1832–3, 406, C98/3055, 1833–5, C98/3065, 417, 1835–6, C98/3080, 388, 1836–1837, 457, C98/3103, 1837–1838, C98/3117, 433, 1838–1839, 437, C98/3130, 1839–1840, 450, C98/3143, 1840–1841, 444, C98/3155, 1841–1842, 435.

[5] John Clapham, *The Bank of England—A History 1797–1914* (Cambridge, 1944), 2, 102.

[6] Clapham (1944), 110.

strongly hint that he was spending money on a collection of books and manuscripts.[7]

Some of the names are easily recognizable, such as Ackerman, who must be the well-known engraver Rudolph Ackerman; Cullingford, the auctioneer John Cullingford; and Gullan, the engraver John Gullan. Other names fall into place, such as Hawkins, with whom he had a large number of transactions between 1830 and 1834. This is almost certainly the bookbinder and seller William Hawkins. Spooner must be the bookseller William Spooner; Mansell, the engraver John Mansell; Nelson, the bookseller Edward Nelson; and Walter, the bookseller William Walter of Drury Lane.[8] Nearly all of these transactions are for round sums of either guineas or pounds, suggesting that they were not running accounts for necessities. He also seems to have sold items from his collection, as some of these names appear on the other side of his account. Between 1837 and 1839 Spooner paid him £160. Since books and manuscripts were not expensive, expenditure on this scale reflects a handsome library. Unfortunately, virtually nothing further is known of its contents. Beatty certainly owned an early fifteenth-century lectionary of the gospels in English for the first three Sundays in Advent, today in the British Library. The fact, too, that it bears at the back what appears to be a press-mark in his hand—manuscript 1347—seems to suggest that he had a large collection of rare books.[9] But this is the only tantalizing glimpse of his library holdings. Presumably the collection was broken up and sold, but it has been impossible to find evidence of its auction. No catalogue survives, and there is no sign that he corresponded with any of London's leading antiquarians— except Pettigrew. Moreover, he was never a member of the prestigious Roxburghe Club, although he was acquainted with its secretary, the biblio-grapher Thomas Frognall Dibdin.[10]

Other aspects of Beatty's private life are a matter of pure speculation. It is tempting to imagine that he and Lady Hamilton were more than just good friends, and that the daughter of his housekeeper, Mrs Jane Jones, whose education was paid for out of Beatty's estate, was the result of an extramarital

[7] £70 was the sum left in the customer ledger account. The inventory of his goods (see above p. 191) says the amount was £80.

[8] The names of London's booksellers and engravers can be found in *Slater's London Directory* for the 1830s.

[9] BL Add MSS 30358: the MS bears Beatty's autograph. It was bought by the British Museum at Sotheby's on 5 June 1877, but we have been unable to trace its provenance.

[10] Clive Bigham, *The Roxburghe Club: Its History and Members, 1812–1927* (Oxford, 1928). For Pettigrew's relations with Beatty, see above, p. 180. Dibdin was one of the guests at the Burneys' dinner-table in 1831.

liaison late in life; but there is no speck of evidence to support the idea. Beatty's personal life is a closed book. And it seems more than plausible that he intended it to remain unopened. Just as he hid his roots, so he was careful to leave little record of his day-to-day life. The very fact that no will has been found, given his prominence and that he died in London, is indicative of a man who wanted to give nothing of himself away. So, too, his burial in Kensal Green in an unmarked vault suggests that he wanted Beatty the individual to leave no visible trace in the world. It is as if he were determined that William Beatty should only survive in the national imagination as Nelson's surgeon, a purely public figure. Such reticence in a sociable, likeable man is peculiar, but it possibly reflected an understandable fear of his life (and death) becoming a subject for popular titillation in the way that his friend and commander's had done. The hero had been a colossus with a feet of clay. Even before Nelson died, his private as well as his professional life had become public property, his relationship with Emma cruelly exposed in the media spotlight. Beatty had manipulated his association with Nelson to his professional advantage and become a minor celebrity, but it is arguable that he was anxious that his own private life should not be similarly picked over and his carefully fostered reputation mauled. Perhaps he too had interesting skeletons in the cupboard.

It was as Beatty the public figure, then, that he wanted to be remembered and that he asked to be judged. This being so, he could not but have been satisfied by the two tributes that appeared in the press, even if he might have been somewhat surprised that his passing was not more widely acknowledged. The *Annual Register*, in particular, provided him with the perfect epitaph by praising his commitment to duty and at the same time linking him indissolubly with the afternoon of 21 October 1805: 'It may justly be said of Sir William Beatty that the whole of his professional life seemed to accord with the sentiment expressed in Nelson's last and ever memorable signal to the fleet'—that is: 'England expects that every man will do his duty.'[11]

---

[11] *Annual Register* (1842), pt. ii, p. 260. The sentence was lifted from the obituary in the *Londonderry Sentinel* of 2 Apr. 1842. Beatty cites the signal correctly in the *Authentic Narrative*, but on the next page interestingly talks about the duty of every British sailor.

Select Bibliography

MANUSCRIPT SOURCES

The following collections and series have been consulted completely or in part:

Bank of England Archives, London

Beatty's Bank Account
Bank of England Archives, drawing office customer account ledgers, C98/3010, 1828–1829, 254, C98/3018, 1829–1829, 370, C98/3024, 1829–1830, 576, C98/3035, 1830–1831, 558, C98/3044, 1831–1832, 529, C98/3091, 1832–3, 406, C98/3055, 1833–5 C98/3065, 417, 1835–6 C98/3080, 388, 1836–1837, 457, C98/3103, 1837–1838, C98/3117, 433, 1838–1839, 437, C98/3130, 1839–1840, 450, C98/3143, 1840–1841, 444, C98/3155, 1841–1842, 435.

Beinecke Library (Yale University, New Haven)

Burney Family Collection, Series 1, Box Folder 1/101

British Library, London

ADD MSS 29915: Earl St Vincent Papers
ADD MSS 34992: Viscount Nelson Papers
EG 3782: Lady Emma Hamilton Correspondence

Clerical, Medical and General Life Assurance Archives, Bristol

Minute Books 1–6 and B1–B3

Edinburgh University Library

Faculty of Medicine, Index of Matriculands
Faculty of Medicine, Class Lists

King's College London

FP1/1: Index of Pupils, Guy's and St Thomas's Hospitals, 1723–1819
FP3/1: Guy's Hospital Entry Books, 1778–1813

Minterne Magna, Dorset

Papers of Sir Henry Digby

The National Archives (formerly Public Records Office), Kew

ADM 1: Captain's Letters and Court Martial Proceedings

ADM 1/407–11: Correspondence, Commander-in-Chief, Mediterranean

ADM 6: Commission and Warrant Books, Pensions to Widows and Orphans

ADM11/40: Surgeons' Service Records

ADM 22: Pensions to Widows and Orphans

ADM 24: Surgeons' Full Pay Records

ADM 25: Surgeons' Half Pay Records

ADM 35: Pay Books

ADM 36: Muster Books

ADM 51: Captains' Logs

ADM 52: Masters' Logs

ADM 97/88: Correspondence of the Physicians of the Fleet

ADM 101: Medical Logs

ADM 102: Surgeons' Succession Books and Free Gifts

ADM 104: Surgeons and Assistant Surgeons' Service Records, Seniority Lists, Pension Records, Succession Books

ADM 106: Surgeons' Succession Books

ADM 196: Commissioned and Warrant Officers' Service Records

HO: 1841, 1851 Censuses

IR 26, 27: Death Duty Registers

LC: Lord Chamberlain's Office

PRO/11: Probate Records

PMG 15: Pensions

PMG 50: Probate and Administration Records

WORKS6/119: Nelson Memorial Committee Minute Book

National Archives of Ireland, Dublin

Philip Crossle, Beatty Genealogical Notes

National Library of Ireland, Dublin

MS 32509: Philip Crossle, Beatty Genealogical Notes

National Maritime Museum, Greenwich

AGC/0/2: Benjamin Outram Correspondence

CRK: Phillipps–Croker Papers

ELL/245: William Burnett, Report on Medical Officers 1831

IGR/22: Journal of Peter Cullen

HSR/U/24: William Beatty Papers

MRF/105 and MSS/89/044: Correspondence of Thomas Masterman Hardy

STO: Sir Robert Stoppard Papers
Wel/30: William Rivers Notes

Nelson Museum & Local History Centre, Monmouth

E214: Viscount Nelson Papers

Private Collection

William Westenburg's account of Trafalgar

Public Record Office of Northen Ireland, Belfast

D/607, 671: Downshire Papers
D/623: Abercorn Papers
D/642: Hill Papers
DOW5/3/1: Freeholders Registers
MIC 5A/6–7: 1831 Census, City of Londonderry
SCH 1298: Londonderry School Records
T307: Hearth Money Rolls
T808/15258: 1740 List of Protestant Householders
T808/15264–7: 1766 List of Householders
T3419: 1796 Spinning Wheel Entitlement Lists

Royal College of Surgeons of England, London

Examination Books

Royal Naval Museum, Portsmouth

MS 1963/1: Benjamin Stevenson, Letter
MS 1984/494: Richard Francis Roberts, Journal
MS 1998/41/1: William Rivers, Gunnery Notebook
MS 418/88: William Beatty, Physician of the Fleet Correspondence

Royal Society Library, London

EC/1818/02: Fellowship Election Lists

St Andrews University Library

UY452/131–2: Senate Minute-book

Wellcome Library, London

L19: Longmore Papers
MS 3367–81: Viscount Nelson Papers

MS 5141: Report on the Post-mortem Examination of Viscount Nelson
MS 6242: Sir William Beatty Correspondence

PERIODICALS AND NEWSPAPERS

Annual Register
Army List
Belfast Newsletter
Bell's Weekly Messenger
Chambers' Journal
Cholera Gazette
European Magazine and London Review
Exeter Times
Gentleman's Magazine
Lancet
London Gazette
Londonderry Journal
Londonderry Sentinel
Mid-Ulster Mail
Morning Chronicle
Notes & Queries
Navy Chronicle
Navy List
Proceedings of the Royal Society
Royal Kalendar
Slater's London Directory
Steel's Original and Correct List of the Royal Navy
The Times

BOOKS AND ARTICLES

ACERRA, MARTINE, 'Le Scorbut', *L'Histoire*, 36 (1981), 74–5.

ACKROYD, MARCUS, BROCKLISS, LAURENCE, MOSS, MICHAEL, RETFORD, KATE, and STEVENSON, JOHN, *Advancing with the Army: Professionalization and Social Mobility in the Army Medical Corps 1790–1850* (Oxford, 2006).

ADDIS, C. P., *The Men Who Fought with Nelson in HMS Victory at Trafalgar* (London, 1988).

ADKINS, ROY, *Trafalgar: The Biography of a Battle* (London, 2004).

Admiralty, *Regulations and Instructions relating to his Majesty's Service at Sea* (London, 1731).

Admiralty, *Regulations and Instructions* (London, 1806).

ALLEN, JOSEPH, *Life of Lord Nelson* (London, 1852).

—— (ed.), *Memoirs of the Life and Services of Sir William Hargood* (Greenwich, 1841).

Army Medical Department, *Fifth Report of the Commissioners of Military Enquiry: Army Medical Department* (London, 1808).

ARTHUR WILLIAM DEVIS, Exhibition Catalogue, Hariss Museum & Art Gallery (Manchester, 2000).

ASPINALL, A., *The Later Correspondence of George III*, Vol. 4 (Cambridge, 1968).

ATKINS, JOHN, *The Navy Surgeon* (London, 1742).

The Authentic History of the Gallant Life, Heroic Actions and Sea Fights of the Right Honourable Horatio Lord Viscount Nelson, K.B. (London, 1805).

AYSHFORD, PAM and DEREK, *The Complete Trafalgar Roll* (Brussels, 2004).

BARDON, JONATHAN, *A History of Ulster* (Belfast, 1992).

BEATTY, WILLIAM, *Authentic Narrative of the Death of Lord Nelson* (London, 1807).

—— *Authentic Narrative of the Death of Lord Nelson* (London, 1825).

BELL, JOHN, *Memorial Concerning the Present State of Military and Naval Surgery* (Edinburgh, 1800).

BENNETT, GEOFFREY, *The Battle of Trafalgar* (London, 1977).

BESANT, ARTHUR DIGBY, *Our Centenary, Being the History of the First Hundred Years of the Clerical, Medical and General Life Assurance Society* (London, 1924).

BESTERMAN, THEODORE (ed.), *The Publishing Firm of Cadell and Davies: Select Correspondence and Accounts, 1793–1836* (London, 1938).

BIGHAM, CLIVE, *The Roxburghe Club: Its History and Members, 1812–1927* (Oxford, 1928).

BLAGDON, FRANCIS WILLIAM, *Edward Orme's Graphic History of the Life, Exploits, and Death of Horatio Nelson, etc.* (London, 1806).

BLANE, GILBERT, *Observations on the Diseases Incident to Seamen* (London, 1799).

—— 'Statement of the Comparative Health of the British Navy from the Year 1774 to the Year 1814', *Medico-Chirurgical Transactions*, 6 (1815).

—— *Select Dissertations* (1822), in C. Lloyd (ed.), *The Health of Seamen.*

—— *A Brief Statement of the Progressive Improvement of the Health of the Royal Navy* (London, 1830).

BOLD, JOHN, *An Architectural History of the Royal Hospital for Seamen and the Queen's House* (London, 2000).

BOURCHIER, JANE, *Memoir of the Late Admiral Sir Edward Codrington* (London, 1873).

BOWN, STEPHEN R., *The Age of Scurvy: How a Surgeon, a Mariner and a Gentleman Helped Britain Win the Battle of Trafalgar* (Chichester, 2003).

BREWER, JOHN, *The Sinews of Power* (London, 1989).

BROADLEY, A. M. and BARTELOT, R. G., *Nelson's Hardy: His Life, Letters and Friends* (London, 1909).

BROADLEY, A. M., *Three Dorset Captains at Trafalgar* (London, 1906).

BROCKLISS, LAURENCE, 'Medicine and the Small University in Eighteenth-Century France', in G. P. Brizzi and Jacques Verger (eds.), *Le università minori in Europa (secoli XV–XIX)* (Soveria Mannelli, 1998), 263–4.

—— 'Organisation, Training and the Medical Marketplace in the Eighteenth Century', in Peter Elmer (ed.), *The Healing Arts: Health, Society and Disease in Europe, 1500–1800* (Manchester, 2004), 346–71.

—— and JONES, COLIN, *The Medical World of Early Modern France* (Oxford, 1997).

Burke's Peerage and Baronetage (London, 1938).

BURTCHAELL, G. D., *Alumni Dublinenses: A Register of the Students, Graduates, Professors and Provosts of Trinity College in the University of Dublin (1593–1860)* (Dublin, 1935).

CARPENTER, KENNETH, *The History of Scurvy and Vitamin C* (Cambridge, 1986).

CHARTERS, ERICA, ' "The Most Inveterate Scurvy": Disease and the British Garrison at Quebec, 1759–1760', unpublished paper, 2004.

CHEVERS, F. M., 'Memories of the Battle of Trafalgar', *Notes & Queries*, 6th ser., 4 (1881), 503–5.

CLAPHAM, JOHN, *The Bank of England—A History 1797–1914*, 2 vols. (Cambridge, 1944).

CLARK, Sir GEORGE, *A History of the Royal College of Physicians of London*, 2 vols. (London, 1964).

CLARKE, J. S. and MCARTHUR J., *Life of Lord Nelson*, 2 vols. (London, 1809).

CLARKSON, LESLIE and CRAWFORD, ELIZABETH, *Ways to Wealth: The Cust Family of Eighteenth Century Armagh* (Belfast, 1985).

CLAYTON, TIM and CRAIG, PHIL, *Trafalgar: The Men, the Battle, the Storm* (London, 2004).

CLIPPINGDALE, S. D., 'Sir William Beatty', *Journal of the Royal Naval Medical Service* (Oct. 1916), 455–65.

COLEMAN, TERRY, *Nelson—The Man and the Legend*, new and rev. edn. (London, 2001).

COLLINGWOOD, ADAM, *Anecdotes of the late Lord Viscount Nelson; including copious accounts of the three great victories obtained . . . off the Nile, Copenhagen & Trafalgar, also, of the various engagements and expeditions wherein his Lordship signalized his courage. An authentic account of his death . . . To which is added, the ceremonial of his funeral . . . Also, select poetry, etc.* (London, 1806).

COLLINGWOOD, CUTHBERT, *Life and Letters of Vice-Admiral Lord Collingwood*, ed. O Warner (London, 1968).

COOKE, JOHN and MAULE, JOHN, *An Historical Account of the Royal Hospital for Seamen at Greenwich* (London, 1789).

COOKSON, J. E., *The British Armed Nation 1793–1815* (Oxford, 1997).

CORBETT, JULIAN, *The Campaign of Trafalgar*, 2 vols. (London, 1919).

CORFIELD, PENELOPE J., *Power and the Professions in Britain 1700–1850* (London, 1995).

A Correct Account of the Funeral Procession of Lord Nelson (London, 1806).

COTTON, HENRY, *Fasti Ecclesiae Hibernicae: The Succession of the Members and Prelates of the Cathedral Bodies of Ireland*, 3 vols. (Dublin, 1845–78).

COURT, W. E., '18th Century Drugs for the Royal Navy', *Pharmaceutical History*, 17 (1987), 2–6.

CUMBY, W. P., 'The Battle of Trafalgar: An Unpublished Narrative', *The Nineteenth Century*, 46 (1899), 718–28.

DESBRIÈRE, E., *The Naval Campaign of 1805: Trafalgar*, trans. C. Eastwick, 2 vols. (Oxford, 1933).

A Description of the Royal Hospital for Seamen, at Greenwich (London, 1846).

DIGBY, ANNE, *Making a Medical Living: Doctors and Patients in the English Market for Medicine, 1720–1911* (Cambridge, 1994).

DILLON, WILLIAM HENRY, *A Narrative of My Professional Adventures 1790–1839*, ed. Michael A. Lewis, Navy Records Society, 2 vols. (London, 1953–6).

DOW, DEREK and MOSS, MICHAEL, 'The Medical Curriculum at Glasgow in the Early Nineteenth Century', *History of Universities*, 7 (1988), 227–58.

DRAPER, J. N., 'With Nelson in the Mediterranean: Private Papers of Dr Leonard Gillespie', *Chambers's Journal*, 14 (1945), 229–33, 317–19.

DUNCAN, ARCHIBALD, 'A Correct Narrative of the Funeral of Horatio Lord Viscount Nelson', in *The Life of Lord Horatio Nelson* (London, 1806).

DUFFY, MICHAEL, *Soldiers, Sugar and Seapower: The British Expeditions to the West Indies and the War against Revolutionary France* (Oxford, 1987).

DUNNE, CHARLES, *The Chirurgical Candidate* (London, 1808).

ELLIS, HAROLD, 'Famous Trauma Victims: Nelson', *Trauma*, 3: 2 (2001), 127–31.

ERFFA, H. VON., *The Paintings of Benjamin West* (New Haven, Conn., 1986).

EVANS, ERIC, *The Forging of the Modern State: Early Industrial Britain 1783–1870* (London, 1983).

FOSTER, JOSEPH, *Alumni Oxonienses*, 4 vols. (Oxford, 1888).

GALT, JOHN, *The Life, Studies and Works of Benjamin West* (London, 1820).

GATTY, M. and A., *Recollections of the life of the Rev. A. J. Scott, D. D., Lord Nelson's Chaplain* (London, 1842).

GEGGUS, DAVID, *Slavery, War and Revolution: The British Occupation of Saint Domingue* (Oxford, 1982).

GEYER-GORDESCH, J., *Physicians and Surgeons in Glasgow: A History of the Royal College of Physicians and Surgeons of Glasgow, c. 1599–1868* (London, 1999).

GIBNEY, WILLIAM, *Recollections of an Old Army Doctor* (London, 1896).

GILL, CONRAD, *The Naval Mutinies of 1797* (Manchester, 1913).

GILLESPIE, LEONARD, *Advice to Commanders of HM Fleet in the West Indies* (London, 1798).

—— *Observations on the Diseases which Prevailed on Board a Part of His Majesty's Squadron, on the Leeward Island Station, between Nov. 1794 and April 1796* (London, 1800).

GRAHAM, JOHN, *Derriana* (Londonderry, 1823; repr. Toronto, 1851).

Greater London Industrial Archaeology Society, *Notes and News* (June, 1996).

GREIG, JAMES (ed.), *The Farington Diary*. 8 vols. (London, 1922–8).

GRAVES, ALGERNON, *The British Institution 1806–67: A Complete Dictionary of Contributions* (London, 1908).

—— *The Royal Academy Exhibitions*, 8 vols. (London, 1906).

HAMILTON, ROBERT, *The Duties of a Regimental Surgeon Considered*, 2 vols. (London, 1787).

HAMON, JEAN PIERRE, 'Les Chirugiens navigants français de la bataille de Trafalgar, 21 octobre 1805', unpublished thesis, Nantes (1983).

HARBOUR, JOHN, *Trafalgar and the Spanish Navy* (London, 1988).

HARRISON, JAMES, *The Life of Horatio Lord Viscount Nelson*, 2 vols. (London, 1806).

HILL, J. R., *The Prizes of War: The Naval Prize System in the Napoleonic Wars, 1793–1815* (Stroud, 1998).

HILLS, A.-M. E., 'Nelson's Illnesses', *Journal of the Royal Naval Medical Service*, 86 (2000), 72–80.

Historical Sketch and Laws of the Royal College of Physicians of Edinburgh from its Institution to 1925 (Edinburgh, 1925).

HOOCK, HOLGER, 'The British Military Pantheon in St Paul's Cathedral: The State, Cultural Patriotism and the Politics of National Monuments, *c.* 1795–1820', in Matthew Craske and Richard Wrigley (eds.), *Pantheons: Transformations of a Monumental Idea* (Aldershot, 2004).

HOWARD, HENRY, 'The English Illustrated Bible in the Eighteenth Century', D.Phil. thesis, University of Oxford (2005).

HUTCHINSON, A. C., *Some Further Observations on the Subject of the Proper Period for Amputating in Gun-Shot Wounds* (London, 1817).

IVES, EDWARD, *A Voyage to India* (London, 1773).

JACKSON, Sir LOUIS C., *History of the United Service Club* (Aldershot, 1937).

JAMES, W. M., *The Naval History of Great Britain* (London, 2002).

JENKS, TIMOTHY, 'Contesting the Hero: The Funeral of Admiral Lord Nelson', *Journal of British History*, 39 (2000), 422–53.

LAMBERT, ANDREW, *Nelson: Britannia's God of War* (London, 2004).

LAMBERT, GAIL, *Peter Wilson: Colonial Surgeon* (Palmerston North, NZ, 1981).

LAWRENCE, SUSAN, *Charitable Knowledge: Hospital Pupils and Practitioners in Eighteenth-Century London* (Cambridge, 1996).

LEADBETTER, CHARLES, *The Royal Gauger*, 3rd edn. (London, 1750).

LE QUESNE, L. P., 'Nelson and His Surgeons', *Journal of the Royal Naval Medical Service*, 86 (2000), 85–8.

'Lewis Rotely', *Nelson Dispatch*, 6 (1999), 383–5.

LINDEMANN, MARY, *Medicine and Society in Early Modern Europe* (London, 1999).

LLOYD, C. (ed.), *The Health of Seamen: Selections from the Works of Dr. James Lind, Sir Gilbert Blane and Dr. Thomas Trotter* (London, 1965).

—— and COULTER, J. L. S., *Medicine and the Navy 1200–1900*. vol. 3, *1715–1815* (Edinburgh, 1961).

LODY, JOY, 'Treasure in a Parish Chest', *Nelson Dispatch*, 6 (1999), 434–5.

LOUDON, IRVINE, *Medical Care and the General Practitioner, 1750–1850* (Oxford, 1986).

LOVELL, W. S., *Personal Narrative of Events from 1799 to 1815* (London, 1879).

MCBRIDE, IAN, *The Siege of Derry in Ulster Protestant Mythology* (Dublin, 1997).

MCGRIGOR, Sir JAMES, *The Scalpel and the Sword: The Autobiography of the Father of Army Medicine*, ed. Mary McGrigor (Dalkeith, 2000).

MCILRAITH, JOHN, *Life of Sir John Richardson* (London, 1868).

MACKENZIE, JOHN, *Narrative of the Siege of Londonderry* (London, 1690; repr. Belfast, 1861).

MCKENZIE, R. H., *Trafalgar Roll* (London, 1913).

MCMAHON, A. T., Captain, *The Life of Nelson* (London, 1899).

MCPHERSON, CHARLES *Life on Board a Man of War* (Glasgow, 1928).

MACRORY, PATRICK, *The Siege of Derry* (Oxford, 1988).

MARSDEN, ELIZABETH (ed.), *Brief Memoir of . . . William Marsden* (London, 1838).

MITCHELL, CHARLES, 'Benjamin West's *Death of Nelson*', in Douglas Fraser (ed.), *Essays in the History of Art Presented to Rudolf Wittkower* (London, 1967).

MORRISON, ALFRED, *The Collection of Autograph Letters and Historiographical Documents: The Hamilton and Nelson Papers* (London, 1893–4).

MORRISS, R., 'Practicality and Prejudice: The Blockade Strategy and Naval Medicine During the French Revolutionary War', in P. van der Merwe (ed.), *Science and the French and British Navies, 1700–1850* (London, 2003).

MUNK, WILLIAM, *The Roll of the Royal College of Physicians*, 3 vols. (London, 1878).

NICOLAS, Sir NICHOLAS HARRIS, *The Dispatches and Letters of Lord Nelson*, 7 vols. (London, 1844–6).

[NICOLAS, Lt PAUL], 'An Account of the Battle of Trafalgar', *The Bijou* (London, 1829), 75–6.

NISBET, WILLIAM, *Authentic Memoirs, Biographical, Critical and Literary, of the Most Eminent Physicians and Surgeons of Great* Britain (London, 1818).

NORTHCOTE, WILLIAM, *The Marine Practice of Physic and Surgery*, 2 vols. (London, 1770).

O'BYRNE, WILLIAM RICHARD, *A Naval Biographical Dictionary: Comprising The Life and Services of Every Living Officer in Her Majesty's Navy* (London, 1849).

Official Papers Relating to Operations Performed by Order of the Directors of the Royal Hospital for Seamen at Greenwich on Several of the Pensioners Belonging Thereto (London, 1814).

PAVIERE, SYDNEY H., *The Devis Family of Painters* (Leigh-on-Sea, 1950).

PETRIDES, ANNE and DOWN, JONATHAN (eds.), *Sea Soldier: An Officer of Marines with Duncan, Nelson, Collingwood and Cockburn. The Letters and Journals of Major T. Marmaduke Wybourn, RM, 1797–1813* (Tunbridge Wells, 2000).

PETTIGREW, THOMAS JOSEPH, *Memoirs of the Life of Vice-Admiral Lord Viscount Nelson, KB*, 2 vols. (London, 1849).

PLARR, V. G., *Lives of the Fellows of the Royal College of Surgeons of London*, revised by Sir D'Arcy Power (Bristol, 1930).

PORTER, ROY and DOROTHY, *The Patients' Progress: Doctors and Doctoring in Eighteenth-Century England* (Cambridge, 1989).

RAM, WILLIAM ANDREW, 'Letters of Lieutenant William Andrew Ram Killed at Trafalgar', *Nelson Dispatch*, 6 (1998), 184–7.

Report of the Committee on the Subject of the Burden Sustained by the Parish of Greenwich in Relieving Poor Persons Connected with Greenwich Hospital (Greenwich, 1831).

RISSE, GUENTER, *Hospital Life in Enlightenment Scotland* (Cambridge, 1986).

ROBERTSON, ROBERT, *Observations on the Diseases Incident to Seamen, Retired from the Actual Service, by Reason of Accident, Infirmity or Old Age*, 4 vols. (London, 1807).

[ROBINSON, WILLIAM], 'Jack Nastyface', *Nautical Economy, or Forecastle Reflections of Events during the Last War* (London, 1836).

ROEBUCK, PETER (ed.), *Plantation to Partition* (Belfast, 1981).

RODGER, N. A. M., *The Command of the Ocean: A Naval History of Britain, 1649–1815* (London, 2004).

ROSNER, LISA, *Medical Education in the Age of Improvement* (Edinburgh, 1991).

—— *The Most Beautiful Man in Existence: The Scandalous Life of Alexander Lesassier* (Philadelphia, 1999).

RUSSELL, GILLIAN, *The Theatres of War. Performance, Politics and Society 1793–1815* (Oxford, 1995).

SAMPSON, GEORGE VAUGHAN, *County Londonderry* (Dublin, 1801).

SENHOUSE, HUMPHREY, 'The Battle of Trafalgar', *Macmillan's Magazine*, 81 (1900), 415–25.

SOUTHEY, R., *The Life of Nelson* (London, 1813).

STANHOPE, PHILIP HENRY, *Life of Pitt* (London, 1861).

Statement of the Case on the Part of the Commissioners of Greenwich Hospital in Regard to the Claims Made by the Parish of Greenwich Upon the Institution for Parochial Rates (London, 1838).

TERRAINE, JOHN, *Trafalgar* (London, 1976).

THURSELD, H. G., (ed.), 'Memoirs of Peter Cullen', in *Five Naval Journals, 1789–1817*, Navy Records Society (London, 1951).

THOMAS, R. H. G., *London's First Railway: The London and Greenwich* (London, 1972).

TROTTER, THOMAS, *Medicina Nautica: An Essay on the Diseases of Seamen*, 3 vols. (London, 1797–1803).

TURNBULL, WILLIAM, *The Naval Surgeon* (London, 1806).

UNDERWOOD, E. ASHWORTH, *Boerhaave's Men at Leyden and After* (Edinburgh, 1977).

UWINS, S., *A Memoir of Thomas Uwins RA* (London, 1858).

VENN, J. A., *Alumni Cantabrigienses from 1752–1900*, 6 vols. (Cambridge, 1940–53).

WALKER, GEORGE, *True Account of the Siege of Londonderry* (London, 1689).

WALKER, R., *The Nelson Portraits* (London, 1998).

WARNER, OLIVER, *Nelson's Battles* (London, 1965).

WATT, J., 'The Injuries of Four Centuries of Naval Warfare', *Annals of the Royal College of Surgeons*, 57 (1975), 3–24.

—— 'The Surgery of Sea Warfare from the Galley to the Nuclear Age', *Transactions of the Medical Society of London*, 97 (1980–1), 1–15.

—— 'Nelsonian Medicine in Context', *Journal of the Royal Naval Medical Service*, 86 (2000), 64–80.

WEBB, PAUL, 'Sea Power in the Ochakov Affair of 1791', *International History Review*, 2 (1980), 13–33.

WILLYAMS, COOPER, *An Account of the Campaign in the West Indies in the Year 1794* (London, 1796).

ZUCKERMAN, ARNOLD, 'Disease and Ventilation in the Royal Navy: The Woodenship Years', *Eighteenth-Century Life*, 11 (1987), 77–89.

ZULUETA, JULIAN DE, 'Health in the Spanish Navy During the Age of Nelson', *Journal of the Royal Naval Medical Service*, 86 (2000), 89–92.

—— 'Trafalgar: The Spanish View', *Mariner's Mirror*, 66 (1980), 293–319.

WEBSITES

Beatty family, at http://homepages.rootsweb.com/~bp2000 (Jan. 2005).

HMS *Victory*, at http://www.hms-victory.com (Jan. 2005).

Internet Genealogy, Search, at http://www.familysearch.org (Jan. 2005).

Index

Made in the USA
Middletown, DE
27 January 2020